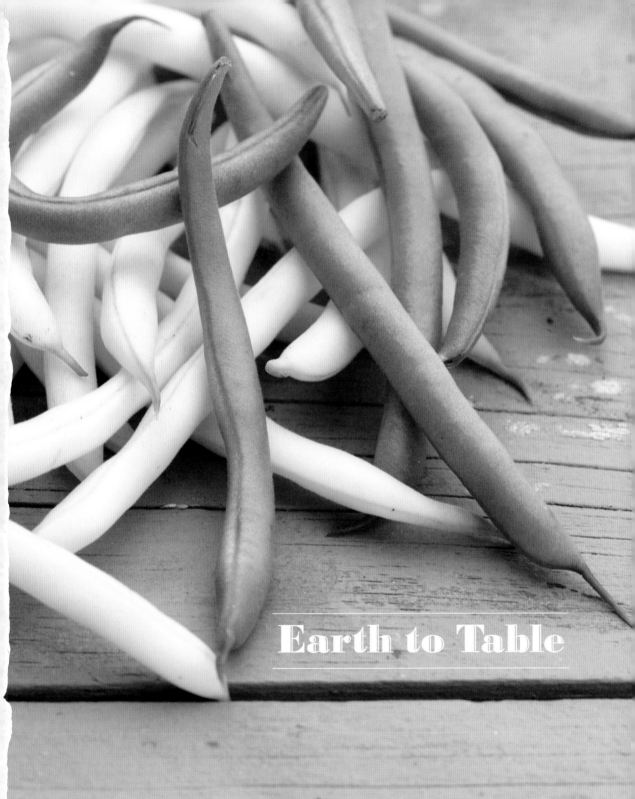

Earth to Table

Seasonal Recipes from
an Organic Farm

Jeff Crump
and Bettina Schormann

EARTH to TABLE

With photographs by
Edward Pond

ecco
An Imprint of HarperCollinsPublishers

Published in Canada in 2009 by Random House Canada.

FIRST U.S. EDITION

PHOTOGRAPHY CREDITS COPYRIGHT:
Page 17, 19, 41–43: Robert Wheeler; Page 28, 110, 155, 157, 166–170, 240–244: Jeff Crump; Page 45: Curt Doughty; Page 99: Jim Fairman, courtesy of Michael Schwartz; Page 156: Bettina Schormann; Page 165: Jen Munkvold; Page 239: Deborah Jones; Page 286: Liliane Calfee Miller

Food Styling and Props: Claire Stubbs
Recipe Editor: Kate Dowhan
Recipe Tester: Mike Vogt

Design by Kelly Hill

Printed in China

Library of Congress Cataloging-in-Publication Data is available upon request.

ISBN: 978-0-06-182594-1

09   10   11   12   13   /TOP   10   9   8   7   6   5   4   3   2   1

For Jules, Maus, Layla & Lawrence with love . . .
and Gunner, always in my heart—J.C.

Scott . to DO . . . .
pretty much everything.
- Pork - brine, bones, stock.
- Ribeye, strip not filet
- Please watch Alex with
                        Gnudi
· fish is in today
  I will pick-up miso
for Sablefish
  Sockeye is now out of
season . . . .
See you @ 3   JC.

"Eating is an agricultural act."
WENDELL BERRY

CONTENTS

Fall 149

Winter 221

Conclusion

Introduction

Everybody has some sense of what good food is.

What many of us actually eat may not taste especially good, may not be particularly good for us, and probably comes from a farm or factory we don't want to even imagine. But that's not because we don't know what we want. It's just that we always seem to end up eating something else.

After all, marketers know what we want. There is hardly an industrial-grade fast-food burger that is not advertised with images of dewy, plump tomatoes, wholesome bread straight from the oven, some kind of premium beef. The reality of flaccid vegetable matter, a soggy bun and tasteless meat is, of course, rather different. But that's not really news—jokes about fast food that doesn't look anything like the commercials aren't even funny anymore. What is significant is that we are so mesmerized by the promise of fresh, wholesome food that we can be tricked into eating something else. Packages wouldn't be decorated with images of traditional farms and contented animals, and commercials wouldn't depict chefs and Italian grandmothers carefully tasting this or that "authentic" recipe, if these weren't the things we all think of as important.

The desire for food grown and prepared with care is not elitist or limited to a band of hippies. It's what we *all* want.

Similarly, just as no one says they want tasteless, truck-ripened vegetables or feed-lot beef, no one deliberately plans a rushed meal. And yet, again, that is what we end up eating, wolfing down burgers in our cars or slurping a plastic tray of microwaved pasta as we stand hunched over the kitchen sink. Fast-food companies rarely show lonely people eating in their cubicles at work, or solitary figures heedlessly munching as they watch television at night. As usual, the marketers seem to know what we really want: they show smiling families gathered around the dining-room table. Talking, laughing, spending time together. If marketers know what we want, why don't we get what we want?

In other words, we're promised one thing, and we get something else. We end up gulping down food of dubious provenance when what we really want is to linger with friends and family over a meal of fresh, wholesome ingredients, carefully prepared. Fast food is sold to us on the merit of its illusory resemblance to Slow Food.

In any case, there is no point complaining about the food we don't want to eat. No point being negative or wringing our hands about what other people eat. Besides, I am not invulnerable to the seductions of certain burgers. So I'm not here to wag my finger at anybody. I just wanted to make the point that I probably don't have to convince anyone that fresh, wholesome, carefully prepared food, enjoyed in a civilized manner with people we care about, is the way to go—it's what everyone already wants. In fact, paying attention to what we want is a good way to figure out what's right to eat: tomato salad in August, fish and chips by the sea, a cold beer with lime on a hot summer day, even chicken wings with friends while watching football. Strawberries in February? Beef stew in July? Forget it.

Of course, paying attention to our hankerings won't tell us everything we need to know, partly because industrial-scale farming, shopping and eating have permitted our culture to forget a great deal that we once knew about food, and it's hard to have a craving for something you've never thought of or even really noticed. If you're accustomed to eating fast-food french fries, you'd never know that even fries are seasonal (potatoes are not at their best between January and March). And if you're used to nuking your dinner in a microwave, you might not have developed a longing for the experience of a kitchen filled with the aromas of cooking, the warmth of the stove, the steamy clatter of pots or the satisfaction of washing up. There are some things we have to remember *how* to want if we want to do it right.

There are a few basic skills that all people should have: communication, personal finance, basic auto repair and cooking. These have all been slipping through our fingers as we become more and more specialized and dependent on specialists for everything. (I won't comment on my financial acumen, but I can tell you I don't change my own spark plugs.) I'm not sure which came first, the loss of our skills in the kitchen or convenience food that replaces the need for skill. I imagine they happened together. In any case, a couple of generations after the arrival of the TV dinner and the Radar Range, it's pretty clear that big business has given us the tools never to really cook again. Whole generations of kids are growing up without a need to cook, much less shop, thoughtfully.

I was giving a cooking demo one year in a ski resort in the Rocky Mountains, a corporate team-building event that featured hands-on cooking. The teams received a recipe and ingredients, then were instructed to cook the dish. Each group was allowed to ask me only one question. After much debate, a team of men approached me with their question, and a head of garlic. The question was, "Is this a clove?" The recipe was roast chicken, to serve six people, and it called for five cloves of garlic. Now, I would have thought it was obvious that nearly a whole head of garlic per person would taste pretty devastating. But I guess not.

Back when food was made by hand, with ingredients offered up seasonally by the landscape around you, it was pretty easy to know what to eat. You ate what was at hand. You ate what your parents ate, and what their parents had eaten before them. That's what culture is, I suppose: a way of formulating and storing knowledge.

It hardly needs to be said that this is not the way we eat today. To a large degree, we have a food culture only by default; we eat whatever we feel like eating, and that often means that we eat whatever happens to be available. The fact that what is available includes an astonishing array of foods doesn't change the reality that we're often lost as we negotiate the choices we stumble across in the supermarket.

If we don't know how to cook, then we lose the power of choice. You can't buy local, seasonal produce if you don't know what it is or what to do with it. Fast food becomes the only option, and that means allowing agribusiness and marketers to make our decisions.

And then the smells of the kitchen and the pleasure (and freedom) of putting together a meal will be lost.

IF THE WORLD WERE FAIR, we'd have celebrity farmers.

We have celebrity chefs, after all. People stay up late into the night, watching transfixed as charismatic men and women prepare enticing meals on television. It's not hard to figure out why. Food is important. It puts in physical form many of the things we value in life. It tells us who we are, and what kind of lives we dream of living. Food is all about what's best in life.

So I wish the world were ready for the first celebrity farmer.

Here's why. If you don't give the farmer credit for the taste of the food, then you're not giving the food credit either. I once did an externship at the famed restaurant Chez Panisse in Berkeley, California. Of course, the whole point of being an apprentice is to learn something, probably in the course of performing some humble task. I was instructed to shuck and clean a few cases of corn. As I sat there sullenly ripping the waxy green husks from the cobs, the head chef, Russell Moore, approached me and asked how the corn tasted. Since I was an apprentice, I gave the wrong answer. "It's not cooked," I said. "Why would I taste it?"

He snatched a cob from my hand and took a big bite, chewed reflectively for a moment, then told me to prepare the corn for the staff meal and wait for the "real good stuff" that was coming tomorrow. I tasted it myself and thought, "Tastes like corn to me."

The next day, there was a new delivery of corn at my station. It had come from Chino Ranch, a farm that has become justly famous for the excellence of the food it produces. The first thing I did was tear open a cob and take a bite. I still get chills when I think about it. It was one of those rare moments when you discover sheer perfection: the crisp, slightly starchy sweetness was heavenly. I looked up and saw that Russell had been watching me with the knowing smile of a kung fu master. Without a word, he turned and continued his day.

So *that's* what corn tastes like.

Still, it wasn't as though I'd learned all there is to know about

food from a single bite of corn. Most of us have already figured out that corn has to be eaten at the right time, and it's one vegetable that tends to be grown locally. No one in their right mind eats Argentinean corn in February. It would taste like porridge, and it would feel wrong. We wait for corn season, and for a few weeks we revel in the perfect confluence of weather and taste. Then it's gone for a year. We have only so many corn seasons in our lives.

We're a little less rigid with strawberries and tomatoes, but most of us get it. If you want a plump, sweet strawberry, grab one in early summer. If you want a fleshy, blood-red tomato, wait a few weeks more. At the right time of year, you might even find ripe, flavorful local produce in your supermarket. But many of us can't wait for those few weeks when strawberries and tomatoes are available at farmers' markets or in the little stalls on the side of the road. Some of us might even get so impatient that we pick up the pale, mealy strawberries and tomatoes that are available year-round, along with apples that have traveled halfway around the globe and avocadoes that taste like glue. Unnaturally symmetrical, and gleaming like children's toys under the halogen lights, this stuff doesn't taste nearly as good as it looks. In fact, for the most part, it tastes terrible.

Even worse, some people don't know the difference between the exquisite, local, seasonal food around them and the tasteless, rigid fare on offer in the supermarket.

It's the farmers who make good food taste good. They do it not only by taking care of the planting and weeding and harvesting (and peering inscrutably at the horizon, watching for signs of rain), but by doing it right, and simply by doing it at all. A day can make all the difference, and a farmer's life is a year of those days.

I'm grateful that farmers go to all this trouble. Without the men and women who grow and sell fresh produce, or raise range-fed animals, we'd all be doomed to eating bleak, industrial food. I'm not saying I would never eat a chocolate bar or a takeout burger. But without produce and meat from properly managed farms, life would be pretty grim.

Here's what I mean. We already take for granted that we can buy the food we want: organic beef, non-pasteurized local cheese, pesticide-free seasonal produce and so forth. We think we're entitled to it. But I keep reminding myself that, not that long ago, this stuff just wasn't available, at least not on any scale, unless you grew it or made it yourself. It simply wasn't there. What was available was processed, industrial output (what might be called post-food). You couldn't choose to eat what you wanted, any more than a citizen of the USSR could choose to buy a new car. If what you want isn't available, you're not quite as free as you would otherwise be.

Farmers produce some of the most amazing things in life, and they don't get much credit for it. How heartbreaking it must be to work your ass off in the hot sun, fighting weather, time, bugs and weeds to grow something as simple as arugula, then to cut it, wash it, pack it and drive it all the way to a restaurant—only to have some chef reject it because of a few holes, or because the leaves are too big or small, or simply because it's not on the menu right at that moment. Once, when I told a farmer I didn't need anything that week, he responded acidly that he would tell the plants to stop growing. On the other hand, an unfortunate cook once asked me what gardening has to do with cooking (I never said I was the *only* person who was foolish when he was young). Just as cooking means everything to the farmer (obviously, that is the destiny of the food he or she grows), farming means everything to the cook.

So, would I watch a reality TV show that followed the trials of an articulate farmer pursuing the perfect heirloom tomato? Absolutely.

I COUNT MYSELF LUCKY that I don't have to wait for a smart television executive with a taste for good food to come up with a series like that. I get to watch it nearly every day, and the main character is a farmer named Chris Krucker.

I met Chris in the summer of 2005 when I had been the executive chef at the Ancaster Old Mill for a couple of years. I have to admit that when I got a letter from a local organic farmer, I thought "hippie." And when I first shook hands with a guy who wore his grey-flecked hair in a ponytail under a floppy hat, well, it's safe to say I found little reason to revise my preconceptions.

(Incidentally, even other local organic farmers think Chris has a few things in common with his sixties predecessors. Once, I was working in the field with him when a truck full of guys from a rival farm sped by with their windows down, shouting the inevitable taunt "Get a haircut!" When organic farmers think you're a hippie, you've probably got a little hippie in you.)

However, I quickly learned that Chris was not all peace and love. He was already suspicious of me, having been warned that chefs are a pain in the neck. For my part, I knew for a fact that farmers can be impossible. And this wasn't just stereotyping—for as long as I've been washing dishes or peeling potatoes, I've always sought out restaurants that source their produce carefully and locally. I had met enough stubborn, idealistic and ornery farmers to know that Chris might not be easy to get along with.

All the same, ManoRun Farm was everything industrial monoculture is not. Chickens, ducks and turkeys waddled around merrily in the shade of a big red barn. Horses stood at the fence, absentmindedly flicking at flies. Cats wandered in and out of a sprawling Victorian house. A few cows and pigs clustered in a small grove of trees as if they were gossiping.

And the fields were a riot of growth. Towering stands of flowering Jerusalem artichokes. Carpets of various lettuces: cavolo nero, red and green oak leaf, romaine, curly endive, spinach. Sprawling nests of pumpkin and squash vines, ranks of corn, a kaleidoscope of beet greens. There was a lot going on. Of course, there were also weeds growing stubbornly amidst all this food, but as enticing as a prim garden can be, I'd rather see an abundance of life than a weed-free expanse from which all but a single species has been chemically exterminated.

All of which is to say that Chris's farm was just what I had been looking for for ten years. And so had my friend and colleague Bettina, the Old Mill's Pastry Chef. Bettina and I wanted to create an earth-to-table experience that would not only endow the Old Mill's restaurant kitchen with delicious seasonal produce, but would also allow the chefs to gain from the hands-on experience of working the land. To our delight, we discovered that we were becoming part of something even greater: a sustainable system that now nourishes our community, our traditions and our environment.

Little did Chris know what he was getting into.

We ended up settling on a trial order: fingerling potatoes, spinach, beets, radishes, French beans and heirloom tomatoes. Of course, Chris grows much more than this, but we agreed this would be a good place to start. We'd take it from there.

One thing I soon figured out is that farms have an important difference from restaurants: you don't order from a menu. What you get is what comes out of the ground. If we get a lot of spinach (and spinach is one of those foods that doesn't really have a season—it just keeps growing), we have to be creative enough to accommodate it. We watch the deliveries happen in order to analyze the spinach and review our mental menu items for a dish that suits that particular spinach on that particular day. Do we have a big party who would love a good soup? Are we short on arugula—in other words, can we substitute spinach for arugula in our dinner salad? Is the spinach pristine and small enough that we can keep it as is and simply dress it, or do we have to stew or cream it?

Chris, for his part, learned that restaurants have an important difference from his family kitchen: you can't make people eat something just because you did a great job growing it. One year, he had a bumper crop of radishes and kept showing up with bushels of the things. Now, I don't care how good a radish is, or how much you love them—you can eat only so many. We could use about two bunches a week, which meant that some of Chris's radishes were going to meet a bad end.

Chris brought us a lot of stuff that year that didn't get used: kale, beet greens, rainbow Swiss chard, big overgrown greens. My cooks didn't know what to do with it all at first, and I had to witness the horror of boxes of produce wilting in the fridge. But that was my problem; I had told Chris that if he got me the goods, I would cook

Clockwise from top left: Bettina Schormann; Jeff Crump; Kaleb and Chris Krucker.

them. I'd had hopes of putting cavolo nero on the map (partly on the strength of its cool name, but more for its robustness and addictive bitterness), but I'm afraid much of it went to waste.

So at first we were paying for food we didn't use, and paying a premium for the food we did serve—even if was not quite what we ordered. In fact, we still do. The reason we don't order food the way another business might order microchips, or fuel injectors, or lumber, is that food is not just another commodity, and farming is not just another way of producing something. Farmers take risks that other businessmen do not, and they are custodians of an important heritage that they should not be called upon to subsidize out of their own pockets. There were once hundreds of varieties of apples grown in Ontario; now we can buy six in the supermarkets. Many delicious apples, with exotic and enticing names like Foxwhelp, Sheep's Snout, Bastard Rough Coat and Bloody Turk, have been lost forever, displaced by the shiny billiard balls we now think of as fruit. (Similarly, there are hundreds of types of cheese made in Italy and France, some only in a single village, by a lone cheesemaker; if one of these artisans dies without training an apprentice, a cheese could be lost forever.)

We want farmers to grow and market high-quality, local, seasonal produce and provide us with tasty, healthy, humanely raised meat. Yet our industrial food system gives them every incentive to get bigger, more energy-intensive, more global. Why on earth would I, either as a chef or as a cook at home, throw in my lot with a food system I know to be destructive, one that leaches the life out of local economies? The answer is, I wouldn't. And I don't.

We get our produce from Chris the same way people in cities around the world are now getting theirs: we belong to a Community Shared Agriculture program (CSA). The idea is simple. Customers don't buy produce from the farmer; they buy a share of his crop. This brings the farmer crucial capital early in the year, and spreads the risk that the crop might not turn out as planned. In other words, CSAs mimic living on the farm. You take the good with the bad, and if bugs eat all the zucchinis in August, you get no zucchinis in August. Of course, the more likely outcome is that you'll get a box of delicious, ripe zucchinis (and heaps of other stuff), but still, if something does go wrong, Chris is not the only guy left holding the bag. If he were, he might be tempted to pursue a less labor-intensive line of work. Like farming with chemicals.

And of course, this is not just about zucchinis. It's about supporting the local economy. In a world without CSAs, if Chris's farm were to fail, no one would even notice; we'd just get our zucchinis at the supermarket. This way, Bettina and I and everyone who belongs to the CSA have a stake in the local landscape. We are invited to open houses and even to work in the fields.

We accepted the latter invitation eagerly. In fact, we made sure that everyone involved with the restaurant had a chance to go out to the farm to roll up their sleeves and help out. No one was forced to pull weeds or feed pigs on their day off, and I doubt Chris would have wanted his farm overrun by people who had no idea what they were doing. But we wanted everyone on board. Chefs don't make food, and farmers don't make food— food is the result of a long and largely hidden process, and I found this process fascinating enough to assume that everyone working in the restaurant would be equally interested. If I was wrong, no one has told me yet.

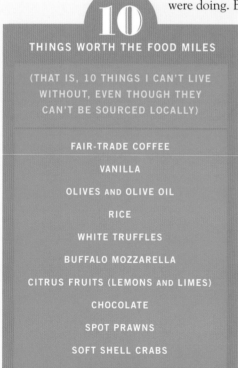

10
THINGS WORTH THE FOOD MILES

(THAT IS, 10 THINGS I CAN'T LIVE WITHOUT, EVEN THOUGH THEY CAN'T BE SOURCED LOCALLY)

FAIR-TRADE COFFEE

VANILLA

OLIVES AND OLIVE OIL

RICE

WHITE TRUFFLES

BUFFALO MOZZARELLA

CITRUS FRUITS (LEMONS AND LIMES)

CHOCOLATE

SPOT PRAWNS

SOFT SHELL CRABS

This insistence on working with and protecting local producers is the key to the Slow Food movement. Slow Food is not about foie gras and caviar; it's about carrots and potatoes. It's about *quality* food, but that's not the same thing as expensive food. The way I see it, Slow Food is the way to defend the world against everything that's wrong with the way we tend to eat.

There are many strange ideas out there about Slow Food, so I will clarify a couple of points. First, it is not an ideological position; I certainly don't turn up my nose at a suspect plate of food and announce, "Sorry, can't eat that—I'm Slow Food, you see." Second, Slow Food does not mean slow cooking; it's just not fast food (globally sourced, industrially produced, unappetizingly prepared and unhealthy). Third, it's not necessarily "health food." There is nothing quite as delicious as lardo, a Piedmontese delicacy, which some people are alarmed to discover is pure cured pork fat. (Even people who would eat a six-piece packet of Chicken McNuggets, which contains eighteen grams of fat, would shrink from the idea of a paper-thin slice of lardo.) Fourth, Slow Food is not anti-globalization; it just struggles to control the exchange of ideas, rather than be controlled by it—in other words, it is an effort to forestall the complete homogenization of taste.

Perhaps I should simply call Slow Food "good food." One of my chefs once complained, "You're always just handing me food." I replied, "That's because I want you to know what it tastes like." There is no argument for good food quite as powerful as tasting it. I sometimes hold classes for kids, in which I prepare both Kraft Dinner and a proper Slow Food version of macaroni and cheese. Most kids are astonished to learn that the bright orange powder in the foil envelope is not, in fact, cheese in any meaningful sense. And I am happy to report that, as much as kids love Kraft Dinner, they love real macaroni and real cheese even more.

Adults are no different. I once had a customer send back a crème brûlée because she'd detected small dark flecks in the custard and assumed it had gone bad. I went out with a vanilla bean in hand and encouraged her to smell it and tease out a few of the seeds—the brothers and sisters of the seemingly ominous dark flecks. She ate the crème brûlée happily, and I'd like to think that, now that she knows what the real item tastes like, she'll never settle for the ersatz version so many of us are accustomed to.

Think of all the food that is more familiar as a counterfeit: Black Forest cake, trifle, ice cream, cheese, ham, mortadella, shepherd's pie. If you've never had the real thing, you have no idea what you're missing. The same goes for new foods. You probably had to learn to like many of the most delicious things in life: olives, oysters, wine and beer, for example. If you don't try lardo, that's one less thing for you to enjoy in life.

In the end, I hope it becomes clear that what Bettina and I advocate when we encourage people to close the gap from earth to table is not that we all adopt some regimen of food purity, or that we abstain from certain foods. This is not about sacrifice (something I confess I have little talent for), it's about discovery. And what you discover may well be right around the corner, or just outside your door.

THERE IS MORE THAN ONE WAY to enjoy this book.

You may not try all the recipes, and you may not be interested in everything we have to say about this or that. What we set out to communicate is not the definitive set of answers to all of the questions surrounding our food culture, but a year's worth of our experiences as we did our best to answer them for ourselves. We have talked to a lot of people doing something similar, many of them among the world's best chefs, and we discovered that everybody's take on the issues is at least a little bit different. You'll meet some of these people as you read through the book, and learn what they think about farming and food. Some are animated by big ideas; some are just striving for the highest level of excellence their vocation can take them to. But the fact that so many brilliant chefs are heading in the same direction tells me that we're definitely on to something.

For my part, I can't claim to be an expert on anything but cooking. I'm not in any position to lecture you on farming, or the environment, or questions of sustainability. But I do think and read about these questions a lot, and looking for answers (or at least understanding the questions) made up a significant part of my relationship with the farm over the year described in the book. There are reasons we do what we do, and I thought it made sense to share them with you in each chapter's "spotlight."

We also figured this book would appeal not only to people who like to cook (and read) but also to people who like to *do*. (Not that cooking and reading aren't *doing*.) A lot of what we talk about falls outside of the familiar trip to the supermarket to pick up ingredients, so each chapter includes a "how-to" section that gives you an introduction to a new way of getting food from the field to your dinner table. I hope you are at least tempted to try some of this yourself.

Bettina kept a diary of our earth-to-table experience growing, harvesting and baking with Red Fife wheat, a nearly forgotten heirloom variety that has recently begun to enjoy something of a renaissance. (Bettina also wrote all of the dessert recipes in the book.)

We can't tell you how to read the book, of course. Now that it's in your hands, it's out of ours. But we would like to pass on a suggestion: Don't set your menu by leafing through the book. Instead, first see what's out there—in the garden, in the market, even in the woods. Once you know what nature has put on the menu, come back and investigate how we would cook it. Of course, the food you find may be a little different from what we have available to us—indeed, you may have more choices than we do here in Ontario, with our relatively short growing season. You will figure it all out.

Everywhere is local to someone. The neighborhood around our restaurant, the Old Mill, and ManoRun Farm is our idea of local, but everyone has local sources of food. Every strawberry has to be plucked somewhere, by someone. Every farm has a landscape that looks enticing in the morning sunlight; every field has weeds, and every laborer eventually has a sore back. But no farm is exactly like any other. That uniqueness is worth holding out for.

What To Cook With
WHEN WE MENTION

SALT, WE MEAN KOSHER

BUTTER, WE MEAN UNSALTED

OLIVE OIL, WE MEAN EXTRA-VIRGIN

EGGS, WE MEAN LARGE AND ORGANIC

PARSLEY, WE MEAN BROAD-LEAF ITALIAN

YEAST, WE MEAN INSTANT

CHEF HESTON BLUMENTHAL

THE FAT DUCK, BRAY, U.K.

It may seem like a long way from a muddy field to the tables of the best restaurants in the world. But when you think about it, every vegetable has to come from *somewhere*. And if there is one thing every forward-thinking chef I speak with has in common, it's the belief not only that great dishes are made with great food (no surprise there) but that great food is, for the most part, local and seasonal. No surprise there either, really. But good to know.

The ideas and philosophies of this book are fairly simple, and there is no reason we can't all go about cooking and eating not only deliciously but also sustainably, at least much of the time. But it occurred to me that the link between the world of Michelin-starred restaurants and the shopping you do at the farmers' market each weekend is not all that distant. We see this in the world of fashion all the time—the ideas that come to life in exotic ateliers and first see the light of day on runways in Milan (or wherever) soon end up in local stores, at affordable prices. Most of us will never wear $10,000 gowns, but we may well see dresses that resemble them when we go to the mall (if we go to malls). Even french fries were once haute cuisine.

My point, of course, is not that following trends is a good way to be popular, or that seasonal, local cooking is just another fashion. (Indeed, it's the way our species has eaten for well over 99 percent of its history—hardly a passing fad.) But good ideas do often start off in studios and laboratories and ivory towers before making their way into the mainstream, and great chefs' kitchens can be all of those things.

And none more than Heston Blumenthal's kitchen at the Fat Duck, the restaurant deemed the best in the world by *Restaurant* magazine in 2005 (and second-best in 2006, 2007 and 2008). It's an unprepossessing restaurant in a quiet, tidy village not far from Heathrow Airport, but make no mistake: this place is a chef's dream. So, rather than just dream, I headed over to work there for a month.

Was I nervous? Let's say I was eager to see it all. The legendary "bacon and egg ice cream," the "snail porridge," the now classic dish called "sound of the sea," which comes with an iPod—working in Heston's kitchen would mean preparing the food that earned the Fat Duck its three Michelin stars. Many cooking techniques, such as *sous vide* and something called fluid gel, have been developed in this kitchen. This is not a restaurant known for local, seasonal fare; its reputation is for wild innovation and a sort of mad scientist's enthusiasm for new ideas and techniques. But I wasn't there to have my own thoughts about

Heston Blumenthal (left), showing the author around Laverstoke Park Farm.

food and agriculture confirmed. I was there to learn from a chef running perhaps the most exciting kitchen in the world.

It was about three days in when I actually met Heston. I was shucking my hundredth oyster and was about to gently cover it with passion-fruit gel when I felt a hand on my shoulder. "You're Jeff, the Canadian."

I turned and was face to face with the most dynamic chef in the world. There he was: nattily dressed, built like a rugby player, his trademark shaved head gleaming. Instantly likable. "Thanks for coming to the Fat Duck."

He was thanking *me?* I was sure the place would do fine without my help. A few weeks at the Fat Duck can make a young cook's career.

The line cooks at the Fat Duck are the rock stars of the food world. There are only ten or so spots on the hotline, and the apps and pastry positions are coveted the world over. Everyone is under thirty, all hard-partying perfectionists, a rare combination. I thought to myself that most of my kitchen staff would be right at home here. The music blares during preservice—Amy Winehouse to techno to Johnny Cash. But when service starts, everyone is deadly serious. The hours are brutal, even for someone like me who works sixty-hour work weeks. My shift was from 8 a.m. till 11 p.m. But morale was extraordinarily high.

The kitchen is absurdly tiny—about one-tenth the size of my kitchen, with the same number of cooks—and working in it was a little like playing tag in a phone booth. My motto was: Just watch your back all day and keep super-clean.

Once I had managed to prove that I knew what to do in a kitchen, I was given some interesting tasks, like receiving deliveries of whole squabs, guts and feathers included. We evis-cerated the birds and hung them in the fridge to "ripen." I also found myself on snail duty one morning before I'd had a chance to grab a coffee. There was a knock at the back door, and when I opened it I was handed about a hundred pounds of snails. I had never met a snail farmer until that moment, and was struck by how much he actually looked like a snail! Short and plump, not the cleanest chap in the world. (Difficult to stay clean in his line of work, I would imagine.) In any case, I cleaned snails for the first time in my life. Yes, there is a part of the snail that you don't want to eat. It is called the sac (you can guess what it holds). Snails are a cinch to clean, but there were a lot of them. We blanched and marinated them for the signature dish on the menu.

Was it worth a trip across the Atlantic to gut birds and clean snails? Well, yes, it was. Though my feet often ached and my eyes were pretty bleary by closing time, I found it exhilarating to get back to basics—not only the basics of execution as a line chef but the basics of food itself. Whether I was confronted with a feathery bird or a pail of gastropods, it was galvanizing to be reminded that the world-famous dishes these animals would soon become began as living things. We all know this, of course, but you know it more acutely somehow when you've experienced it up to your elbows.

Still, what I really wanted was a chat with Heston, and I didn't have to wait long. We met for tea at his pub, the Hind's Head. As I was waiting for him in the bar, I exchanged a few words with the hostess, who got a little flustered when she discovered whom I was meeting. When he arrived, he asked for tea before we sat down in a private room to talk. A few minutes later, the hostess arrived with a whole tray of tea. "So sorry," she said. "I forgot which type of tea you wanted, so I made them all!"

Heston manages to be a flurry of activity even when he's sitting still. You can see his mind racing. He speaks with infectious energy, his thoughts galloping away in all directions. His phone vibrates every two minutes, and he takes his glasses

off at regular intervals to think or to make a particularly important point.

Sustainable gastronomy is clearly an idea dear to his heart, because we ended up talking for twice as long as his assistant had allotted me, and we could have gone on much longer (particularly if he didn't have a book to write, a BBC television show to produce and a column to write, not to mention a family and two restaurants demanding his attention). He made it clear he wanted to support the earth-to-table project.

The thing that struck me most was that, while the Fat Duck is not known for its earth-to-table credentials, Heston is quietly very committed to local food—something I saw first-hand when I visited Laverstoke

What Heston Cooks With His Son

The dish Heston's son has taken to is a simple carbonara pasta—he thinks it will help get the girls! In a skillet, sauté onions, garlic, bacon and chilies. In a bowl, whisk two eggs with Parmesan cheese. Boil some pasta, then combine all of the hot ingredients with the egg mixture. Season, stir and serve.

Park Farm, the farm his food comes from (see page 41). The reason is simple: it tastes better.

"We all *want* to eat wholesome food, but sometimes we just don't," he admits. Part of the problem is that we're busy. Fair enough. But part of the problem, he says, is that we're being manipulated. "Imagery is used to make us think we're buying local" is his way of putting it. You look at a package of sliced ham, admire the family farm featured on its label and assume the pig was raised in that kind of rustic Eden. But you'd be "seriously shocked," he argues, if you knew the reality.

That is not to say that it has to be difficult to eat good food, or to shop for it. The key, he says, is to "look for quality over quantity." Not that your dinner

has to be expensive; start with basic but local, seasonal produce and perhaps a cheaper cut of meat from a good butcher, and you're better off than you would have been with something more convenient but less nutritious.

This approach is going to involve more cooking, of course, but as he says, you're cooking for the soul as well as the stomach. And why not involve the whole family? Heston calls cooking with his kids an "incredibly rewarding and satisfying experience." (Indeed, his first book was called *Family Food*—a pretty surprising subject for a guy considered the foremost chef on the planet.)

Cooking with your family may seem like a small thing, but in the end, how you *feel* about your food is the tip of a huge ethical iceberg. If you make food an important part of the life of your household, chances are you will make choices that will lead to a more sustainable food system. If, on the other hand, you're just looking at price, it makes sense to assume that the people who produce your food will take the same approach. Heston points out that the race to lower costs will eventually hit rock bottom, with disastrous results. But once people finally see where their food system is heading, improvement becomes all but inevitable.

"In the U.K. to begin the change, we have had to eat a very strong pill with BSE [bovine spongiform encephalopathy, or mad cow disease] and avian flu. But now people are starting to ask questions."

That's another way of saying that people in the U.K. are growing and selling better food because people are demanding it. Now, Heston feels, the U.K. is a world leader in food culture. Supermarkets are carrying more local, organic produce, more high-quality meat. Chefs like Jamie Oliver are growing their own food. Heston exudes optimism about British food.

And, of course, he's leading the way. I wanted to work at the Fat Duck because it is the most progressive kitchen in the world. What I discovered was that the Michelin three-star experience is still rooted in the earth-to-table idea, and that the most creative and advanced chef working today is a family man who loves good old-fashioned food.

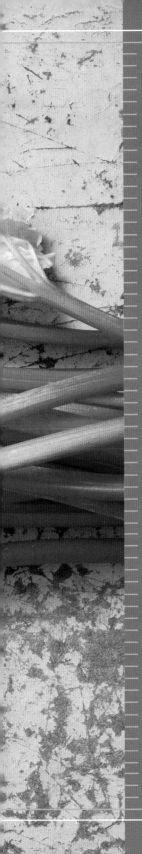

ASPARAGUS

CHERRIES

DANDELION GREENS

FAVA BEANS

WHAT TO EAT

SPRING

FIDDLEHEADS

HERBS

KING SALMON

LAMB

MAPLE SYRUP

MOREL MUSHROOMS

NEW POTATOES

PEAS

RADISHES

RAMPS

RHUBARB

SOFT SHELL CRAB

SPINACH

YOUNG LETTUCES

The most welcome of seasons needs no introduction from me. We may enjoy each of the seasons, but none provokes the same giddy excitement as spring. (No one throws on a sweater in September and sighs, "Thank *goodness* it's autumn!") We all know the signs of spring, and even the mention of them can make the heart beat a little faster: flowers pushing though the snow, buds appearing on the trees, birdsong returning in the mornings. No season yields pure joy the way spring does.

We think of spring as the moment of relief from the long days of winter, but if you eat locally, and you live anywhere it gets cold in the winter, you've still got some waiting to do. In fact, for all animals who depend on what the earth offers up, and that includes farmers and CSA members, spring is the leanest season of the year. The deer have stripped the landscape of every last edible morsel, the livestock have likely eaten through all the previous summer's hay and the farmer's family may well have emptied the larder. (It was not so long ago that many of us lived on farms and knew what it meant to be hungry in the spring.)

The first edibles to appear are not even crops, they are wild growth. Fiddleheads, nettles and dandelions are among the season's first yield, and their earthy, bitter flavor is nearly as refreshing as the first warm days. For me, ramps are the season's highlight. A wild version of leeks, ramps are versatile and delicious. I use them in soups, in risotto and grilled on their own. My favorite way to eat them is how I first had them at Craft Restaurant in New York City: simply stewed and covered in *beurre blanc*, then served with toasted brioche. Heavenly. One of our closely guarded secrets is the location of a patch of ramps in the woods near the restaurant. Every spring I am out there with the woodland creatures, prying ramps out of the cold earth. It's not as easy as trolling the aisles of the supermarket, but nature writes the menu, not me. Ramps are the first vegetable on the menu, and chefs are excited to hear that they are "up."

Morels are a little harder to come by, but they are one of the great gifts of the mushroom family. They are earthy, with a distinctive nutty taste. Like most mushrooms, morels soak up the flavor of butter or cream beautifully. Unfortunately, our local forest doesn't provide us with morels. However, I do find them growing in my backyard. We also grow our own shiitakes in bucked-up sections of timber.

Rhubarb may not be everybody's favorite vegetable, but it is certainly something I look forward to during the bitter Canadian winter. From the small, tender shoots that you can eat like sour candy to thick woody stalks that get cooked for jams and compotes, rhubarb is surprisingly versatile. It's on the menu in a few different places, just like the ramps.

I can't think of a single vegetable that heralds spring more than asparagus. Its tender flesh and subtle flavor deliver promise of the garden riches to come. Meanwhile, the menu at the Old Mill changes. Everything lightens up along with the weather; it's sautéed, steamed, poached. It's tender, herbaceous. Just like what we see out the window.

MY FIRST IMPRESSIONS OF LIFE AS A FARMER are auditory: the crackle of my car's tires on gravel, then an unfamiliar hiss of grass brushing under the car as I drive to park at the edge of the field. It is cool but promises to be sunny and the dawn sun is casting long shadows from the tops of furrows.

There are signs of young life all around me; everything is baby. Baby ducks, tiny vegetables, awkward calves, tiny shoots of fiddleheads.

For my part, I'm sluggish, and holding my Starbucks coffee protectively. I'm gazing at what seems to be a vast expanse of turned earth, but I'm thinking of tonight's specials and the fact that I'm going to be on the line, which would be tough enough even without a day of what I assume will be back-breaking labor. That is to say, I'm regretting the decision to get here so early in the morning when I was at the restaurant until eleven last night.

But then it strikes me: Chris was here long before I arrived. In the same way that we have been working for hours by the time customers get to the restaurant, Chris has been preparing the soil, nurturing the seedlings in his greenhouse and planning the operation in which I will be only a foot soldier. The ground has been worked to the point that we can walk only between rows. I feel a surge of guilt when I accidentally sink my shoe into a mound of exquisitely tender earth.

My job today is to get plugs of young onions into the ground, and after I part from my half-finished coffee and get to work, I feel as though I'm on vacation. Though the task is repetitive, I find it refreshing not to think. I slip into a sort of trance and find myself appreciating the moment, something I seldom do. I enjoy the fresh air, the near-silence. A deer pokes its head out of the treeline. I spot a

tiny purple flower growing out of a manure pile, and I see in this a kind of lesson. I realize I'm not going over the tasks that await me at the restaurant; instead, I am fully participating in the everyday miracle of life itself.

Fifteen minutes later, the vacation is over. There is no doubt about it: this is work. My knees have already begun to ache, and the soil has worked its way so far under my fingernails that it hurts. It's still early morning and the sun already feels like a wool sock wrapped around my neck. I'm ready to pack it in.

What keeps me on my knees in a patch of dirt is the realization that, for Chris, this was never meant to be a vacation. For him, it's the main event. He has one chance to get it right each year, and he has rain, snow, frost, bugs and ill-tempered chefs all working against him. This is one way his job is different from mine. In the kitchen, if you make a mistake you may curse for a moment but you can quickly start again. Out here, you have to wait another year for your next chance.

So it is with some panic that I realize no one has shown me how to actually plant an onion. Am I doing it right? I hope I am, or Chris's onion harvest is going to be a bust. This is his livelihood, and I'm just some chef joking around in the sun. I certainly would not let Chris near my hotline, much less let him cook for customers. Time to get serious now. Do it right or don't do it at all.

Four inches apart, root down, sprout up. The soft bulbs with a long, limp sprout are no good, firm bulb and small sprout . . . that's the one. In they go.

We plant six beds of onion, three white and three red. That's about six thousand onions, each planted by hand. I'm aching and spent, but farmhands John and Richard tell me this is not really the hard work. I have to agree that, despite my creaking joints, it is very enjoyable. Once I figure out what I'm doing, we joke and talk about food and stuff. For the first time in my life, "stuff" includes bugs and other things we come across in the soil. Is this a good bug or a bad bug? The more onions I plant, the more important this becomes.

Finally, mercifully, it's lunch time, and it is just like staff meal at the resto. Everyone stops what they're doing and congregates around a communal table. My hands reek of onion, but that does nothing to blunt my appetite. Today it is salad, cheese and salami, all from the farm. Chris is quite talented at charcuterie. Perhaps it's just modesty, but he claims he's "just making sausages." To me, it is pure art. I can't resist. My mind turns to the restaurant and the thought of putting a local charcuterie platter on the menu. I may be tired, but I'm clearly just getting started.

AND SO IT WENT. We still had the bok choy, mesclun and kale to get into the ground over the next few days, and it all had to be bedded in straw to keep the weeds down. The bok choy was also shrouded in ground cover (which looks like cheesecloth to me) to keep the hungry bugs out and invite in just the right amount of sunlight to keep it from bolting.

Nothing was quite as labor-intensive as planting the asparagus, which requires a lot more than the patience required to nestle a tender shoot into the cool, welcoming earth. Instead, Chris dug three-foot-deep trenches into the field with a Bobcat, which roared around and spewed black exhaust in a way I hadn't previously associated with organic farming. But I certainly wasn't going to volunteer to dig those trenches myself.

The asparagus roots emerged from burlap bags looking like stringy ginseng—in other words, nothing like the delicate green spears we think of. We covered the roots with earth at the bottom of the trenches, but we did not fill the trenches back in. That we would do gradually, over the course of the season, giving the increasingly familiar-looking shoots a chance to reach for the surface before we backfilled a little more. It began to make sense: asparagus is so tender because we cut off only the very tip of the shoot.

The thing is, it *all* makes sense. For all its mysterious unpredictability, farming, like nature, is a relentlessly logical process. Perhaps I shouldn't make a distinction between farming and nature. In fact, farming is where the distinction between nature and culture breaks down. I am reminded of the spectacle of a tomato plant growing lustily in a pile of compost. No one had planted it there. Presumably, a sheep had eaten a tomato and left its seeds in the manure, which had been piled and composted. There, the seed had done the only thing it knew how to do: it started turning itself into a plant, which would make more seeds and entice animals to carry them around by packing them in fruit. All very logical, but in this instance unforeseen.

I should be careful when I get lyrical about farms and the mystery of growth. From what I've seen of them, farms are not places for dreaming or coming up with theories about things. On a farm, the things themselves are important, and they're right in front of you. Cows caked in their own manure. Problems that need to be solved, decisions that have to be made. Farmers are intensely practical people. But that doesn't mean they're not participating in something mysterious, something they don't quite control. They are, and I'd guess that's why they do it, despite all the difficulties of their way of life.

Bettina's Wheat Story

I'm a pastry chef, so I can't be expected to be unbiased when it comes to bread. But I still have to say it: bread is civilization. A loaf of bread is the product of a whole way of life. It's about taking a handful of seeds in the spring and turning them into a delicate, fragrant, delicious loaf sometime later—something you can do only if you have farms and infrastructure and division of labor and cooperation. In short, civilization.

I know, I take bread and wheat pretty seriously. But that's the direction your thoughts take you when you're kneading and rolling dough. And I do a lot of that.

In any case, it's not just me. I worked for a summer as a cook in tree-planting camps and made bread for the planters every day. The one day I couldn't get the yeast to rise for whatever reason, some of the planters had tears in their eyes when they realized there wouldn't be fresh bread that day. It broke my heart. People have a very strong connection to bread.

I wanted to make bread that I could trace right back to the soil, so that the incomparable aroma of the loaves in the oven would be, in a sense, the scent of the turned earth. I wanted to make the whole thing, from start to finish. (I'm a Slow Food member, after all, and practicing tastes a lot better than preaching.)

It wasn't hard to settle on a variety of wheat to plant. The strain known as Red Fife was brought to Canada by a man named David Fife in 1842 and was first grown in the Otonabee region of Ontario, now known as Central Ontario. Legends place the origin of these seeds in either Scotland or Ukraine; still others believe that Red Fife is a hybrid of seeds already found in Canadian soil and seeds from Ukraine. In other words, the exact origin is unknown. But it has been grown here in Canada for a long time. If there is a Canadian wheat, it's Red Fife.

Red Fife flourished for many decades across Ontario and into the American Midwest. This grain has a unique ability to adapt to different growing conditions, so it made itself right at home in climates as different as the east coast and the prairies. Wheat, however, is like everything else: eventually, even the mightiest fall. It's a timeless story, really. Red Fife is the King Lear of grain. It was toppled from its pedestal by varieties of which it was the genetic parent. Just about every variety of wheat grown in Canada today comes from Red Fife. Thanks to Red Fife, Canada produces some of the finest wheat in the world.

Unfortunately, the original grain almost became extinct. What is so enticing about these new varieties of wheat that farmers abandoned Red Fife? They yield more. Red Fife is what is called a "landrace," which means it is not a variety in the usual sense. A landrace is a domesticated plant (or animal) that can adapt to its local environment; it is able to do this by relying on genetic variability. The seeds produce a little bit of everything, and the most viable genetic combinations for one particular time or place are the most successful. If that sounds a little like natural selection, it's because it *is* natural selection. (This is perhaps a way of saying that landraces are more natural than developed varieties of crops or breeds of animals.)

What this means in practice is that if you plant Red Fife, you stand a good chance of harvesting some wheat, since whatever comes up will adapt to the conditions. It's a kind of crop insurance. Humans have been depending on landrace wheat for ten thousand years—as long as wheat has been domesticated. If you depend on the wheat you grow to feed your family, you could do a lot worse than Red Fife.

But it also means that you may not harvest as much wheat as you would have if you'd planted a variety designed for your specific conditions. Landraces provide high yield stability, but only intermediate yield levels—you know you're going to have something to harvest, but it's not going to be as much as it could be.

Modern farming is about increasing yields, mostly through genetic engineering and chemical inputs. So it's not surprising that an old-fashioned wheat like Red Fife grew less and less popular, until it was pretty much forgotten.

In 1988, the Heritage Wheat Program began to reintroduce Red Fife commercially. One pound of the wheat was planted that year, and in 2004 seventy tons was harvested. Farmers in Saskatchewan and the Maritimes led the way.

In 2003, the Canadian Slow Food Ark of Taste adopted Red Fife wheat as its first presidium. What that means is that people (like me) who make it their business to protect foods that are in danger of being pushed aside by the global process of homogenization—and being forgotten or lost—decided that this variety of wheat was worth protecting. A presidium is a strategy Slow Food members deploy to help local artisans or farmers overcome some of the hurdles they face in pursuing their vocations. This could mean help dealing with bureaucracy, with technical problems, with marketing and even with financial challenges. (*Presidium* is Latin for "fort" or "garrison"; its role is protection.)

One of the leading growers of Red Fife in Canada is Marc Loiselle. In 2004, we contacted him about buying some flour so we could start making Red Fife bread for the restaurant. Marc is a no-nonsense Saskatchewan farmer who has been on the front lines of the fight between organic farmers and the massive agricultural companies that sell genetically modified seeds. (Because pollen from genetically modified crops migrates to surrounding fields, organic farmers face the constant threat of contamination, which could result in loss of market access, loss of income and loss of the freedom to grow what they choose. Marc and his allies took their grievance all the way to the Supreme Court of Canada.)

Marc is also a powerful advocate for Red Fife. He represented the presidium in October 2004 at the biannual *Salone del Gusto* (Hall of Taste) in Turin, Italy, where about five thousand farmers, chefs and other experts from 130 countries and 1,250 food communities got together to compare notes and enjoy good food. Artisanal Red Fife sourdough bread was reportedly a hit.

Marc was able to supply us with only ninety pounds of flour and twenty pounds of seed. We used the flour in about a day—and loved it. Although I personally can't pick out a distinguishable taste, the flour is said to have an earthy nuttiness. I think this has more to do with the wild yeast method of baking than the wheat itself; a conventional loaf made with yeast seems to taste the same. I can get behind an earthy nuttiness if others can taste it. But for me, the heritage is really the most important part.

Which brings me to that bag of seed we set aside. There it sat in a corner of the broom closet until the next spring.

We started our bread project when there weren't any leaves on the trees, and there was still a little frost on the ground. A farm can be a bleak place before the weather turns and the fields come to life. There we were, standing around at the edge of what seemed to be a vast expanse of mud, with little sense of how to turn a bag of kernels into a field of golden wheat. All we knew was that something almost magical was about to happen (though frustratingly slowly, I could tell even then).

Red Fife or otherwise, when you look at a grain of wheat, you see potential—of the stalk, of the harvest, of the bread. You think about how much work and time and energy and knowledge it takes to develop that potential. The science involved. The care involved. These are things that are completely lost with institutional farming and milling and baking. Bread doesn't work every time, and looking at the dusty little seeds and the cold mud, I had to wonder whether seeds are any more guaranteed than the bread they would hopefully become.

In any case, we had a farmer, two farmhands, the farmer's son and two chefs—and what looked like a lot of work to do. We had two very different methods of planting designed for the two beds that had been prepped for the wheat. The first we "broadcast," meaning we just tossed the seeds in the general direction of the bed and crossed our fingers. The other we planted with a contraption that resembled a bike. We put the seeds in a hopper, which tucked them directly into the ground. I'm sure this device has a proper name, but we just called it "the wheat bike."

Not only was this the first crop we planted but it was also our first opportunity to spend time with the man who would be growing our produce for the next six months. This was the very beginning of our relationship with Chris Krucker. We hit it off right away and seemed to share the same sense of humour, and we quickly made friends with his mischievous son, Kaleb, and his farmhand John. We were immediately taken by their sincerity and their infectious energy.

Once you've run a wheat bike with a guy for a while, you have a pretty good sense of whether you're going to get along.

The bike was a little tough to navigate. Getting a straight line was tricky, but since we'd already seen the broadcast method (that is, tossing handfuls of seed around onto prepared soil), how important could a straight line be anyway? We did our best and got the seeds in the ground, but even though this was fun, it was far from easy. I don't know if planting's the type of hard that begins to seem easy once you've been doing it for a while—I don't think so. Planting is hard work. You need to pay attention to what you are doing, and you can't really put it off until the next day, or week. You have a window of weather opportunity, and once the window has closed, you have to wait until next year. This makes you aware of how important it is to get as much work done as possible on the days you have. Not *exactly* making hay while the sun shines, but the same idea.

By the end of the day, we had begun to feel like farmers, not so much because we were tired and muddy, but because from the moment the crop was in the ground, we began to will the little seeds to germinate. Once you've planted a seed, you start thinking about it, especially in the days or weeks before it pushes out of the mud. How long does it take for wheat to grow? I was hoping it would be ready the next week.

A few weeks later, all we had was long grass that looked like it needed mowing. The weather seemed to be in our favor. It was a fairly wet spring, giving our wheat all the moisture it needed to be as lush as a beautiful lawn. It wasn't until the summer that our tender shoots really began to look like wheat.

FORAGING

Your neighbors may wonder what you're doing, but you can find the ingredients for a great salad in your front yard each spring, particularly if you don't use herbicides. If you do, it shouldn't be difficult to find dandelion greens somewhere else. Tender, a little bitter, delicious with crusty bread, dandelions are so addictive you may find yourself plucking your lawn before you mow it so that none of the distinctive serrated leaves go to waste.

Foraging for food is the opposite of a trip to the supermarket. Instead of having ingredients shipped from halfway around the world so you can make dinner, the forager visits each spot where the ingredients grow. It's not just local, it's micro-local. No food miles, no pesticides, no exploitation, no middleman and no markup. In fact, foraging takes money out of the equation just as it reintroduces the specificity of place and season.

It is also a fascinating window to the world around you. Even in the city, we are surrounded by food we seldom notice. There are the dandelions, of course, but also huckleberry trees in schoolyards, rosemary bushes, day lilies, juniper berries and fruit trees that no one seems to know what to do with. Apart from the raccoons, that is; they gorge each year on the cherries and apples that people can't be bothered to pick. Once you start foraging, you see the world differently— you start wondering what you can eat.

I try very hard to include a bit of foraged food in our menu, just to keep thing interesting. We're lucky to have a forest across the street—my idea of convenience food.

I began my foraging career while I was working as a chef on the west coast. We started with fiddleheads in March, added morel mushrooms and miners' lettuces through the spring, then moved on to wild huckleberries, raspberries, Pacific dewberries, lobster mushrooms, chicken-of-the-woods mushrooms and matsutake mushrooms through the summer months. The berries start fading out in the fall, just as the last mushroom varieties come to the surface. One thing about poking around in the bush, looking for tasty morsels, in the northern forests of British Columbia—there are other animals doing the same thing, and some of them are much bigger and hungrier than the average chef. One afternoon, a friend and I had to abandon our bikes when a black bear laid claim to the area we'd chosen to comb for mushrooms.

There are no bears around our current restaurant, so it is much safer to go looking for seasonal treats. We can reliably find dandelions, fiddleheads, all kinds of edible flowers (nasturtiums, chive flowers, marigolds, rose petals), milkweed, mushrooms, cedar sprouts, maple syrup and wild mustard.

Personally, I love stinging nettles. Yes, I mean the weeds with the tiny stinging hairs. To remove the sting, simply boil the nettles in water for three minutes. These weeds are densely rich in vitamins and minerals. Look for them around the perimeter of fields and along fences, and enjoy them with the pasta on page 63, or pureed and stirred into chicken noodle soup, or in an omelet or frittata.

Mushrooms are the quintessential wild food. The culinary possibilities are endless, but my favorite is the most simple:

pan-roasting with butter and herbs. Of course, there *are* mushrooms out there that you don't want to eat. Identification is key, and it's pretty straightforward once you learn it. One of the tricks to mushroom identification is to be able to identify trees. The same mushrooms always grow under the same trees. Still, you don't want to roll the dice with mushrooms. Luckily, most mycological societies hold guided foraging trips and identification seminars for neophyte mushroom gatherers.

The forest near the restaurant is also very close to my house, and I've been using it for various purposes for a long time, but it recently unveiled a secret I'm not sure I should share—but I will. I was riding my bike through the trails, and I noticed a patch of ramps, also known as wild leeks. Now, ramps are a culinary dream food, a treasure among chefs, but they are particularly hard to come by. They are available for only a few weeks in the spring, and this was the first time I had found my own. They are versatile and have a delicate oniony, garlicky flavor. They are absolutely delicious in soups, stirred into mashed potatoes, blended into a vegetable mix or simply grilled and eaten on their own. Not surprisingly, they sell for a premium across the country for four weeks a year.

And there I stood, in the dappled shade of a forest morning, in the midst of what, as far as I knew, was the largest patch of wild leeks that ever existed—right across the street from the restaurant. It was a dream come true. I couldn't imagine whom I could share this discovery with. Chef friends would be desperately jealous; others would hardly care. It was like standing alone at the edge of the Grand Canyon.

It is uniquely satisfying to wash a colander full of greens and berries you've harvested from the largely forgotten spaces of the familiar world. I suggest you try it.

COMPOST

There is a big difference between soil and dirt. A handful of fertile soil is bursting with life. It is spongy and dark, which means that it is full of carbon and organic matter, things plants need to grow. But roots don't soak up the nutrients directly. They depend on microorganisms to break down the bits of stuff in the soil, and they reward the microorganisms by offering up tiny doses of sugar in exchange. These minute creatures are often thought of as microscopic livestock. If you're going to farm, these are the animals you need to feed.

For thousands of years, farmers have maintained the fertility of their soils by adding organic matter to feed the microscopic livestock (not that they thought in these terms). By mixing together plant and animal waste—compost—and adding it to their fields the way a baker adds yeast to dough, they managed to keep their farms going year after year. Those who didn't compost quickly exhausted their fields, as their crops soaked up the soil's nutrients, leaving little but dirt behind.

This traditional method of soil improvement was one of the unintended casualties of the First World War, as leftover munitions were recycled into fertilizer (the same chemicals that make artillery shells explode also make plants grow). By the end of the Second World War, munitions factories turned to making fertilizer directly. Today's chemical fertilizers— let's call them artificial compost—depend on natural gas to the degree that fertilizer prices track gas prices.

But while chemical fertilizers allow farmers to keep yields high, they disrupt the chemical processes that keep the soil alive. In fact, much agricultural soil is little more than a dirty sponge that soaks up the fertilizer's blend of nitrogen, phosphorus and potassium each year and releases it to the growing crops. This might not be a problem if there were an infinite supply of fertilizer, if nitrogen runoff from farms didn't cause such troubling environmental problems, from algae-choked rivers and estuaries to global warming, and if the artificial version of compost actually worked. But it doesn't. Not only does it leave the soil devoid of biological life, but it deprives the produce of the complex variety of vitamins and minerals that have been leached out of the soil. (Trace mineral levels in food have fallen by about 75 percent since 1940.)

If you don't use chemical fertilizers, on the other hand, you have to find a way to supply the soil with the nutrients it needs. And if you are farming land that was once farmed chemically, you have to find a way to bring it back to life. So anyone involved in sustainable farming tends to take compost pretty seriously.

Chris Krucker calls the manure pile the "engine that drives the farm." He piles up all the manure he can find and "cooks" it for about eight months, turning it every now and then, until it becomes a crumbly, sweet-smelling black batter that he doesn't hesitate to sink his hands into.

Any extra produce goes into the pile as well. Or it's fed to the pigs and ends up in the pile eventually. Chris is always surprised when someone tells him this is a waste. The way he sees it, everything that leaves the farm has to be replaced. If you take away ten turnips, then you have to put back ten turnips' worth of nutrients. So the turnip that goes onto the compost pile isn't a waste. It's just going to feed the microorganisms rather than a CSA member. And it will be a turnip again next year anyway.

Composting happens on a rather larger scale at Laverstoke Park Farm, which I visited with Heston Blumenthal when he recommended it as the place that is "setting the bar" in agriculture. Run by former Formula One driver and massive celebrity

Jody Scheckter, Laverstoke is 2,500 acres of cutting-edge farm—in fact, it's the largest freehold private farm on the planet. There are pigs, chickens, cows, lambs and the largest herd of water buffalo in the world. Jody also grows Chardonnay grapes to make sparkling wine.

Jody exudes confidence and is obviously driven. The first thing he did was show us his books on grass—old historical books, something only a farmer could love. But he hasn't yet adjusted to the slow pace of a farmer's life. He drives like a maniac; as we toured the farm in his SUV, he almost drove away while I still had one foot out the door.

At the heart of the farm is a state-of-the-art soil laboratory. As Jody explains, if you're going to be a farmer, you need to start with soil. Soil determines what will grow and, more impor-tantly, what the livestock will eat. At Laverstoke, the animals feast on gourmet pastures where the menu includes cresses, kales,

herbs and grasses. Their diet is more complete than the average human diet. You are what you eat. And it follows that you are what your food eats as well.

But when Jody took over Laverstoke, the land was in a state of exhaustion. Conven-tional farming had depleted the soil so much that nothing would grow. Since then, the land has been in "rehab," recovering from years of chemicals under a supervised regimen of top-quality compost.

I wasn't really prepared for the sheer scale of the compost operation at Laverstoke. It sprawls over an impressive three acres. That's twenty towering rows of steaming poop, each about two hundred yards long. Each row is meticulously labeled according to the ratio if its com-ponents, so that the men and women in the lab coats will be able to keep track of which mix-ture works best. According to Jody, there is more life in a handful of compost than there are people on earth.

However, I found myself alone amidst the seemingly endless rows of steaming manure—with a mischievous smile, Heston refused to set foot into the compost area and gave me a good-natured shove so that the photographer could get a shot of at least one chef. But once I was in there, I was relieved to discover that that aroma was actually quite pleasant—musty-sweet and wholesome. Chris would have been proud of me, as I stuck my hand right in.

Inside one of the many outbuildings, technicians are hard at work on "compost tea," which is not nearly as unpleasant as it sounds. This tea is a brew that contains nutrients, enzymes, natural hormones and the complex set of bacteria and fungi that plants depend on to absorb what they need from the soil. The tea can be poured into the soil around plants that need extra nutrition, or it can be sprayed onto a plant's leaves, where the helpful microorganisms establish colonies that prevent infection.

A day at Laverstoke Park Farm is a glimpse into the future of agriculture. Like traditional farms all over the world, it is a closed loop, in which the waste of one process is the beginning of another. But Jody's farm adds a twist to the past: he has enlisted science to undo the damage that industrial farming has done and to make the farm sustainable into the future. By treating farming as an ecological rather than an industrial system, Laverstoke represents a viable model for others to aspire to.

I was lucky to spend the day with these two groundbreakers. As I listened to Jody and Heston tell stories about how they have both lost their driver's licenses for one reason or another, I realized that, although their lives seem completely different from what I do every day, they are just ordinary people doing extraordinary things.

CHEF MATTHEW DILLON

SITKA AND SPRUCE, SEATTLE, WASHINGTON

"I'm totally in!" read the email I received from Matthew Dillon when I first approached him to talk about the earth-to-table idea for this book.

It seemed like an unusually laid-back response from a guy named one of *Food & Wine*'s ten best new chefs. But once I had spoken to him, I realized this informality is not only characteristic of Dillon, it's what makes him, and his food, so irresistible. He's famous for saying that he wants his restaurant, Sitka and Spruce, to feel more like a dinner party than dining out, and that he wants to feel as though he's cooking for friends rather than patrons. He doesn't mind taking orders or serving the food himself.

"We don't have people going around filling water glasses and asking you how's your meal," he says. "I'd rather see people sitting around, having a great time, maybe eating with their hands or whatever, sharing their food."

This informal charm extends to the restaurant itself. Housed in a former doughnut shop in a strip mall, Sitka and Spruce features a very inexpensive blackboard menu that changes daily, if not more frequently—an arrangement all chefs fantasize about. Whatever is fresh and "amazing" at that moment is what gets served.

It's a style of running a restaurant that requires a lot of thought, and I ask him why he cooks this way. His answer is disarming: "It's the only way I know how—it just comes naturally to me as a chef." Dillon's training has been earth-to-table from the beginning. He started out at a well-known Seattle-area restaurant called the Herb Farm, where for the first time

Jeremy Faber, forager (left), and Matt Dillon outside Dillon's new restaurant in Seattle.

he encountered foragers walking in the back door with the day's harvest. There was dirt still on their hands, and dirt on the food: weeds, berries, fiddleheads, matsutake mushrooms. If that's what the foragers found, that's what the guests would be eating.

He has been foraging for years himself. And his friend Jeremy Faber, a former cook, now does it full-time with a company called Foraged and Found Edibles. On any given day, Faber will pull up at the restaurant with a load of, say, cauliflower mushrooms, and the chalkboard will change accordingly. You might find a nettle frittata, pan-fried sorrels, or fiddleheads with halibut, but whatever gets scrawled in chalk is going to be fresh and difficult to repeat, at least until the following year.

Still, Dillon says, it's not particularly difficult to cook this way. "As a cook, with this type of food, 90 percent of the work is done. A fresh piece of squid doesn't take much to make it tasty." You just need a little knowledge. He concedes that people who are confused in the supermarket (a lot of people, admittedly) might not be ready

to go looking for free food outside—but it's not all that challenging.

Not all of his food comes from woods and ditches, of course. He sources food scrupulously from local producers, with the result that he gets better food and gives back to the local economy at the same time. "We don't do anything fancy," he says. "We buy great food, and we treat it really well. We're not aiming for perfection here. But we know the food is going to be good. That's just a testament to the food we start with."

For Dillon, that's not just a matter of pleasure or taste. It's an example of how doing what feels right *is* right. He says it can be frustrating to overcome what he calls the "barrier of access" to sustainable food: the idea that local, organic food is expensive. Good food isn't expensive; conventional food is artificially cheap. But while it can be a long, slow process to make people understand that, the food itself makes the argument much more convincingly. "When it comes to an evaluation between good food versus conventional food," he says, "we win hands-down every time. For a chef, it is all about taste, and carrot versus carrot, we win, no question."

This battle of the carrots hints at what Dillon sees as his role. "I would like to be portrayed first as a cook, then as an artist, then as an activist working for the good of others." His latest venture is a communal space for cooking classes, readings and general "eat local" information. Like Sitka and Spruce, the new place is a "social statement" for Dillon—his effort to help shape a food culture that will benefit all

those who participate in it. "I want to help the people who are breathing the same air as I am."

Dillon's activism is tinted with an infectious optimism. When I ask him about the future of earth-to-table cooking and eating, he has an upbeat answer. "I think we are there," he says, "or at least we're starting to see the effects." He believes it is a great time to be a chef, particularly in Seattle, home to a roster of farmers and food artisans. He says he'll know that the movement toward a local, seasonal food culture has solidified into real change when the money we all spend on food starts to stick around in the local economy, rather than migrating to corporate coffers far from the markets and restaurants where the profits are collected.

In the meantime, Matthew Dillon is following his own path: raising his own bees, foraging for his own mushrooms, dressing his own meat and musing about one day growing his own produce so he can oversee the entire cycle from earth to table.

SPRING RECIPES

Sparkling Wine and Cherry Juice

Makes 8 5-ounce servings

1 lb very ripe cherries

⅓ cup vodka

1 bottle (750 mL) Prosecco

8 fresh cherries, for garnish

It should be noted that the task of pitting your own cherries is a bit daunting. But if you have a little time, the results of fresh cherry puree added to a bottle of sparkling wine is refreshing and delicious. We suggest using Prosecco, a dry and crisp Italian sparkling wine.

WASH CHERRIES AND PAT DRY. Remove stems and stones. In a food processor, pulse cherries until liquefied, about 3 minutes. Strain and discard pulp. The cherry puree will amount to about 2 cups, but a little more or less won't matter.

In a large pitcher, combine cherry puree, vodka and prosecco. Stir lightly and divide between 8 champagne flutes garnished with fresh cherries.

Salad of Peas, Feta and Mint

Serves 6

2 cups shucked fresh sweet peas

2 tbsp extra-virgin olive oil

1 tbsp red wine vinegar

1 tbsp local honey

2 tsp Dijon mustard

Salt and freshly ground black
   pepper

2 radishes, finely sliced

1 red onion, finely sliced

½ cup fresh mint leaves,
   roughly chopped

¼ cup crumbled feta cheese

Peas and mint are a wonderful combination, refreshing and light. This is a perfect spring lunch with a nice fish or lamb.

IN A MEDIUM POT of boiling salted water, blanch peas until just tender and bright green, about 2 minutes. Refresh under cold water.

In a large bowl, whisk together oil, vinegar, honey and mustard. Season to taste with salt and pepper. Add peas, radishes and onion; toss to coat. Add mint and gently toss. Sprinkle with feta.

Scrambled Eggs with Chives and Caviar

The caviar industry has been hit hard as of late for environmental reasons. Sourcing local caviar was a challenge, but the industry now supplies exceptional sturgeon caviar in the U.S. and Canada.

IN A BOWL, beat eggs with 1 tbsp of the butter.

In a large nonstick skillet, melt 1 tbsp of the butter over medium heat, tilting pan to coat evenly. Add egg mixture and cook for about 3 minutes, gently drawing a rubber spatula across the pan to form soft curds. Add the remaining butter, chives and chive flowers. Season to taste with salt and pepper. Remove from heat when still barely set; the residual heat will continue cooking the eggs.

Serve eggs on top of toasted baguette with smoked salmon and a dollop of caviar.

Serves 4

6 large organic eggs
¼ cup unsalted butter, cut into
  1-inch cubes, divided
1 tbsp minced fresh chives
1 tbsp chive flowers
  (about 2 flowers)
Salt and freshly cracked
  black pepper
4 slices toasted baguette or
  brioche or egg bread
4 thin slices smoked salmon
  (about 2 oz)
1 tbsp North American caviar
  (optional)

For a more soufflé-like version of scrambled eggs, try cooking them in a bowl over steaming water.

Grilled Asparagus with Fried Egg and Parmesan Frico

Serves 6

PARMESAN FRICO

1½ cups freshly grated
    Parmesan cheese

ASPARAGUS

1 lb fresh spring asparagus
    (about 1 bunch), woody ends
    snapped off

2 tbsp extra-virgin olive oil

1 tsp salt

1 tsp freshly ground
    black pepper

FRIED EGGS

Canola oil

6 large organic eggs

Salt and freshly cracked
    black pepper

An interesting twist on this recipe would be to substitute duck eggs; however, we have been receiving organic eggs from free-range chicken from a woman who lives about 20 minutes away. This dish is an excellent way to present these wonderful eggs.

Asparagus is the first spring vegetable, and this may be your opportunity to dust off the barbecue! Heat the grill 30 to 40 minutes before you are ready to cook.

PREPARE THE PARMESAN FRICO: Preheat oven to 350°F and line a baking sheet with a nonstick baking mat or parchment paper. Divide Parmesan into 6 distinctive piles on baking sheet, and slightly flatten each pile into a 2-inch circle. Bake until cheese is crispy and slightly browned, about 7 minutes. While still warm, remove Parmesan clusters from baking sheet to a wire rack and let cool completely. (*Make ahead: Store in an airtight container for up to 2 days.*)

Prepare the asparagus: Preheat grill or barbecue to high. On a large baking sheet, toss asparagus, olive oil and half each of the salt and pepper. Grill asparagus, turning occasionally, until slightly charred and tender, about 5 minutes. Season with remaining salt and pepper, then set aside to cool at room temperature.

Prepare the eggs: In a small skillet, heat 1 tbsp canola oil over medium heat. Break 2 eggs into a small bowl, then slip into skillet. Cook until egg whites start to firm, about 3 minutes. Season lightly with salt and pepper, and cook until whites are just firm and yolks are still soft and runny, about 1 minute. Loosen edges with a small palette knife and remove eggs to a plate. Repeat with the remaining eggs. >>>

To assemble: Divide asparagus evenly among 6 plates. Place a fried egg on top of each and lean a Parmesan frico against the yolk.

Garden Lettuce Salad

Mixed greens have really become a bit of a bore in most restaurants these days. Forgo the supermarket mixed greens and make your own seasonal blend. We change the salads often in the restaurant to include what comes out of the garden. It is much more interesting than the same old, same old. Simply wash and dry the leaves and toss with Dijon Vinaigrette (see recipe, page 295).

LETTUCE VARIETIES:

Spring and summer: Spinach, dandelion, fine herbs, romaine, red leaf, mâche, Lollo Rosso

Fall and winter: Frisée, Belgian endive, radicchio, escarole

Dandelion Salad with Poached Eggs

Serves 4

CROUTONS

2 cups day-old bread, cut into
    ½-inch cubes

2 tbsp extra-virgin olive oil

1 tsp minced fresh thyme

1 tsp minced fresh rosemary

½ tsp kosher salt

POACHED EGGS

6 cups water

¼ cup white wine vinegar

4 large organic eggs

DRESSING

8 oz slab bacon, cut into ½-inch-
    thick slices, then into 1-inch
    pieces

Canola oil

1 tbsp minced shallots

2 tbsp sherry vinegar

1 tbsp whole-grain mustard

4 cups wild dandelion leaves

This recipe is a dandelion version of Frisée aux Lardons. Wild dandelion leaves are shorter than the ones you see in the grocery store, more reminiscent of arugula. Yes, you can pick dandelions off your front lawn and eat them! The eggs are soft-poached, and if you time it properly, both the egg and dressing will be warm when you serve.

PREPARE THE CROUTONS: Preheat oven to 350°F. On a large rimmed baking sheet, toss bread with olive oil, thyme, rosemary and salt; spread out in a single layer. Bake until golden brown, about 10 minutes.

Prepare the poached eggs: In a shallow saucepan, bring water and vinegar to a boil. Reduce heat to a gentle simmer, stirring water to create a bit of a whirlpool. One at time, break eggs into a small dish, then gently slip into the simmering water. Cook until white is set and yolk is still liquid, about 3 minutes. Remove with a slotted spoon and drain well. Repeat with the remaining eggs.

Meanwhile, prepare the dressing: In a heavy skillet, sauté bacon over medium-high heat until browned and crisp, about 7 minutes. Remove with a slotted spoon to a plate lined with paper towels and set aside. Add enough canola oil to the bacon fat in the pan to equal about ⅓ cup. Add shallots, vinegar and mustard, quickly stirring to combine and scraping up any brown bits on bottom of pan. Remove from heat.

To assemble: In a large bowl, combine dandelion leaves and croutons. Add dressing and bacon pieces; toss to coat. Divide salad among 4 cool plates and top each with a poached egg.

Herbs in Five Sauces

We do not use dried herbs in our restaurant—never have, and never will. Most often, dried herbs taste of dust and can damage a dish. We have three large gardens on our property that supply us with fresh herbs most of the year. Growing herbs in your home is no more difficult than caring for the average houseplant. These plants will not only perfume your home but will also make your food more enjoyable.

Green Goddess Dressing

Makes 2 cups

1 cup Mayonnaise (see recipe, page 293)

3 salt-packed anchovy fillets, rinsed and minced

1 green onion, minced

3 tbsp minced fresh flat-leaf (Italian) parsley

2 tbsp minced fresh chives

1 tsp minced fresh tarragon

1 tbsp tarragon-flavored vinegar

Salt and freshly ground black pepper

A cult classic. This creamy, satisfying herb mayonnaise defines retro cool. Feel free to add avocado for a Californian spin.

IN A FOOD PROCESSOR, puree mayonnaise, anchovies, green onion, parsley, chives, tarragon and vinegar until smooth, about 1 minute. Season to taste with salt and pepper. (*Make ahead: Cover and refrigerate for up to 1 week.*)

TIP: Infusing vinegar is a breeze. Put herbs (tarragon, basil) into a container, like a mason jar. Pour in enough red or white wine vinegar to submerge the herbs. Store in a cool, dark place for at least three weeks. In the restaurant we put whole bunches of tarragon in a jug of white wine vinegar and leave it that way until it is all used up, and then we start again.

Pesto

This one is for pasta, and the key is not to heat the sauce—just use the heat from the pasta. Any additional heat will diminish the freshness and vibrant colour of the basil.

WITH THE FOOD PROCESSOR RUNNING, drop garlic through the feed tube and finely chop. Stop motor and add basil, pine nuts, cheese, salt and pepper. Process until combined and smooth, about 2 minutes. With motor running, slowly add oil through the feed tube, blending until just incorporated but not completely smooth.

TIP: Nuts benefit greatly from a little toasting. Preheat oven to 350ºF. Place desired nuts on an unlined, ungreased baking tray and toast for 5 to 10 minutes. A small nut, like a pine nut, will only take a couple of minutes, while a larger nut, like an almond, will take closer to 10 minutes. A toasted nut will become very fragrant when it is ready to come out of the oven.

Makes 3 cups

3 large cloves garlic
3 cups loosely packed fresh
    basil leaves
½ cup pine nuts, toasted
½ cup coarsely grated
    Parmigiano-Reggiano cheese
1 tsp salt
½ tsp freshly ground
    black pepper
½ cup extra-virgin olive oil

Citrus Gremolata

A great garnish for rich dishes like the Braised Short Ribs (p. 198) or Braised Lamb Shanks (page 250). Helps to cut the fat!

IN A BOWL, combine parsley, lemon zest and garlic. Season to taste with salt and pepper. (*Make ahead: Cover and refrigerate for up to 5 days.*)

Makes ¼ cup

3 tbsp minced fresh flat-leaf
    (Italian) parsley
1 tsp finely grated lemon or
    orange zest
1 medium clove garlic, minced
Salt and freshly ground
    black pepper

Gribiche

This sauce is like a mayonnaise with a twist: instead of using raw egg yolks, it uses cooked. Traditionally, it is meant to liven up cold leftover meat. I love to drape this sauce over boiled asparagus or new potatoes.

USING A MORTAR AND PESTLE, mash egg yolks, gradually adding oil. Once thickened, add vinegar, gherkins, capers, parsley, chervil, tarragon, salt and pepper. Rough chop egg whites and stir into sauce.

TIP: To hard-boil eggs, place in a pot with enough cold water to cover and bring to a boil over medium heat. After 10 minutes, the eggs will be perfectly hard-boiled. Let cool, then peel off shells and separate yolks from whites.

Makes 1½ cups

2 hard-boiled eggs (see tip),
    whites and yolks separated
1 cup extra-virgin olive oil
1 tbsp white wine vinegar
1 tsp chopped gherkin pickles
1 tsp chopped drained capers
1 tsp chopped fresh parsley
1 tsp chopped fresh chervil
1 tsp chopped fresh tarragon
½ tsp salt
½ tsp freshly ground
    black pepper

Salsa Verde

This sauce pairs best with fish. It has quite a tang from the anchovies and capers, but will give your fish a fresh finish.

USING A MORTAR AND PESTLE, in batches if necessary, pound parsley, mint and oregano into a paste. Work in the oil and transfer to a bowl.

Using mortar and pestle, pound garlic and anchovy into a paste; add to herb mixture.

Using mortar and pestle, gently pound capers until slightly crushed; add to herb mixture. Stir in the remaining oil and lemon juice. Season to taste with salt and pepper. (*Make ahead: Cover and refrigerate for up to 1 week.*)

Makes 2 cups

1 cup chopped fresh parsley
¼ cup coarsely chopped fresh mint
1 tbsp coarsely chopped fresh
    oregano
¾ cup extra-virgin olive oil,
    divided
1 small clove garlic
1 salt-packed anchovy fillet,
    rinsed and bones removed
2 tbsp drained capers
Juice of ½ lemon
Salt and freshly cracked
    black pepper

Gnudi with Ramps, Morels and Fiddleheads

Serves 6

GNUDI

1 cup freshly grated Parmesan
    cheese

1 cup fresh ricotta cheese

2 large organic eggs

1 large organic egg yolk

1 tsp ground nutmeg

½ cup all-purpose flour

2 tbsp minced fresh chives

Salt and freshly ground
    black pepper

4 cups semolina

MUSHROOM SAUTÉ

1 tbsp extra-virgin olive oil

1 tbsp unsalted butter

2 cups morels

1 cup chopped ramps

1 cup fiddleheads, blanched

CREAM SAUCE

3 cups whipping (35%) cream

2 cups freshly grated Parmesan
    cheese

This recipe has been made famous by the Spotted Pig in New York City. We were able to take some of our staff there to eat and discovered the secret to their "naked pasta." When you cover the cheese mixture with semolina and chill it overnight, pasta forms around the outside of the gnudi.

PREPARE THE GNUDI: In a large bowl, combine Parmesan, ricotta, eggs, egg yolk and nutmeg. Using a whisk or hand blender, whip mixture until smooth and airy. Fold in flour and chives. Season to taste with salt and pepper.

With floured hands, roll gnudi into 1-inch balls, placing them in a clean bowl. Cover gnudi balls completely with semolina. Cover and refrigerate overnight.

Bring a large pot of water to a boil. Add gnudi and reduce heat to a simmer. Working in batches, poach gnudi until they float to the top, about 4 minutes.

Meanwhile, prepare the mushroom sauté: In a large skillet, heat oil and butter over medium-high heat. Add morels, ramps and fiddleheads; sauté until golden and softened, about 15 minutes. Remove from heat and set aside. Remove the mushroom mixture from the pan with a slotted spoon and drain the fat from the pan before adding the cream in the next step.

Prepare the cream sauce: In the same skillet, heat cream over high heat. Cook until reduced by half, about 5 minutes. Turn heat off and stir in Parmesan until well combined.

To assemble: Divide gnudi evenly among 6 bowls and top with cream sauce, then the mushroom sauté.

Clockwise from top left: cheese and eggs; grating nutmeg; mixing the gnudi; rolling them into balls; placing the balls in semolina; covering the balls with semolina; the finished product.

King Salmon with Spring Salad

Serves 6

6 stalks asparagus, sliced on
　the diagonal

1 cup shucked fresh sweet peas

2 tbsp canola oil

6 pieces wild salmon (preferably
　king) (each 5 oz), skin on

6 large red oak lettuce leaves

3 tbsp Dijon Vinaigrette (see
　recipe, page 295), divided

½ bunch green onions, thinly
　sliced

2 tbsp Salsa Verde (see recipe,
　page 59)

12 nasturtium blossoms

Salt and freshly cracked
　black pepper

This dish appears on the menu when the first salmon arrive at the restaurant. King salmon (also called red spring or Chinook) are large and relatively lean, so roasting the fish after searing for a nice crust is a good option if you have a cast-iron skillet.

IN A LARGE POT of boiling generously salted water, cook asparagus until just tender, about 3 minutes. Using tongs, remove asparagus and plunge into a large bowl of ice water to stop the cooking. Drain and set aside.

Bring the water back to a boil and cook the sweet peas until just tender, about 3 minutes. Remove with a slotted spoon and plunge into ice water. Drain and set aside.

In a large skillet, heat oil over high heat. Add salmon, skin side down, and cook, turning once, until golden and crisp on both sides, about 10 minutes. Set aside.

In a bowl, toss lettuce with 1 tbsp of the vinaigrette. Place a leaf on each of 6 plates. In the same bowl, toss asparagus, peas, onions and the remaining vinaigrette; divide among plates. Place a piece of salmon on each salad and top with 1 tsp salsa. Garnish with nasturtium blossoms. Season to taste with salt and pepper.

Stinging Nettle Linguini

Nettles have bright green leaves that are delicious when cooked. They grow as a weed around the perimeter of the farm, and in the very early spring, they are one of the first things we are able to "harvest" from ManoRun. Be warned, they are named correctly and will sting you. Be sure to wear gloves when picking them. But rest assured, they completely lose their sting when cooked.

IN A LARGE POT of boiling salted water, cook linguini until almost al dente (tender to the bite), about 6 minutes. Add nettle leaves and cook until tender, about 1 minute. Drain and transfer pasta and nettles to a large bowl.

Toss linguini and nettle leaves with butter, chili flakes, oil and lemon juice. Season to taste with salt and pepper. Serve as soon as butter has melted, sprinkled with cheese.

Serves 6

1 lb dried linguini pasta
6 cups young nettle leaves
½ cup unsalted butter,
    chopped into small cubes
1 tbsp chili flakes
3 tbsp extra-virgin olive oil
1 tbsp fresh lemon juice
Salt and freshly cracked
    black pepper
½ cup freshly grated Parmesan
    cheese

Spring Lamb Shoulder

Serves 8

3 lemons

1 lb tomatoes (about 4)

1 boneless lamb shoulder
   (4 to 5 lbs), trimmed

Salt and freshly cracked
   black pepper

10 large cloves garlic (about
   2 bulbs), peeled

2 cinnamon sticks

2 cups port

3 dried bay leaves

2 sprigs fresh thyme

Saffron Rice
   (see recipe, opposite)

The natural life cycle of a lamb starts with birth in the spring, a summer spent in the pasture and arrival on the table in September. This longer life leads to a wonderful depth of flavor, preferred by chefs. In the era where tender meat is king, the notion of spring lamb has become something of a marketing ploy. Spring shoulder is a favorite roast of mine since it seems to attain both tenderness and flavor.

IN A LARGE POT of boiling salted water, cook lemons for 2 minutes. Using tongs, remove lemons, let cool slightly, then cut each into 8 pieces. Set aside.

Cut an X in the bottom of each tomato. Add tomatoes to the pot of water, making sure there is enough water to cover the tomatoes. Bring back to a boil and cook until the skins start to peel back, 30 to 60 seconds. Using tongs, remove tomatoes and plunge into a large bowl of ice water to stop the cooking. The skins should slip off. Cut the peeled tomatoes in half and squeeze gently so that the seeds drip out.

Season lamb generously with salt and pepper. Heat a large, heavy roasting pan over two burners turned to high heat until hot but not smoking. Add lamb and sear, turning occasionally, until well browned on all sides, about 20 minutes. Using tongs, transfer lamb to a baking sheet and set aside. Pour off and discard excess fat and return roasting pan to stovetop.

Add lemons to roasting pan and cook over medium heat, stirring and crushing with a wooden spoon and scraping up any brown bits on the bottom of pan, about 4 minutes. Add garlic and cinnamon; sauté until aromatic, about 6 minutes. Add tomatoes, port, bay leaves and thyme; bring to a boil. Season to taste with salt and pepper. Return lamb to pan. Cover pan tightly with foil   >>>

and cook until lamb is tender, about 2 hours. Remove cinnamon, bay leaves and thyme.

Carve and serve with Saffron Rice.

Saffron Rice

Our version of Indian pilaf, this is a great way to cook rice, and you can add lots of different flavors for variety. I wash the rice to rinse off some of the starch. You don't really have to do this, but it helps create a lighter final dish. Be sure not to add soft herbs until the end, or they will brown.

IN A LARGE BOWL, wash rice in 4 changes of cold water until water is almost clear. Drain and set aside.

In a large saucepan, combine stock with saffron and bring to a boil; reduce heat, cover and keep at a low simmer.

Preheat oven to 375°F. In a large baking dish, heat oil over medium heat for 2 minutes. Add almonds, tossing to coat. Add onion and garlic; sauté until onion is pale golden, about 8 minutes. Add rice, stirring until well coated. Add stock and bring to a simmer.

Cover dish and transfer to oven; bake until rice is tender and liquid is absorbed, about 20 minutes. Let stand, covered, for 15 minutes. Fluff with a fork and season to taste with salt and pepper. Sprinkle with cilantro and paprika.

Serves 8

3 cups white basmati rice
4 cups Chicken Stock
   (see recipe, page 297)
¼ tsp saffron threads
⅓ cup canola oil
¼ cup slivered almonds
1 large onion, minced
1 clove garlic, minced
Salt and freshly ground
   black pepper
¼ cup minced fresh cilantro
1 tsp smoked paprika

Slow-Roasted Pork Shoulder

Serves 6

4-lb boneless pork shoulder
   blade (butt), untied if
   necessary
2 tbsp extra-virgin olive oil
2 tbsp fennel seeds, crushed
Salt and freshly cracked
   black pepper
1 cup barbecue sauce
   (use your favorite)
6 fresh white burger buns
1 recipe Pickled Fennel
   (page 127)

Pulled pork is a personal specialty, but revealing my secret recipe in this book? Impossible. Instead, here is a great version of a favorite. The secret remains safe. This pork can be used on pizza, sandwiches and pasta.

SCORE PORK SHOULDER all over with a sharp knife. In a small bowl, combine oil, fennel, salt and pepper to make a paste. Rub this marinade all over the shoulder. Transfer to a large bowl or resealable plastic bag. Cover or seal and refrigerate for at least 4 hours or for up to 24 hours.

Preheat oven to 300°F. Place pork in a roasting pan and roast, uncovered, until meat is tender and shreds easily or until a meat thermometer inserted in the center registers 160°F, about 6 hours. Transfer pork to a cutting board, tent with foil and let stand for 20 minutes to cool. Slice into thin slices and place in a large bowl. Pour in cooking juices and barbecue sauce, tossing to coat. Serve in burger buns with pickled fennel as a topping or a side dish.

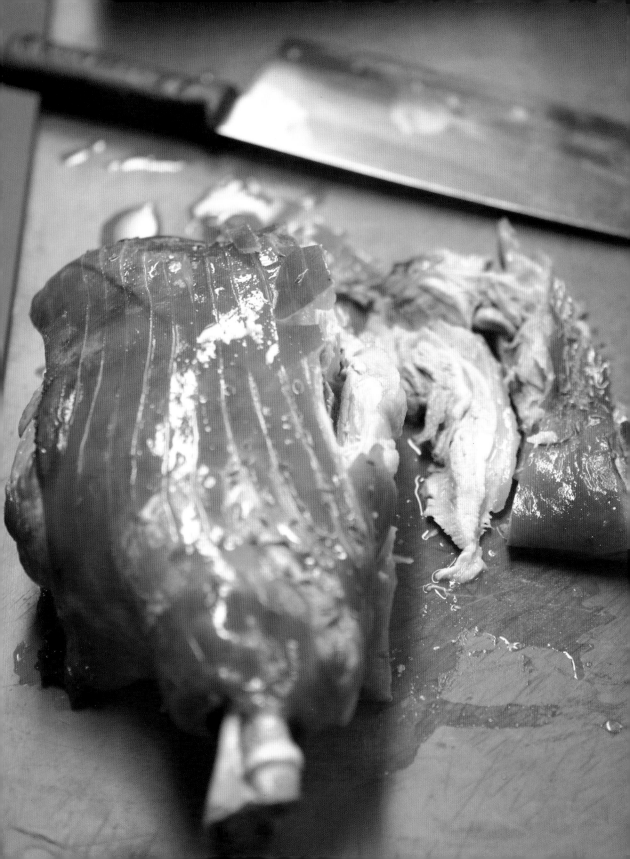

Penne with Asparagus Carbonara

Serves 6

2 lbs asparagus (about 2
   bunches), woody ends
   snapped off
1 lb dried penne pasta
8 oz slab bacon, cut into
   ½-inch-thick slices,
   then into 1-inch pieces
8 large organic egg yolks
1½ cups freshly grated
   Parmesan cheese (about
   5 oz)
½ cup unsalted butter,
   cut into cubes
3 tbsp fresh thyme, minced
3 tbsp extra-virgin olive oil
Salt and freshly cracked
   black pepper

This dish should be saved for fantastic eggs. If you have a chance to purchase organic eggs straight from the farm you should definitely plan on making this recipe that day.

CUT OFF ASPARAGUS TIPS and slice stalks diagonally into ¾-inch pieces. Set aside.

In a large pot of boiling salted water, cook penne until al dente (tender to the bite), about 15 minutes.

Meanwhile, in another large pot of boiling salted water, cook asparagus tips and stalks until tender, about 4 minutes. Drain and set aside.

In a heavy skillet, cook bacon over medium-high heat until browned and crisp, about 7 minutes. Remove with slotted spoon to a plate lined with paper towels and set aside.

In a large bowl, beat egg yolks. Add 2 tbsp of the cheese and the butter. Drain penne, add to egg mixture and toss to coat. Add asparagus, bacon, thyme and oil; toss to coat. Season to taste with salt and pepper.

Serve immediately, sprinkled with the remaining cheese.

Sorrel Frittata

Traditionally, sorrel is identified with spring. In our garden, sorrel flourishes all summer and into fall. The color of sorrel may fade as it cooks, but the flavor hangs on to make this frittata a winner most of the year.

PREHEAT OVEN TO 450°F. In a bowl, lightly beat eggs. Add sorrel and half the goat cheese. Season to taste with salt and pepper.

In a 9- or 10-inch nonstick ovenproof skillet, heat oil and butter over medium-high heat, tilting pan to coat evenly. Pour in egg mixture and cook until almost set, about 3 minutes. Sprinkle with the remaining goat cheese. Transfer to oven and bake until bottom and sides are crisp and golden and top is still slightly runny, about 5 minutes. Let rest for about 10 minutes before slicing into wedges.

Serves 4

6 large organic eggs
1 cup loosely packed fresh sorrel
    leaves, roughly chopped
1 cup soft goat cheese
Salt and freshly cracked
    black pepper
2 tbsp extra-virgin olive oil
2 tbsp unsalted butter

Rhubarb Compote

Cooking this spring compote over low heat, stirring occasionally, helps to release the rhubarb's natural juices and preserve the integrity and shape of the fruit.

Makes 1 cup

1 lb rhubarb, leaves removed,
    stalks cut into ¾-inch
    pieces
¼ cup lightly packed
    brown sugar
2 tbsp water

IN A LARGE SAUCEPAN, combine rhubarb, brown sugar and water, stirring to coat. Cover and cook over low heat, stirring occasionally, until rhubarb is tender, about 5 minutes. Drain fruit and discard juices. (*Make ahead: Cover and refrigerate for up to 2 days.*)

Rhubarb Fool

Serves 6

3 cups whipping (35%) cream
1 cup Rhubarb Compote
    (see recipe, above)

The rhubarb compote is great to serve as a sauce over ice cream, but a simple way to dress it up a little is the Rhubarb Fool. Serve in clear dish to show off the pretty pink swirls.

IN A LARGE BOWL, using an electric mixer or by hand, whip cream until soft peaks form. Gently fold in rhubarb compote, in two batches, leaving some streaks.

Cherries Affogato

Traditionally, ice cream is "drowned" (or *affogato*) with a shot of espresso. So we decided to change it up a little and douse the ice cream in these boozy cherries!

PLACE PITTED CHERRIES in a large bowl and toss with ¼ cup of sugar. Cover and refrigerate overnight.

The next day, strain the cherries with a colander and set juice and cherries aside separately. You should have about ½ cup of juice (a little more or less is not a big deal).

In a medium saucepan, combine the remaining sugar, star anise, cinnamon stick, vanilla bean, cherry juice and lemon juice; bring to a boil over high heat. Reduce heat and simmer until sugar is completely dissolved, about 5 minutes. Allow liquid to cool for 5 minutes, remove the star anise and cinnamon stick with a spoon; stir in Kirsch and cherries. While the cherry sauce is still warm, divide evenly among 6 bowls of vanilla ice cream (page 134).

Serves 6

1 lb sweet Bing cherries, stemmed and pitted

½ cup granulated sugar, divided

2 whole star anise

1 cinnamon sticks

1 vanilla beans, halved

1 tbsp freshly squeezed lemon juice

¼ cup cherry eau de vie (Kirsch)

Maple Shoofly Pie

Makes one 9-inch pie or
eight 3-inch individual tarts

SHELL(S)

½ recipe Pâte Sucrée (page 307)

CRUMB TOPPING

½ cup all-purpose flour

¼ cup lightly packed brown
  sugar

1 tsp salt

½ tsp ground cinnamon

¼ tsp ground nutmeg

½ cup unsalted butter,
  chilled and cut into cubes

FILLING

1 cup pure maple syrup (the
  best quality you can find)

¼ cup mild (light) molasses

¼ cup corn syrup

3 large organic eggs, lightly
  beaten

½ tsp baking soda

¼ tsp salt

Just as winter leaves us, the maple trees start flowing! This classic pie with a maple twist is named for the necessity of shooing the flies away as the sweet, sticky ingredients cool.

PREPARE THE SHELL(S): On a lightly floured surface, roll out pâte sucrée to fit a 9-inch pie plate or eight 3-inch tart pans. Press into plate or pans, leaving a ¾-inch overhang. Run overhang under and crimp edges. Prick all over with a fork. Chill shell(s) for at least 30 minutes or for up to 12 hours.

Preheat oven to 325°F, with rack placed in the bottom third.

Prepare the crumb topping: In a bowl, whisk together flour, brown sugar, salt, cinnamon and nutmeg. Cut in butter and work mixture with your fingers until it forms a fine, crumbly texture; set aside.

Prepare the filling: In a bowl, combine maple syrup, molasses and corn syrup. Stir in eggs, baking soda and salt. Pour into prepared pie shell(s) and sprinkle evenly with crumb topping.

Place pie(s) on a rimmed baking sheet and bake until pastry is golden and topping is crisp and golden, about 50 minutes. Let cool on wire rack for at least 30 minutes or for up to 2 hours before serving.

Buttermilk Panna Cotta

Makes 6 individual desserts

¼ cup cold water

1 packet (½ oz) powdered
 unflavored gelatin

2 cups buttermilk

2 cups whipping (35%) cream

1 cup granulated sugar

1 vanilla bean, split lengthwise
 and seeds scraped out

Panna cotta, a custard set with gelatin, is an excellent way to present fruit all year round. The tartness of the buttermilk will complement both sweet summer compotes and sugary winter preserves.

IN A SMALL BOWL, combine cold water and gelatin; let bloom for 10 minutes.

 Meanwhile, in a saucepan, combine buttermilk, cream, sugar and vanilla bean and seeds. Bring to a boil over high heat. Remove from heat and let stand for 5 minutes, allowing vanilla flavor to infuse the mixture.   >>>

Strain through a fine-mesh sieve into a bowl and discard vanilla. Stir in gelatin mixture.

Divide mixture among 6 lightly oiled ½-cup ramekins (or 6 4-ounce Rum Baba molds, as we use in the restaurant for a tall, commanding presence—see photo, opposite). Refrigerate until set, about 4 hours. (*Make ahead: Cover and refrigerate for up to 2 days.*)

Turn out of ramekins, if desired, when serving. Serve with rhubarb compote or your favorite fresh fruit sauce.

TIP: Gelatin will continue to set for up to 2 days after its initial incorporation, so you can play with the texture and solidity of your panna cotta by serving it earlier or later. Leaving it to bloom for too long will give you a bouncy, rubbery product. On the other hand, if you do not let it set for long enough, the custard will be impossible to turn out of the ramekins. The ideal texture is firm enough to jiggle on a spoon but soft enough to melt on your tongue. Gelatin can be found in the baking section of most grocery stores.

TIP: Vanilla is the second most expensive flavor in the world. It is nice to know that there are a few ways to make the flavour last. What we usually do at the restaurant is make vanilla sugar. Once you've used the bean to flavor your recipe, rinse and dry it, add it to a container of granulated sugar and leave it there for about two weeks to flavor the sugar. This sugar can then be used to sweeten coffee or tea, or added to cookie recipes and other baked goods and desserts. Vanilla sugar will keep indefinitely in an airtight container.

Milk and Honey Bread

Makes 2 loaves

6 cups all-purpose flour
   (approx.), divided
2 tsp kosher salt
1 tsp dry instant yeast
1 cup whole milk
¼ cup local honey
2 tbsp unsalted butter, melted

Our restaurant has a long history of bread-making; we have been selling loaves of bread for many years now and roll 70 loaves each day. Milk and honey bread is our standard white loaf. The milk and honey give the crust a beautiful dark color and add to the delicious texture of the bread.

IN A BOWL, whisk together 2 cups of the flour, salt and yeast.

In a large bowl, whisk together milk and honey. Beat in dry ingredients until combined. Using a spoon, gradually work in the remaining flour until dough pulls away from the sides of the bowl.

Turn out onto a lightly floured surface and knead until dough is smooth and elastic, about 10 minutes. Place in a large greased bowl, turning dough to grease all over. Cover with a tea towel and let rise in a still oven, with light on and door closed, until doubled in size, about 1½ hours.

Punch down dough and turn out onto a lightly floured surface. Divide in half, roll into two loaves and place into two lightly oiled loaf pans. Cover with tea towels and let rise in still oven until doubled in size, about 45 minutes. Brush tops with melted butter.

Preheat oven to 400°F. Bake loaves until they are golden brown and sound hollow when tapped on the bottom, about 30 minutes. Let cool on wire racks.

WHAT TO EAT

SUMMER

If spring is green, summer is red.

Overnight, it seems, what were once vulnerable little plants flex their muscles and suddenly the farm is crowded with improbably colorful produce: rich, musky tomatoes, sweet, jewel-like strawberries, sleek, plump cherries. Corn, perhaps my favorite, is later. And, of course, it's not red.

The tastes change along with the colors. The delicate shoots of spring give way to the robust, fleshy delights of summer. Nothing compares to a blood red tomato, still warm from the sun, or to a strawberry so perfectly ripe it seems about to burst. The vine vegetables are nearly as assertive: the lemony scent of beans and the floral sweetness of peas.

But nothing announces the arrival of summer quite like strawberries. The fact that there is a bit of a frenzy during strawberry season tells me that seasonal eating is not such a foreign idea, after all. These little gems are available for only about five weeks a year, and while they are around people go crazy. Picking their own berries, making their own jam, serving them in shortcakes and ice cream and pies. I was unbelievably excited when I learned that Chris was growing strawberries—and that I could use these berries for whatever I wanted. And the best part was that they were growing right next to the rhubarb: foods that grow together, go together, and what could be a better summer treat than a strawberry-rhubarb pie?

Cooking is easy in the summer: just don't ruin the way the food already tastes. What is easier than boiling some corn, or preparing some berries? A tomato salad is easy. Grilling is easy. Life is good in the summer. In fact, for a chef, all this abundance makes it tough to settle on a menu, as I don't have enough customers to eat it all. Even if I rule out all the things we eat at other times of year, I could easily have fifty dishes on the menu.

And each of them would be something I could be proud of in a way I hadn't been before. I'd planted some of this food, washed it, weighed it when it arrived from the farm. This mesclun, spinach,

arugula, these onions—they'd passed through my hands and my friends' and colleagues' hands more than once. Every member of the restaurant's staff showed up at the farm at least once a month, sometimes more. One guy, Wyatt, actually gave up the restaurant altogether to try his hand at farming. (It was a trade-off, though, as Chris's daughters, first Naomi and now Nakita, have been working in the kitchen.) But even those of us who didn't go completely over to the other side still found that we have a new attachment to the food—a new kind of satisfaction in a job well done, a new sense of the intrinsic value of food, and even a new kind of hunger.

WHAT I'M STRUCK BY in my first year as a farmhand is this abundance, the way the frosty mud has been transformed in a few weeks into something almost unrecognizable. There is life everywhere. Fat,

assertive chickens fuss all over the farm, everywhere but in the pen, it seems. The trees too, ancient maples that tower over the old farmhouse, are now full of life, and the breeze in their leaves provides the background soundtrack for everything we do around the place (resting in the shade, in particular).

How did there ever come to be such a concept as a "factory farm"? Factories bring in standardized inputs (raw materials), run them through a routinized process and churn out a whole lot of identical things. Now, I know there are monstrous, sprawling farms cultivated by machines the size of houses that produce tons and tons of commodities such as corn and soybeans (which are themselves destined for factories, where they will be turned in sweeteners and ethanol and breakfast cereals). But that's not what people think of when they imagine a farm. Farms have slightly dilapidated barns and listless cows and battered pickups and dusty old tractors that have seen many years of crops come and go. And I'd add this: there is nothing predictable or standardized about a real farm.

It seems to me that farmers don't really grow things. They help some things grow, and they do their best to prevent others from growing, but they're never going to make something grow if it doesn't feel like it. And they're certainly not going to stop anything from growing for long.

Walking around ManoRun Farm in the summer is like stumbling into an exhibit from a biology course. This is life. Somehow, the tiny seeds and feeble seedlings have squeezed their roots into the soil and are reaching for the sun. The muddy fields have disappeared beneath a jungle of green, as leaves unfurl to compete for their share of the sunlight.

Strawberries, for all their delicacy, know how to fight for their place in the sun. Since I was obsessed with getting strawberry dishes on the menu, I was watching the deliveries closely. Chris had set up a pretty good system of dropping off produce to the restaurant, and when that didn't work we always had cooks at the farm to pick up items that might not have made it otherwise. Arugula, mesclun, Swiss chard—all seemed to arrive at the restaurant with ease and in volume. However, the strawberries were somehow being lost in the shuffle. How could that be? If strawberries were the most important thing in the world to me, were they not the most important thing in the world to everyone else? Apparently not.

I took it upon myself to check out the state of the strawberries in the field, and what I found was terribly upsetting: there were more strawberries than anyone knew what to do with. This is not to say that the strawberries weren't being harvested—they were. Chris's CSA customers had to be about the luckiest in the province, each getting a pint or two in their vegetable packages. But there were way too many berries for the farmers to keep up with. Since the end of June and beginning of July had been very hot, the strawberries were growing fast and furious. But then, so was everything else. Chris just couldn't harvest everything as fast as it was growing.

Bettina and I headed out to the field early on a Saturday morning to bring in as many strawberries as we could and save them from turning to mush in the fields. Our spirits were high, but we quickly realized this was not a problem that could be fixed by two people alone—there were a lot of strawberries. At one point, a boy from the farm next door came over to give us a hand, but he was confused by my determination to harvest *all* of the berries.

Then I got it. Some food has to die in the field. And that's fine. For Chris, food that doesn't end up on someone's plate is not necessarily wasted. It may end up as chicken food or pig food, and if it gets left in the field, it is fertilizer for the next year. To be honest, I'd rather not think that the food I worked so hard on (never mind Chris!) might end up feeding livestock or soil bacteria rather than, say, me. But I don't control nature.

AND OF COURSE, not all of the ambitious plants sprouting up at ManoRun Farm are destined for someone's dinner plate. Many of them are weeds. In fact, *most* are weeds. They not only grope their way into ditches and manure piles, but are quite at home in the rich, laboriously tilled earth set aside for the crops. And their will to live is

frightening. They seem to spring up the moment you turn your back, and hang on with the tenacity of a family of cockroaches.

It's not difficult to see the appeal of chemical herbicides or genetically modified strains of crops once you've seen weeds gobble up all your hard work. And when I say all, I mean whole fields. Early that spring, Chris had rented some land nearby to set aside as the "restaurant field." We figured out just how much spinach we'd need, how many carrots and potatoes, and planted them in a field all our own just down the road from ManoRun. Then we all went about our business. When it occurred to us a short time later that we might want to have a look at the field and perhaps pull some weeds, we were in for a disappointing shock. The weeds had recognized a good thing when they saw it and had completely colonized the field. The hapless spinach and carrots never stood a chance.

But that's nature for you. Farming means participating in a wild biological process. And as Chris says, the weeds are indigenous; the cucumbers aren't. The weeds have not only an advantage but a pretty good claim to the land. Farming is a little like trying to protect a minnow in a sea of weeds. You can do it either by paying attention to what is going on in the soil or by soaking everything in toxins.

(On the other side of the ledger, it's usually the case that in addition to getting too much of what you don't want, you get too much of what you *do* want. Then you have to go out into the field and carefully cull the unwanted turnips and carrots and everything else, so that they don't compete with each other and end up stunted.)

I also have to remember how much work the farmer is doing before he even thinks about weeding acres and acres. Consider how much time it takes to care for a dog. Now imagine three pigs, six cows, twenty chickens, eight goats, five horses, an indeterminate number of ducks and turkeys, a temperamental tractor, a thresher that dates from the Summer of Love, a few dozen CSA clients and a couple of high-maintenance chefs. Then keep in mind that weeding is a colossal pain in the neck—you can't just lay waste to the crafty devils. You have to pull them out gently, so as to avoid tearing up the roots of the crops you're trying to protect. No wonder it once seemed a good idea to save some time and drown the weeds in toxic chemicals.

But it's not just about saving time or making things easier. If it were, we could all live on peanut butter sandwiches, I suppose. But we prefer things that are more difficult and take longer. I have no doubt that even the most hard-bitten capitalist would rather drink wine that was exactingly harvested and fermented, and carefully aged. When I get impatient, I think of Paul Bertolli, a big influence on my career. He's a former chef at Chez Panisse and is now an artisanal charcuterie and balsamic vinegar maker. He knows he won't be around to taste his vinegar, since the stuff won't be ready for another fifty years. And he still makes it. All of which is to say that if haste is not even necessarily good in itself, it's certainly not much of an argument for poisoning the soil.

Another thing I try to keep in mind whenever I wish I were free to use chemical weapons on the bloody weeds is that humans are a species like any other, and from the point of view of natural selection, fitness for survival is measured by a species' ability to adapt to its environment. When we're out there in the merciless sun, tugging at goldenrod and thistles and ragweed, that's what we're doing. Adapting to the environment.

Watching Chris, I am struck by how creative this process of adaptation is. Like cooking, farming is all about knowledge and competence. You have to *know* all kinds of things, and then you have to be able to mobilize your knowledge to solve the problems that spring up like weeds. Chris has to know what's important, what to be looking out for, how to fix this or that. Farmers don't have an easy job—I figured that out pretty quickly. And they don't seem to be an especially cheerful bunch, either (though Chris is not a typical farmer in this regard; both he and his wife, Denise, are infectiously energetic). But in my experience, farmers seem happy in some deep-rooted way, and I expect that, as much of a pain in the neck as it may be, adaptation and figuring things out is a very satisfying way to get through each day.

Still, it's not the only way. And it's hard to beat a good lunch. On Thursdays, all of the farmhands and the CSA members who have shown up to pitch in sit down for lunch together. We feel we deserve a bit of a treat after sorting the produce and packing the CSA boxes—indeed, it's just the sort of work you think will never come to an end. After spending a morning doubled over in the field harvesting produce, we then have to divide it all up into packages for the customers to pick up, or for Chris to deliver. And Chris has dozens of customers—that's a lot of dividing!

I am in charge of green onions, but there are also potatoes, carrots, green beans, peas, herbs, tomatoes and the rest of the bounty of the farm to take care of. Each one has to be counted and divided. The packages are then broken down by size (that is, small, medium and large). It is definitely one of those moments when you realize that, though you may be certain *that* you want to do something and know *why* you want to do it, your conviction is not much help when it comes to the question of *how* you're going to do it.

But this is the kind of frustration that lasts only as long as the task at hand. The second you're done, a weight is lifted and you're glad you showed up. And it certainly helps to be working with others who are there for the same reason. Once our work is complete, we take our spots at a long table laden with food produced right there on the farm: tomato and cucumber salads, freshly baked bread, handmade sausages, tender fruit. Not a weed in sight. Unless you look across the road.

Bettina's Wheat Story

I think we all have an image in our minds of a summer wheat field: the clear blue skies, the lazy ripples on the golden sea of grain, the buzz of cicadas, the sun beating down just firmly enough to convince you that work can wait.

In the case of our acres of Red Fife, the sun was right. There was not much we could do but wait for it to mature. But we still had plenty to do, and we had plans for that wheat.

The first time I met Chris, he was interested in bread and wanted to know everything I knew about flour. I imagine my eyes must have lit up at the prospect of a good conversation about the secrets of the arcane world of wheat—information I usually have to keep to myself because most people find it so boring they go cross-eyed! Gluten content, protein content, mineral content, whole wheat, bran, white, rye; it's not very dazzling. But Chris had a ton of questions about the difference between white and whole wheat flours and was determined to get to the bottom of things. We spent some time chatting, and he told me about his plans to sell loaves of bread to his CSA customers.

Good luck, I told him. Give me a call, I added, if there is anything I can do to help. I didn't realize I'd soon be up to my armpits in wet clay.

Chris was building a bread oven. That is, he was finishing one he'd begun the year before. He'd already built the base and ordered the cast-iron door. Wood-burning stone ovens are awesome. We had one built at our sister restaurant in Burlington, and the pizzas that come out of that oven are one of the highlights of eating there. A former chef from our restaurant had a stone bread oven built in his house, with the intention of selling stone-baked bread for a living. The results are amazing.

But those ovens were built by professionals, and Chris is far from a professional wood-burning oven maker. He had some plans, and he talked to anyone who could help fill in the blanks in his understanding. Even so, I wasn't sure his project was going to fly. But Jeff and I were both interested in bread ovens, so we couldn't resist showing up the day Chris and his friends planned to put one together, believing we were there for an exercise in good intentions and high spirits.

When we arrived, there was a mishmash of people willing to help. (That's one thing you don't see with industrial-scale baking: customers showing up on a Saturday afternoon to help build the oven.) Thankfully, it was a nice day, even a bit cool; Jeff and I were wearing jackets.

Chris had already built a form out of slender alder branches. The form would provide the shape of the inside of the oven. What we were there to do was build something like an igloo of clay over the form. Chris had dug the clay from a riverbed in Dundas, sloshed it into the bed of his truck and hauled it back. His daughters were soon up to their knees in gray, cold, slimy Dundas clay, trying to get it to the right consistency to make crude bricks to lay over the wooden skeleton. We also tried to mash in some straw to give the clay a bit more structure.

Like water pistols, clay has the strange property of turning responsible adults into children. I have to admit that I enjoyed mucking around in the gray ooze. Soon, several volunteers had given themselves facials, while others had thoroughly slimed each other and were considering the consequences of letting the clay harden around their fists as they clutched bottles of beer. It was a lot of work, but it was not *all* work.

It takes a lot of clay to make an oven. We used about five hundred pounds of it to build a dome between three and eight inches thick and about three feet high. It took ages to get everything built up and smoothed out and cleaned up.

At the end of the day we had an oven like nothing I had ever seen before. It would take a couple of days to dry, and the wooden skeleton on the inside still had to be burned out, but when we stood back that Saturday afternoon, our handiwork looked just like an oven. A few days later, the Krucker family had their first pizza dinner, and Denise (Chris's wife) told me they were hooked: it was the best pizza they had ever had.

Before this event, I had never even considered that I would be baking bread in an oven I had helped build (even if my help was minimal). But this was where my skills really came in handy for Chris: I actually knew how to bake bread! Chris was interested in sourdough bread, which is leavened by the interaction of naturally occurring yeast and bacteria. But sours can be tricky for a beginner, so I taught Chris how to make yeast-leavened bread. The world of bread is very complicated and this was a time to just keep things simple.

For the first couple of weeks I was very hands-on in getting Chris's bread operation off the ground. He wanted to make about fifty loaves a week for his customers. I would mix the bread the night before at the restaurant, bring it out the next day, roll it and bake it.

Those were some early mornings. Chris would get up at about 4 a.m. to light the fire in the oven so it would be ready to go for 10 a.m. I'm sure those early mornings gave him ample opportunity to question the wisdom of getting into the stone-baked bread business, but Chris is not the kind of guy who backs away from an idea because it promises to be a lot of work.

Wood-fired ovens are not hard to figure out, at least in theory. You heat the oven with the fire, then take the coals out and let the dome cool slightly. It's the residual heat that actually bakes the bread—the first batch of bread is baked at about 680°F for about fifteen minutes and the last batch is closer to 340°F and bakes for close to half an hour. Then it's over and if you have anything else you want to bake, you have to start from the beginning. You're not going to be throwing in a frozen pizza after work.

I was at the farm almost every Thursday morning that first year, trying to help. I got some sense of what tech-support guys must feel like with panicky computer users on the phone—I've never heard Chris more distraught than when he phoned me in the early morning to tell me the bread wouldn't rise. But after a couple weeks, Chris hired a baker named Sarah to come in on Thursdays, and she did a great job. (She was a natural for the role, too; her name was Sarah Baker.) That summer we made multigrain bread with milk and honey. The variety of grains gave the bread a natural earthiness, and the milk and honey guaranteed good crust color.

Chris's customers love the addition of bread to their weekly baskets—the loaves are gorgeous. But it turns out that the oven itself is what people love. I suppose that is not so surprising. The communal oven was for centuries the focal point of village social life, and even today all parties eventually end up in the kitchen and all camping expeditions are centered around a fire. We now use any excuse to go to the farm to make pizzas in the oven, and no matter how many people may be there, they are always clustered around the oven's warm dome.

Chris Krucker firing the pizza oven.

CANNING & PRESERVING

To me, preserving means preserving summer. Each jar of preserves is like a time capsule. When I open it, months later (or perhaps just weeks), I taste terroir and the flavor of long-faded sunshine—in this, a jar of pickled beets is not unlike a bottle of wine.

There is another way that a jar of preserves is like wine: we no longer make it to keep the food from spoiling. We go to the trouble of preparing the food and painstakingly handling the jars so we end up with something delicious. It's really just another way to cook, to bring out the taste of the produce. I am looking to create something new, whether it's tomato sauce or sauerkraut. For me, the art of pickling is as much creation as preservation.

But before I get into the more esoteric forms of preserving, I should mention a pretty simple one: freezing. This is the best way to take care of berries you want to set aside for winter. I lay them out on a tray and freeze them solid, then store them in zip-lock bags. Blackberries, blueberries, raspberries, cherries and strawberries freeze very well and have all kinds of uses: we use the berries in crumbles, tarts and sorbets, and the juice in vinaigrettes. The summer flavor comes through pretty much unaffected and brightens any winter meal.

Pickling, on the other hand, creates entirely new tastes: bright, satisfying and complex. Pickled vegetables are a pure delight on cheeseboards, on charcuterie and meat plates and in salads that need a tart component. Pickling baby carrots, for instance, transforms a humble vegetable into a spicy, tart, completely different dish. Cooking is about contrast in flavors and textures; put a pickled carrot on a salad, and you've got that contrast in spades. Plus, there is something about pickles that makes you hungry. Most chefs love pickles, and just about any vegetable, from carrots to radishes, can be pickled. Maybe that's what we'll do with the big radish delivery next summer!

Though preserves need no further arguments to recommend them, there is still one more: they can be a real pleasure to make. Of course, if you're in a hurry or you have to be somewhere (in other words, if you're thinking about something else), the process of getting food into jars will seem tedious. But I look at the process as something to enjoy. I suppose there is probably some human instinct that takes pleasure from knowing that the harvest has been tucked away and the larder is full. In any case, taking the time to wash and prepare whole bushels of fruit and vegetables that you'll eat much later, sterilizing the jars, watching over bubbling pots in a steamy kitchen—it all adds up to an afternoon to look forward

to, particularly if, like me, you keep a bottle of wine open as you go about the work. And there is a unique pleasure that comes from gazing at the brightly colored jars before you (perhaps reluctantly) store them away.

Canning and preserving is an art, and there is no way I can make you an expert in a few paragraphs (I'm always learning myself). You'll pick up tricks and recipes as you go along.

Nothing can replace experience, and the only way to get that is to start. But before you begin, here are a few things to keep in mind:

- There are many books on preserving—look for recipes that produce small batches, ones you are likely to use.
- Always use the proper method, and follow the recipe. Canning is an age-old technique, so look for canning books in their fifth or sixth printing—they have stood the test of time.
- Choose fresh produce. We are preserving life here, not trying to bring it back.
- Work with sterile equipment. Wash all equipment with soap and water. Sterilize all jars and lids, and don't forget the tongs, spoons and utensils you will be using.
- Store your jars in a cool, dark place—not in your kitchen, where you can look admiringly at them and show them off, but in the basement or a closet. (Again, not unlike wine.)
- Use common sense. If the preserved food doesn't look or smell quite right, don't taste it. Throw it out.

Sterilizing jars is the first and most important step. If your jars are not sterile, you won't preserve anything.

Jars should be free of any chips or cracks. Preserving or canning jars are topped with a glass, plastic or metal lid, and require a rubber seal. Two-piece lids are best for canning, as they vacuum-seal as they cool.

To ensure everything is sterile, wash jars and lids with hot, soapy water. Rinse well and arrange jars and lids, open side up and without touching, on a tray. Set oven to 175°F and heat jars and lids for 25 minutes. Or, boil the jars and lids in a large saucepan, covered with water, for 15 minutes.

Use tongs when handling the hot sterilized jars. Be sure the tongs are sterilized too, by heating the ends in boiling water for a few minutes.

As a rule, hot preserves go into hot jars and cold preserves go into cold jars. All items used in the process of making preserves must be clean. This includes any towels used, and especially your hands.

Some of the recipes in this section call for a boiling water

bath, which is used in canning acidic foods like pickles, tomato sauce and preserves. The boiling water bath eliminates any air-borne microorganisms present in the pickling jar while it is being filled and sealed, and forces the air out if the food and canning liquid, creating a vacuum and perfect seal that prevents spoilage. Processing in a boiling water bath for preservation longer than a few weeks is definitely not optional and should be done with care.

Boiling water baths are sold commercially and are quite reasonably priced as a kit. I suggest you use them. Once filled, the jars must fit in the pot on the rack with 1-inch space at the bottom and enough room at the top to cover the jars by two inches. This allows the water to flow freely around the jars. It is important to remember never to tighten the lid before processing or the air will not be able to escape, and the lid won't seal. Remember it is not you that is making the seal but the jar itself; as the contents of the jar and the air space at the top shrink, the lid is sucked down firmly onto the rim.

Check the seals after one day. A concave lid indicates a proper vacuum. If the lid clicks up and down when pressed, the seal is not complete. You will have to start again.

SEAFOOD

I suppose it is ironic that the one food that is harvested in significant quantities from the wild is one that is not local for many people. I'm talking about seafood, of course.

Fish and shellfish represent a real departure from my love of local, seasonal food. But there is just no way I could give up on seafood, either as a chef or as a cook at home. I personally couldn't live long without the clean, satisfying flavor of fish, and I know my customers would be asking for my head if I ever took salmon off the menu.

I have to admit, though, that our addiction to salmon tells a story about the way we eat and the route our food takes to our table. Most of the salmon on menus around the world is farmed. The reason people turn to aquaculture instead of fishing is that it's cheaper. There is a long-standing and often acrimo-nious debate over whether fishing or fish-farming is the more environmentally friendly way to procure fish—there are serious downsides to both: overfishing, bycatch and damage to the sea floor on one side; toxic effluent and sea lice damaging the local environment and fatally infesting wild fish stocks on the other. I'm not the right person to settle the debate once and for all.

One thing worth pointing out, however, is that the worst thing about fish-farming is that it works, thereby driving down the price of fish. Wild salmon is worth less when farmed salmon is abundant, so fishermen either have to catch more to earn a living or earn a living doing something else. The low price of fish also means that it has to be processed as cheaply as possible to keep costs down. The supposedly fresh fish on the menu or glistening on ice under the

Even though fish is in some ways different from other food, in one important way it is the same: taste should tell you which food is better. Just as an out-of-season tomato on the shelf in the supermarket is never going to live up to the ripe, aromatic version you pick up at a farmers' market in August, a frozen, artificially colored salmon fillet from a fish farm can't compare to the lean, jewel-like flesh of a wild sockeye. At the restaurant, we get excited when the wild salmon is delivered.

We get ours from Terry's Fish in Port Dover, on Lake Erie. He has been concentrating on supplying several southwestern Ontario restaurants with fresh lake and ocean fish and seafood. Your local fish shop will often have a wide selection of fresh fish, seafood and smoked fish, from lake perch, pickerel, smelts and whitefish to ocean-fresh salmon, halibut, cod, mussels and king and snow crab. Even if all of the fish is not from within a hundred-mile radius, the business is. There is a big difference between buying from a place like Terry's and buying

halogen lamps in the supermarket has probably been frozen and shipped thousands of miles to have its pin bones taken out in a vast processing plant in China.

Of course, that's not the sort of fish we serve at the restaurant. When I put proper wild salmon on the menu, customers don't recognize it. Farmed salmon is very fatty. Wild sockeye is so lean you have to cook it to medium-rare or it will be dry (just as a beef tenderloin would be).

from a big chain, and a lot of it comes down to self-interest rather than the ethical high road. One study shows that 45 cents of every dollar spent at a local business stay within circulation in the local economy, while only 13 cents of a dollar spent at a big-box store stick around. Shop locally, and some of the money you spend will come back to you and your neighbors.

What to Look For at the Fishmonger

CATFISH: Because farmed catfish eat a primarily vegetarian diet of corn, soybeans and rice, choosing this tender, savory fish actually reduces the number of wild fish caught to process as fish feed. Catfish are farmed in closed inland ponds, which all but eliminates the possibility of domesticated fish mingling with wild populations and possibly spreading disease.

ARCTIC CHAR: Like catfish (and unlike most salmon), most Arctic char is farmed in ponds located safely away from natural bodies of water, so the risk of wild stocks being affected by aquaculture are nearly nil. In fact, some Arctic char operations raise only sterile fish, which ensures that even if some do somehow escape, there is no chance they will be able to interbreed with their wild cousin.

STRIPED BASS: When you buy farmed striped bass, what you're actually taking home is a hybrid between wild striped bass and white bass, so there is no risk of genetic disease. They are raised commercially in ponds and tanks located well inland, so that there is no risk of ocean pollution from runoff of wastewater from the farms.

TILAPIA: Tilapia may well be the food of the future, since tilapia consume less protein than they yield—that is, they provide a healthy protein profit.

CHEF MICHAEL SCHWARTZ

MICHAEL'S GENUINE FOOD & DRINK, MIAMI, FLORIDA

Eating locally sometimes means enjoying frog's legs.

Chef Michael Schwartz lives and works in Miami, and there are plenty of frogs in the Everglades. Hence his classic American version of a classic French dish: hot Buffalo frog's legs.

Schwartz runs Michael's Genuine Food & Drink, named one of the top ten new restaurants in the U.S. by the *New York Times*, and listed among America's "Best Farm-to-Table Restaurants" in 2007 by *Gourmet* magazine. *Bon Appétit* calls it "the hottest indie act" in Miami. What everyone seems to love about Michael's is what Schwartz loves about food. The restaurant's motto is "Fresh. Simple. Pure." The servers wear T-shirts splashed with the word "genuine."

"'Genuine' summed up everything we were doing,"

Schwartz tells me. "So we ran with it."

What genuine means to Schwartz is local, seasonal, unpretentious food and a dining experience that's meant to be social, informal, unpretentious and warm. As a young chef, he tells me, you want to dazzle with exotic ingredients and sophisticated plating. As you mature a little, he goes on, you develop a more "sensible" relationship with food. You concentrate on the basics—the food itself and the experience of eating it.

Not that Schwartz is a grizzled old veteran by any means. His burly frame and impressive goatee give him a slightly dangerous air, but his infectious smile makes him look like a kid.

At Michael's, unpretentious food takes the form of crispy hominy with chili and lime, *poulet rouge* from Louisiana and, of course, local favorites such as swordfish and grouper. There is pizza from a wood-fired oven. And the kitchen is open, so diners can see exactly what goes on and what goes into their meals.

This is a key point for Schwartz. Like so many of the chefs I spoke to in the course of researching this book, he considers himself a disciple of Alice Waters, the owner of Chez Panisse, and arguably the most influential chef in America among chefs. She is the godmother of local, sustainable gastronomy. Like anyone working in that tradition, he goes out of his way to source and to feature top-quality seasonal food, and to work carefully with like-minded producers.

He gets as much as he can from Paradise Farms, a lush, five-acre tropical garden that supplies fruit, vegetables, greens and edible flowers to area restaurants. As with other farm-restaurant partnerships, Paradise invites chefs out to the farm for classes. And one of the highlights of Miami's culinary scene is the series of regular Dinners in Paradise, prepared by area chefs to raise money for charity. Schwartz is a cofounder of the series. He

jokes that he may have been a farmer in another life.

But Schwartz veers from optimism to pessimism and back when I ask him how he sees the future of earth-to-table cooking and eating. When I tell him he *sounds* like a farmer (I have yet to meet an openly optimistic farmer), he says, "I know, but it is hard to stay enthusiastic when I can buy food from California cheaper than from right here in Florida. Some days it is *only* available from California."

In fact, his biggest challenge in strengthening the earth-to-table link, he says, is that his sprawling urban environment gobbles up farm land, and small-scale farms are very scarce. Despite the fact that Florida has two growing seasons and is one of the continent's biggest growers of food (or perhaps because of this fact), Schwartz is envious of our relationship with Chris's farm, and even more envious of Blue Hill's relationship with Stone Barns (see page 164). "Dan Barber is living my dream," he says with a sigh. I wondered what Dan would say about the opportunity to live near the beaches of Florida.

What troubles Schwartz is that the whole food system is rigged against chefs and businessmen like him. First, he cannot simply get the things he wants—if no one is farming an item locally, it ceases to be one of his local options for the menu. But what is even more exasperating is that produce shipped in from thousands of miles away is generally cheaper than the same thing grown down the road. What that means is that he has to compromise just to keep the doors open. "I am a businessman as well as a chef," he says, "so the food must be utilized on the menu well." He is forced to "splurge" on local produce he can highlight.

He would love for the earth-to-table idea to take hold in the mainstream—to move out of the gourmet circuit. That would mean economies of scale, local food available widely and affordably. It would mean healthier, better-tasting food and a healthier environment.

He's clearly on a roll as he lists the benefits of a local, seasonal food culture. So I ask what he'd say to a room full of people if he had the podium. "I'd say,

'Spend five minutes and think about the cost of conventional food, both environmentally and on our children's health. Sourcing local is the only sustainable and reasonable answer for our food system.'"

For Schwartz, as for everyone I spoke to, eating sustainably and supporting local producers is not an ideological crusade. Nor is it a marketing ploy or a branding exercise. It's simple common sense.

And simplicity, once again, is one of his bywords. I ask him what comes to mind as the simplest, most delicious seasonal dish. He stares at a delivery of plump tomatoes that sits displayed on his open kitchen bar before answering. He can't decide. Is it an heirloom tomato simply served with olive oil and salt or, later in the season, cherry tomatoes roasted on the vine with a soft white cheese, such as buffalo mozzarella or ricotta. In the end, what matters is not the dish he chooses, but the idea that directs his decision. As he says, "Let the food speak for itself."

SUMMER RECIPES

Beer with Ice and Lime

Yes, everyone knows Corona goes best with lime, but few know that all lagers taste better with lime. That citric zing takes it from bland to boastful. In the summer heat, add one more trick to your bag: ice cubes.

That's right, I just suggested you add ice to your beer. I'll stand my ground. Go ahead, try it, just once when the hot sun is beating down, and you'll understand. The slight addition of water will not compromise the taste so much as help you stay hydrated and, most importantly, keep your beverage ice cold to the last drop.

Local Fruit Sangria

Serves 6

1 bottle (750 mL) fruity red wine
   (such as Beaujolais or
   Zinfandel)
1 lemon, cut into wedges
1 orange, cut into wedges
5 cherries
3 plums, sliced
2 tbsp granulated sugar
2 tbsp brandy
2 cups club soda
Ice cubes

Don't get stuck on the ingredients for this recipe; you can add whatever fruit is ripe and juicy—just toss it in. In our area, plums and cherries rule in the middle of summer. Find out what is best in your area and use that. This recipe is meant to be a fun way to enjoy wine in the middle of summer, when cocktails should be casual and refreshing!

POUR WINE INTO A LARGE PITCHER. Squeeze juice from lemon and orange wedges into wine. Add wedges to pitcher, leaving out seeds, if possible. Stir in cherries, plums, sugar and brandy. (*Make ahead: Cover and refrigerate for up to 12 hours.*)

Add club soda and ice just before serving.

Watermelon Agua Fresca

Mexican in origin, this sweet drink is both refreshing and beautiful. Don't be afraid to add some tequila or vodka for a cocktail version.

IN A BLENDER, working in batches, process watermelon until smooth. Pour through a strainer into a large pitcher. You should have about 8 cups of juice. Stir in lime juice, honey and ginger. Pour into ice-filled glasses and garnish with lime slices and mint.

Serves 6

1 large seedless watermelon
   (about 8 lbs), peeled and cut
   into 2-inch pieces
1 cup freshly squeezed lime
   juice (about 10 limes)
1 cup local honey
1½-inch piece of gingerroot,
   grated
Ice cubes
Lime slices and fresh mint
   leaves, for garnish

Leek Mimosa

Serves 4

8 medium leeks (about 2½ lbs)

10 cups Chicken Stock (see
  recipe, page 297)

¼ cup red wine vinegar

2 tbsp minced shallots

1 tbsp Dijon mustard

6 tbsp extra-virgin olive oil

Salt and freshly cracked
  black pepper

3 hard-boiled organic eggs
  (see tip), coarsely chopped

2 tbsp chopped fresh flat-leaf
  (Italian) parsley

Generally relegated to a simple ingredient in a main dish, the leek is a noble vegetable that deserves the spotlight from time to time. Leeks can be served this way for a lunch main course. Once you have completed this recipe, you will have about 8 cups of stock left over. Keep it: it freezes well for about 3 months and can be used in a number of the recipes in this book.

PREHEAT OVEN TO 400°F. Trim off roots and dark green tops of leeks, leaving about 6 inches of pale green leek. Halve lengthwise and rinse well under lukewarm water to remove any dirt. Drain and pat dry.

Arrange leeks cut side up in a single layer in a large baking dish. Pour in stock, cover with foil and bake until tender, about 1 hour. Using tongs, lift leeks from dish, letting stock drain into dish. Arrange leeks on a serving platter. Reserve 2 tbsp of the stock. (Let the rest of the stock cool, then transfer it to an airtight container and freeze it for another use.)

In a small bowl, combine vinegar and shallots. Whisk in mustard and reserved stock. Add oil in a slow stream, whisking to combine. Season to taste with salt and pepper.

Pour vinaigrette over leeks, tossing gently to combine. Sprinkle with egg and parsley.

TIP: To hard-boil eggs, place in a pot with enough cold water to cover and bring to a boil over medium heat. Boil for 10 minutes. Let cool, then peel off shells and coarsely chop.

New Potato Salad with Green Beans and Shallots

This salad, which is great for a picnic, is best served freshly made, but can be refrigerated for up to 1 day. Toss well before serving.

IN A MEDIUM POT, cover potatoes with cold salted water. Bring to a boil over high heat, reduce heat and simmer until potatoes are tender, about 30 minutes. Add beans and cook until tender, about 3 minutes. Drain potatoes and beans and let cool.

Meanwhile, in a large bowl, whisk together lemon juice, mustard, salt and pepper. Stir in sour cream, fennel tops and shallots.

Cut potatoes in half. In a large bowl, toss beans and potatoes with dressing. Season to taste with salt and pepper.

Serves 4

1 lb small new potatoes (about 5)
8 oz green beans, trimmed
2 tbsp freshly squeezed lemon juice (about 1 lemon)
1 tbsp Dijon mustard
¼ tsp salt
¼ tsp freshly ground black pepper
2 tbsp sour cream
1 tbsp minced fennel tops or fresh dill
2 shallots, sliced

Heirloom Tomato Salad
with Buffalo Mozzarella

This is it: tomato salad is the quintessential earth-to-table recipe. It's a fresh-off-the-vine kind of dish. Tomatoes are sweet and tart, juicy and colorful. What more could you ask for? Okay, maybe some fresh buffalo mozzarella.

CORE TOMATOES and cut some into wedges or slices. In a bowl, gently toss heirloom tomatoes and cherry tomatoes with oil, basil and salt.

Arrange tomatoes on a platter and sprinkle mozzarella evenly over tomatoes. Season to taste with salt and pepper. Take a bow.

Serves 6

3 lbs heirloom tomatoes,
    assorted shapes, sizes and
    colors
1 cup cherry tomatoes, halved
½ cup extra-virgin olive oil
¼ cup packed small basil leaves
1 tsp kosher salt
1 lb buffalo mozzarella cheese,
    sliced or torn thin
Salt and freshly cracked
    black pepper

Slow-Roasted Roma Tomatoes

This is a great way to make a luscious Roma tomato even better. Basically, we are slowly removing the water, leaving nothing but sweet tomato goodness. At the restaurant, we take this one step further and pack our tomatoes with a portion of the tomato vine, which contains most of the famous tomato aroma. You can use these tomatoes on Make-Your-Own Pizza (page 190), Tomato Confit (page 301) or in Whole Wheat Focaccia (page 146).

PREHEAT OVEN TO 200°F. Place tomatoes cut side up on 2 large rimmed baking sheets. In a bowl, combine oil and garlic; drizzle over tomatoes. Season to taste with salt and pepper. Roast until tomatoes are shriveled, about 6 hours. (*Make ahead: Pack into resealable plastic bags and refrigerate for up to 2 weeks.*)

Makes about 40 pieces

4 lbs plum (Roma) tomatoes,
    quartered
½ cup extra-virgin olive oil
6 cloves garlic, very thinly sliced
Salt and freshly cracked
    black pepper

Zucchini and Eggplant Carpaccio

Serves 6

1 lb green zucchini (about 3)

1 lb yellow zucchini (about 3)

1 lb small Italian eggplants
(about 2)

⅓ cup extra-virgin olive oil

2 tsp grated lemon zest

Juice of 1 lemon

2 shallots, minced

Salt and freshly cracked
black pepper

1 habanero chili pepper, seeded
and minced

1 cup grated pecorino cheese
(about 4 oz)

½ cup minced fresh flat-leaf
(Italian) parsley

What grows together, goes together. This is a great way to think about food. Zucchini and eggplants grow side by side on the farm. Because these vegetables can be bland alone, I grill them for smokiness and pair them with some heat in the chilies for zing. This salad can be served hot or cold, and it is perfect for picnics or light lunches.

IF GRILLING VEGETABLES, preheat grill or barbecue to medium.

Slice zucchini and eggplants lengthwise into wafer-thin slices. Place in a bowl if serving raw, or grill until softened and grill-marked, about 1 minute per side.

In a large bowl, whisk together oil, lemon zest, lemon juice and shallots. Season to taste with salt and pepper. Add vegetables and toss gently to coat. Let stand for 5 minutes.

Carefully arrange vegetables on plates and sprinkle with chili pepper, cheese and parsley.

Deep-Fried Zucchini Blossoms

If you grow zucchini in your yard, you will have these beauties for about a month or two in the summer. Be sure to pick only the male flowers—the ones that do not have baby zucchini attached. If you pick the females, you will not have zucchini to eat later. Check inside the flower before cooking; a little black bug usually resides there.

IN A LARGE, wide, heavy saucepan, heat 1 inch of oil over high heat until it registers 375°F on a candy/deep-fry thermometer, about 10 minutes.

Meanwhile, in a bowl, whisk together flour, club soda and salt until smooth.

Working in batches of 3, dip zucchini blossoms in batter, turning to coat. Brush blossoms against side of bowl to remove excess batter. Carefully transfer blossoms to the hot oil and fry, turning occasionally with a slotted spoon, until golden, 1 to 2 minutes per batch. Transfer to a plate lined with paper towels and season to taste with salt and pepper. Serve warm.

Makes 15 pieces

4 cups vegetable oil (approx.)
$\frac{2}{3}$ cup all-purpose flour
$\frac{2}{3}$ cup club soda
$\frac{1}{4}$ tsp kosher salt
15 zucchini blossoms
Salt and freshly cracked
    black pepper

Peperonata

⅓ cup extra-virgin olive oil,
  divided
2 cloves garlic, minced
1 tbsp chili flakes
4 large sweet red peppers (about
  1¾ lbs), thinly sliced
  lengthwise
3 cups sliced red onions
1 tbsp fresh thyme leaves,
  chopped
2 tbsp capers
3 tbsp red wine vinegar
2 tbsp fresh oregano leaves,
  chopped
Sea salt and freshly ground
  black pepper

This spicy dish goes very well with silky smooth buffalo mozzarella and crusty fried bread.

IN A LARGE SKILLET, heat 3 tbsp of the oil over medium-high heat. Add garlic and chili flakes; sauté until aromatic, about 1 minute. Add peppers, onions and thyme; reduce heat to medium and sauté until peppers are softened, about 6 minutes. Add capers and the remaining oil; sauté until flavors are combined, about 1 minute. Transfer pepper mixture to a shallow plastic or stainless steel dish.

Turn off heat, add vinegar to skillet and reduce by half. (The residual heat will be enough to reduce this small amount.) Using a rubber spatula, scrape vinegar over pepper mixture. Stir in oregano. (The heat from the peppers will help release the flavor of the oregano.) Season to taste with salt and pepper. (*Make ahead: Let cool, cover and refrigerate for up to 3 days.*)

Panzanella

Serves 6

2 sweet red peppers

2 sweet yellow peppers

2 lbs mixed tomatoes (about 5
   medium), chopped into
   1-inch pieces

1 lb stale French baguette (about
   1), torn into 1-inch cubes

7 anchovy fillets, rinsed and
   minced

1 red onion, finely sliced

¼ cup drained capers

½ cup Red Wine Vinaigrette
   (see recipe, page 295),
   divided

1 cup packed fresh arugula
   leaves

Salt and freshly cracked
   black pepper

I first enjoyed panzanella at the world-famous Zuni Café in San Francisco. It is now one of my favorite salads, but it should be made only when tomatoes are at their ripest. It's garlicky, salty and oily, with loads of flavor. It's best served with chicken.

I prefer using baguette for the bread because there is salt in it, and therefore more flavor. The bread must be at least a day old so it will soak up the flavor.

Don't worry about the small bits of charred skin that come off the roasted peppers—they will only add to the flavor of the dish!

PREHEAT GRILL OR BARBECUE to high. Grill red and yellow peppers, turning often with tongs, until blistered and blackened on all sides, about 10 minutes. Transfer to a large bowl and cover with plastic wrap. Let steam for 20 minutes, then peel skins and chop peppers into 1-inch pieces.

In a large bowl, combine tomatoes, bread, anchovies, onion and capers. Drizzle with 2 tbsp of the vinaigrette and let stand until bread has absorbed dressing, about 5 minutes. Add roasted peppers and toss to coat. Drizzle with the remaining vinaigrette. Add arugula and toss to coat. Season to taste with salt and pepper. Serve immediately.

Corn on the Cob with Chili Lime Butter

Granted, sweet corn at the end of summer is absolutely delicious with nothing more than butter and salt. But the chili lime butter will put a refreshing twist on this summer classic, particularly if you pair the corn with the cold beer recipe on page 102.

IN A BOWL, combine butter, shallot, chili, lime zest, lime juice and salt. Cover and refrigerate for at least an hour before using. (*Make ahead: Place butter in plastic wrap, roll into a log and refrigerate for up to 1 week or freeze for up to 3 months.*)

In a large pot of boiling unsalted water, cook corn until tender, about 3 minutes. Using tongs, remove corn from water and, while still hot, spread with chili lime butter.

Serves 4

¼ cup unsalted butter, softened
1 tbsp finely minced shallot
1 tsp minced Thai or serrano
    chili pepper (preferably red),
    including seeds
1 tsp finely grated lime zest
2 tsp freshly squeezed lime juice
½ tsp sea salt
4 ears corn, husked and cleaned

Corn Soup

Serves 6

5 ears corn (about 1½ lbs)

2 tbsp unsalted butter

1 medium onion, minced

1 clove garlic, minced

1 tbsp white wine vinegar

4½ cups Chicken Stock
(see recipe, page 297)
or water

Salt and freshly cracked
black pepper

1 tsp cayenne pepper

This recipe is straight out of my beat-up notebook from my time at Chez Panisse. Corn, as I noted earlier in this book, was one of my earliest food epiphanies. In this recipe, the freshness of the corn is of utmost importance. If you didn't just pick up your corn from a farmstand, put this recipe down!

CLEAN THE CORN of its husks and silks. Using a sharp knife, remove the kernels from the cobs and set aside.

In a medium saucepan, melt butter over medium-high heat. Add onion and garlic; sauté until onion is golden and softened, about 20 minutes. Add corn kernels and vinegar, stirring to coat. Add stock, reduce heat to medium and simmer until corn is tender, about 10 minutes. Using a slotted spoon, remove 1 cup of the corn-onion mixture and set aside.

Working in batches, transfer the remaining soup to a blender and puree until completely smooth, about 3 minutes per batch. Return to the saucepan and stir in the reserved corn-onion mixture; reheat until steaming. Season to taste with salt and black pepper. Serve with cayenne sprinkled on top.

Grilled Corn on the Cob with Chilies and Cheese

A typical street food in Mexico is this grilled corn, rolled in crema or mayonnaise and cheese. I have used the king of cheese, Parmesan, as a sharp note that goes well with chili powder and mayo. Serve with beer with ice and lime (see page 102).

Serves 4

4 ears corn

¼ cup Mayonnaise (see recipe, page 293)

1 cup freshly grated Parmesan cheese

1 tsp chili powder

Salt and freshly cracked black pepper

4 lime wedges

PULL HUSKS BACK FROM CORN, leaving them attached at the bottom, and remove silks. Wrap husks back over corn. Soak corn in water for at least 10 minutes before grilling (so the husks don't burn on the grill). Drain well. Meanwhile, preheat grill or barbecue to high.

Lightly oil the grill racks and grill corn (in husks), uncovered, turning often, until slightly charred, about 15 minutes. Carefully pull back husks and grill corn, turning often, until corn is slightly charred and becomes bright and glossy, about 5 minutes.

Let your guests brush their corn with mayonnaise and sprinkle it with cheese, chili powder, salt and pepper. Serve with lime wedges for guests to squeeze over their corn.

Eggplant Caponata

2 large eggplants (about 2½
   lbs total), cut into 1-inch
   cubes

2 tbsp kosher salt

1½ cups olive oil (not
   extra-virgin), divided

6 stalks celery, cut into ½-inch
   dice

½ bulb fennel, cut into ½-inch
   dice

1 zucchini, cut into ½-inch
   dice

2 cloves garlic, minced

1 medium onion, cut into ½-inch
   pieces

3 medium tomatoes, cut into
   ½-inch dice

1 cup drained green olives,
   coarsely chopped

½ cup drained capers

½ cup sultana raisins

½ cup pine nuts

½ cup white wine vinegar

2 tbsp granulated sugar

Salt and freshly cracked
   black pepper

¾ cup whole raw almonds,
   lightly toasted

½ cup minced fresh basil

Most of the chefs that have taught me to cook have been women, and I owe a particular debt to chef Anne Yarymowich of Toronto. She is a great advocate of traditional recipes and big bold flavours. Whenever I presented her with a dish that I had "invented," she would immediately ask me, "Where did this dish originate?" If I didn't have a certain country or region in mind, well, I could just forget it. The dish would never make it to the menu. It was Anne who introduced me to eggplant caponata (it's Sicilian by the way). This rich, garlicky side dish is delicious with fish, beef and lamb. Chilling it for at least 8 hours before serving allows the flavours to really develop.

IN A COLANDER set over a bowl, toss eggplants with salt. Let drain for 1 hour. Rinse well and pat dry with paper towels.

In a large, deep pot, heat 1 cup of the oil over medium heat until hot but not smoking. Add celery and fennel; sauté for 1 minute. Add zucchini and sauté for 3 minutes. Add eggplant and sauté until vegetables are golden brown and tender, about 10 minutes. Using a slotted spoon, transfer vegetables to a plate lined with paper towels; set aside.

Add the remaining oil to the pot and sauté garlic and onion over medium heat until golden, about 5 minutes. Stir in tomatoes, olives, capers, raisins, pine nuts, vinegar and sugar; cook for 10 minutes. Add reserved vegetables and cook, stirring occasionally, for 10 minutes. Season to taste with salt and pepper.

Transfer to a wide, shallow dish and let cool for 1 hour. Cover and refrigerate for at least 8 hours. (*Make ahead: Refrigerate for up to 1 week.*)

>>>

About one hour before serving, remove from refrigerator and bring to room temperature. Serve sprinkled with almonds and basil.

Iceberg Wedge
with Green Goddess Dressing

This is one classic retro salad. We serve it at our more casual restaurant, Spencer's on the Waterfront, and it's a perennial favorite! An important note before you begin the recipe: the first step is to pickle the onions, a process that takes 3 hours.

IN A BOWL, combine red onion and vinegar; let stand for 3 hours. (*Make ahead: Cover and refrigerate for up to 3 days.*)

In a heavy skillet, sauté bacon over medium-high heat until browned and crisp, about 7 minutes. Drain on a plate lined with paper towels.

On each of 4 plates, cross 2 lettuce wedges on their sides. Pour dressing evenly over wedges. Sprinkle with pickled onions, bacon, tomatoes, blue cheese and chives. Season to taste with salt and pepper.

Serves 4

1 small red onion, thinly sliced

1 cup red wine vinegar

1 cup chopped double-smoked bacon

1 head iceberg lettuce, cut into 8 wedges

4 cups Green Goddess Dressing (see recipe, page 56)

8 Yellow Pear cherry tomatoes, halved

½ cup crumbled blue cheese

¼ cup minced fresh chives

Salt and freshly cracked black pepper

Bistecca

¼ cup smoked paprika

¼ cup ground cumin

¼ cup freshly cracked
   black pepper

3 tbsp kosher salt

2 tbsp ground coriander

1 tbsp packed brown sugar

¼ cup extra-virgin olive oil

1 bone-in porterhouse steak
   (about 3½ lbs)

So you feel like steak? Try this monster, but be sure to have a bunch of friends around. In Italy, quality rules over quantity, so this is not a giant steak for one; it is meant to be grilled or roasted for a party. This cut of meat is thick, so it will take a while to cook it properly. Once cooked, the steak can be treated like a roast, sliced thin and served on the cutting board with a variety of dipping sauces (see caption on opposite page), so everyone has a choice.

IN A SMALL BOWL, combine paprika, cumin, pepper, salt, coriander and brown sugar. Stir in oil. Cover steak generously with rub. Let stand at room temperature for 1 hour, or cover and refrigerate for up to 24 hours.

Preheat two-burner barbecue to high. Just before cooking steak, turn off one side. Sear steak on hot side, turning once, about 10 minutes. Move steak over unlit side. Close lid and cook, adjusting heat as necessary so that the temperature remains at about 400°F and does not drop below 350°F, until a meat thermometer inserted in the center of the steak registers 125°F for rare, about 45 minutes, or until desired doneness. (Remember that the internal temperature of the steak will rise slightly while it is resting.) Let rest for at least 15 minutes before slicing.

Sauces from top to bottom: Dijon mustard, Fresh Horseradish Cream (page 301), Our Steak Sauce (page 300), Maple Mustard Sauce (page 300), Garlicky Rouille (page 294).

Chicken Under a Brick

Serves 4

1 whole chicken (about 3 lbs)
1½ cups Piri Piri Sauce
  (see recipe, opposite)

Start planning this dish a day ahead so you can marinate it overnight. The brick is only there to keep the chicken flat and ensure even cooking—don't eat it! I like to serve the crisp chicken with a side of Panzanella (page 114).

RINSE CHICKEN UNDER cold water and pat dry. Using a chef's knife, cut off wing tips on each wing. Using kitchen shears, cut chicken down each side of backbone; remove backbone and save for stock. Turn bird breast side up and press firmly on the breastbone to flatten. Tuck wings behind back. Place in a shallow glass dish and brush with piri piri sauce. Cover and refrigerate, turning occasionally, for at least 4 hours or for up to 24 hours. Thirty minutes before grilling, remove chicken from refrigerator and place on a baking sheet.

Prepare a medium-hot charcoal fire with coals banked to one side, or heat a gas grill or barbecue to high on one side and to medium-low on other side. Place chicken, breast side down, on the hottest part of the grill. Place a brick on the chicken to weigh it down for even cooking. Cook chicken, turning once, until skin has deep golden grill marks, about 5 minutes. Move chicken to cooler side of grill. Cover and grill chicken indirectly, turning every 5 minutes, still using the brick to hold it down, until juices run clear when the spot between thigh and breast is pricked and an instant-read thermometer inserted in the thickest part of a thigh registers 165°F, about 30 minutes. Transfer chicken to a serving platter and tent with foil. Let rest for 10 minutes before carving.

Piri Piri Sauce

This versatile hot sauce is delicious with chicken, burgers and potato salad. It is a good idea to keep some handy in the fridge for hot-sauce emergencies.

The most basic piri piri sauce recipe calls for oil, salt and cayenne pepper or minced fresh hot chili pepper. I've added a couple more ingredients to mine. I suggest using serrano chilies, which are both spicy and fruity at once, and go well with vinegar and herbs.

IN A BOWL, combine chilies, oil, vinegar, paprika and salt; stir well. Pour into a jar, close tightly and let flavors blend overnight in the fridge. (*Make ahead: Refrigerate for up to 1 month.*)

Makes 1½ cups

6 hot red chili peppers (such as serrano or Thai), seeded and minced
1 cup extra-virgin olive oil
⅓ cup cider vinegar
2 tsp paprika (preferably smoked paprika, for more body)
1 tsp kosher salt

Korean-Cut Ribs with Honey and Soy Sauce

Korean-cut ribs are beef short ribs cut across the bone ¼ inch thick, 2 inches wide and 5 bones across. They are simple to prepare and finger-licking good, so if you are serving them at a barbecue party, make lots. Be a star and pretend you invented them—I won't tell. This recipe pairs well with Pickled Fennel.

IN A BOWL, combine honey, soy sauce, vinegar and sambal, mixing well. Place ribs in a large resealable bag and pour in marinade. Seal, toss to coat ribs and refrigerate for 12 hours.

Preheat grill or barbecue to high. Remove ribs from marinade and discard marinade. Grill ribs, turning occasionally, until golden and crisp, about 3 minutes per side. Remove ribs from grill, season with salt and pepper and sprinkle with chili. Serve immediately.

Serves 6

¼ cup local honey
¼ cup soy sauce
2 tbsp rice vinegar
1 tbsp sambal oelek hot sauce
4 lbs Korean-cut short ribs
Salt and freshly cracked
    black pepper
1 small Thai chili pepper,
    seeded and minced

Pickled Fennel

Once again, fennel shows off its versatility. All the best flavors—sweet, sour and spicy—combine to provide a counterpoint to fatty cuts of meat such as short ribs or pork belly.

IN A SAUCEPAN, combine garlic, vinegar, sugar, salt and chili flakes. Bring to a boil over high heat. Reduce heat and simmer until sugar is dissolved, about 10 minutes. Transfer to a large bowl and let cool slightly. Stir in fennel, cover and refrigerate for at least 2 hours or for up to 12 hours.

Serves 6

4 cloves garlic, smashed
4 cups rice vinegar
1 cup granulated sugar
¼ cup kosher salt
1½ tbsp chili flakes
2 bulbs fennel, thinly sliced

Whole Roasted Sockeye Salmon with Romesco

Serves 8

4 cups Romesco stuffing (see
    recipe, page 131)
1 whole wild sockeye salmon
    (about 5 lbs), scaled and
    gutted
2 tbsp extra-virgin olive oil
Salt and freshly cracked
    black pepper

Ask your fishmonger to scale, gut and remove the pin bones from your salmon. Once that task is done, this recipe is dead easy and a real showstopper. Serve with a green salad.

PUSH STUFFING INTO cavity of salmon, being careful not to overstuff it. Cut 4 lengths of butcher string to wrap around width of fish (see photo). Tie salmon tightly at 3-inch intervals and place on a baking sheet lined with parchment paper. (*Make ahead: Cover and refrigerate for up to 24 hours.*)

Preheat oven to 350°F. Brush salmon with oil and season with salt and pepper. Bake until an instant-read thermometer inserted into side of salmon registers 130°F for medium, about 30 minutes. Slide fish, on parchment, onto a wire rack and let cool for 10 minutes. Cut into 1½ inch slices.

Romesco

Here's another great recipe from my time at Chez Panisse. Romesco can be used as an accompaniment to fish, shellfish or potatoes, and is wonderful with grilled steak. Garlicky and spicy, it's an easy crowd pleaser. When peeling the peppers, don't worry about small bits of charred skin—they add flavor.

PREHEAT GRILL or barbecue to high. Grill red peppers, turning often with tongs, until blistered and blackened on all sides, about 10 minutes. Transfer to a large bowl and cover with plastic wrap. Let steam for 20 minutes, then peel skins and chop peppers into ½-inch pieces.

In a large skillet, heat 2 tbsp of the oil over medium-high heat. Add bread and fry, turning once, until golden brown, about 4 minutes. Remove bread and let cool. Cut into ½-inch cubes and set aside.

Return pan to medium heat and add garlic, tomatoes and almonds; sauté until juices have evaporated, about 2 minutes.

To make a stuffing: In a large bowl, combine garlic mixture, roasted peppers, bread, the remaining oil, parsley, vinegar and lemon juice; mix well. Season to taste with salt and pepper.

To make a smooth sauce for dipping: In a food processor, pulse garlic mixture, roasted peppers and bread until coarsely chopped. With the motor running, slowly add the remaining oil through the feed tube, processing until smooth. Transfer to a large bowl and stir in parsley, vinegar and lemon juice. Season to taste with salt and pepper. (*Make ahead: Cover and refrigerate for up to 2 weeks.*)

Makes 4 cups

5 sweet red peppers (about 1½ lbs)

1¼ cups extra-virgin olive oil, divided

1 slice country-style white bread, about 1 inch thick

1 clove garlic, minced

1 cup roughly chopped tomatoes (about 2 medium)

4 tbsp slivered almonds

1 tbsp minced fresh flat-leaf (Italian) parsley

1 tbsp sherry vinegar

Juice of ½ lemon or lime

Salt and freshly cracked black pepper

Pickled Beets, Shallots, Pearl Onions or Carrots

Makes two 8-ounce jars

10 to 15 small fresh beets

   or

20 large shallots, peeled

   or

4 cups pearl onions, peeled

   or

1 lb baby carrots, peeled

2 cups cider vinegar

1½ cups granulated sugar

½ cup water

2 tbsp whole peppercorns

2 tsp pickling salt

2 tsp fennel seeds

8 sprigs fresh rosemary

8 sprigs fresh thyme

8 dried bay leaves

Pickles are something to be craved. The tart crunch of a good pickle always adds an edge to my hunger for dinner, and I am sure I am not alone. Although these recipes are meant to preserve the vegetable, I'm afraid they are seldom actually called upon to do that—we tend to crack open the jars as soon as they are made. We add pickles to salads, arrange them on top of soups and feature them on charcuterie platters. Every year we make more, yet rarely do they make it into winter.

STERILIZE TWO 8-OUNCE CANNING JARS and lids (see page 92).

For beets: Scrub and trim beets, leaving ½ inch of stem and top root attached. Place in a large saucepan, cover with water and bring to a boil over high heat. Reduce heat, cover and simmer until tender, about 45 minutes. (The time will vary depending on the size of the beets.) Drain and rinse under cold water. Remove skins by rubbing beets with a paper towel and cut beets into bite-size pieces, if necessary.

For shallots: Place in a large saucepan, cover with water and bring to a boil over high heat. Reduce heat, cover and simmer until tender, about 10 minutes. Drain and rinse under cold water. Cut each shallot in half.

For pearl onions: Place in a heatproof bowl and pour in boiling water to cover; let stand for 2 minutes. Drain and chill in cold water.

For carrots: Place in a large saucepan, cover with water and bring to a boil over high heat. Reduce heat, cover and simmer until tender, about 6 minutes. Drain and rinse under cold water. Leave whole.

In a large saucepan, combine vinegar, sugar, water, >>>

peppercorns, salt and fennel seeds. Bring to a boil over high heat, stirring occasionally. Remove from heat.

Using a slotted spoon, pack vegetables into canning jars to within ¾ inch of rim, gently pushing down to fit. Add rosemary, thyme and bay leaves. Pour in vinegar mixture, leaving ½ inch headspace. Slide a clean spatula between the food and the jar, gently moving the food, to release any air bubbles. Wipe rims with a clean, damp cloth. Cover jars with lids and screw on bands until resistance is met. Process in a boiling water bath for 30 minutes (see page 90 for details on canning and preserving).

French Vanilla Ice Cream

Makes 4 cups

2 cups whipping (35%) cream

2 cups milk

½ cup granulated sugar, divided

1 vanilla bean, split lengthwise and seeds scraped out

6 large egg yolks

In case you are feeling adventurous, I've included this recipe for French vanilla ice cream. Basically, if you have an ice cream maker and can make a custard sauce, you can make your own ice cream. Please feel free to be as creative as you like with the recipe; you can add fruit or nuts and create any combination you like.

IN A MEDIUM SAUCEPAN, combine cream, milk and half the sugar. Add vanilla bean and seeds. Bring to a boil over high heat without stirring. Remove from heat and let stand for 30 minutes, allowing vanilla flavor to infuse the mixture.

In a bowl, whisk together egg yolks and the remaining sugar. Gradually whisk in cream mixture. (If the hot liquid is added too quickly, you may end up with scrambled eggs.)

Return mixture to saucepan and cook over medium-low heat, stirring constantly with a wooden spoon, until thick enough to coat the back of the spoon, about 5 minutes. Strain through a fine-mesh sieve into a bowl and discard vanilla. Let cool at room temperature for 30 minutes. Place plastic wrap directly on surface and refrigerate until chilled, about 2 hours.

Transfer to an ice cream maker and process as directed in the manufacturer's instructions.

Smash-In Ice Creams

The idea behind smash-in ice creams is that good-quality French vanilla ice cream can become your canvas for ice cream creations, and you won't have to learn how to make ice cream or buy an ice cream maker. Of course, if you want to make your own ice cream, go right ahead. Famous smash-ins include Cookie Dough and Cookies and Cream, but I've given you four variations that you may not be able to buy in the store. Branch out on your own, and experiment with Maple Shoofly Pie Smash-In Ice Cream or Sticky Toffee Pudding Smash-In Ice Cream.

RHUBARB SMASH-IN ICE CREAM: Using a stand mixer, a hand mixer or a potato masher, combine ice cream and compote. Top with a little more compote or ice cream, or serve with any spring or summer dessert, such as Cherry Clafoutis (page 141).

ALMOND SMASH-IN ICE CREAM: Using a stand mixer, a hand mixer or a potato masher, combine ice cream, almonds, cardamom and ginger. Serve with Plum Tarts (page 142).

CINNAMON SMASH-IN ICE CREAM: Using a stand mixer, a hand mixer or a potato masher, combine ice cream, cinnamon and nutmeg. Serve with Sticky Toffee Pudding (page 276) or Mile-High Pumpkin Pie (page 212).

PUMPKIN SEED BRITTLE SMASH-IN ICE CREAM: In a food processor, pulse brittle 5 times. Using a stand mixer, a hand mixer or a potato masher, combine ice cream and brittle. Serve topped with Caramel Sauce (page 305).

Makes 2 cups

2 cups good-quality French vanilla ice cream

½ cup Rhubarb Compote (see recipe, page 70)

½ cup sliced toasted almonds
1 tsp ground cardamom
½ tsp ground ginger

1 tbsp ground cinnamon
¼ tsp ground nutmeg

½ cup Pumpkin Seed Brittle (see recipe, page 215)

Shortcakes with Chantilly Cream and Macerated Strawberries

Makes 8 individual cakes or
20 mini cakes

SHORTCAKES

2 cups all-purpose flour

3 tbsp granulated sugar

1 tbsp baking powder

1 tsp salt

¼ cup unsalted butter, chilled

1¼ cups whipping (35%)
    cream

Additional whipping cream,
    for brushing

Icing sugar, for dusting

MACERATED STRAWBERRIES

½ vanilla bean (or ½ tsp pure
    vanilla extract)

4 cups fresh summer
    strawberries, hulled and
    quartered

½ cup granulated sugar

CHANTILLY CREAM

1 cup whipping (35%) cream

1 tbsp icing sugar

½ tsp pure vanilla extract

We feature these shortcakes on our summer dessert menu each year. I love to use strawberries at the height of the summer season, and these shortcakes highlight their natural flavor—there is so much of it in each little berry! We macerate the berries, creating an easy, natural sauce. The buttery, rich shortcakes provide a home for the strawberries and absorb their juice.

PREPARE THE SHORTCAKES: In a large bowl, whisk together flour, granulated sugar, baking powder and salt. Using a stand or hand grater, grate in butter. Using a wooden spoon, mix in cream until dough comes together.

Turn out onto a floured surface and pat dough into a 1-inch-thick circle. Using a round cutter, cut into 3-inch rounds (for mini cakes, use a 2-inch cutter). Transfer dough circles to a baking sheet lined with parchment paper and refrigerate for at least 20 minutes. (*Make ahead: Cover and refrigerate for up to 2 hours, or freeze in an airtight container for up to 1 month. When baking from frozen, increase baking time to 25 minutes, 20 minutes for minis.*)

Preheat oven to 400°F. Brush tops of dough circles with cream and dust with icing sugar. Bake until golden brown, about 15 minutes, 10 minutes for minis.

Prepare the strawberries: Using a paring knife, split vanilla bean in half lengthwise and gently scrape seeds into a large bowl. Add strawberries and sugar; toss to combine. Let stand for at least 30 minutes to blend the flavors. (*Make ahead: Cover and refrigerate for up to 3 hours.*) Makes 4 cups.   >>>

Prepare the Chantilly cream: In a bowl, whip cream until soft peaks form. Add icing sugar and vanilla; whip until just combined. Makes 1 cup.

To assemble: Cut shortcakes in half horizontally. For each serving, place the bottom half of a shortcake on a plate and generously spoon on strawberries and juices. Dollop with Chantilly cream and cover with top half of shortcake. Dust with icing sugar.

Blueberry Upside-Down Cake

Serves 8

BERRIES

¼ cup unsalted butter

½ cup lightly packed brown
sugar

3 cups fresh wild blueberries

CAKE

1½ cups all-purpose flour

¾ cup yellow cornmeal

1 tbsp baking powder

1 tsp salt

1½ cups granulated sugar

1 cup unsalted butter, softened

4 large eggs

2 tsp pure vanilla extract

¾ cup plain yogurt

Blueberries, like strawberries, have a short but sweet season. If you can wait for the tiny wild blueberries that are only available a few weeks of the year, this delicious cake will be even more special. When Chef Susur Lee visited our restaurant for an event, he enjoyed the cake so much he asked if he could put it on his own menu— what an honour.

Be sure the cake is still warm when you try and release it from the pan, otherwise it may stick—you can warm it up again if needed. Serve with a dollop of fresh Chantilly cream (page 137) or your favorite ice cream.

PREPARE THE BERRIES: In a 10-inch cast-iron skillet, melt butter over medium heat. Add brown sugar and cook, stirring constantly, until sugar is completely dissolved, about 8 minutes. Remove from heat and distribute blueberries over butter-sugar glaze; set aside.

Prepare the cake: Preheat oven to 350°F. In a large bowl, sift together flour, cornmeal, baking powder and salt; set aside.

In a stand mixer fitted with paddle attachment, cream sugar and butter until very light and fluffy. Add eggs, one at a time, beating after each addition. Add vanilla and mix until smooth. On low speed, mix in flour mixture. Fold in yogurt. Spread batter evenly over blueberries in skillet.

Bake until a toothpick inserted in the center of cake comes out clean, about 50 minutes. Let cool for 15 minutes, then run a knife around the inside edge of the skillet. Invert a large plate over skillet and, using oven mitts, turn skillet upside down to flip cake onto plate.

Cherry Clafoutis

This recipe seems to make its way on and off the menu all the time. I love it. I've substituted a number of different fruits—raspberries and peaches, for example—for the cherries, but I think the cherries give the best results. The custard-like batter works best if you let it stand for about 30 minutes before use, and even better if you let it rest overnight.

The recipe can be presented in six individual ½-cup ramekins, or in a 3-cup baking dish; it's your choice. I've also presented it in an 8-inch cast-iron skillet, which is quite lovely—a real showstopper. Serve topped with Chantilly cream (page 137) or Rhubarb Smash-In Ice Cream (page 135).

IN A FOOD PROCESSOR, combine flour, sugar, almonds and salt; pulse to combine. Add eggs, cream, vanilla, orange zest and lemon zest; pulse to combine, scraping down sides of bowl. Pour into a bowl, cover and refrigerate for at least 30 minutes or for up to 12 hours.

Preheat oven to 350°F. Arrange cherries in six ½-cup ramekins or one 3-cup baking dish. Stir chilled batter, then pour evenly over cherries. Bake until golden brown and puffed, about 40 minutes for ramekins and 1 hour for baking dish. Let cool for 20 minutes before serving.

Serves 6

½ cup all-purpose flour
½ cup granulated sugar
3 tbsp ground almonds
½ tsp salt
4 large eggs
1½ cups whipping (35%) cream
1 tsp pure vanilla extract
Grated zest of 1 orange and 1 lemon
1 lb sweet cherries, stemmed and pitted

Plum Tarts

Makes 8 individual tarts

8 plums, cut into wedges

⅔ cup granulated sugar,
   divided

1 tbsp ground cinnamon

All-purpose flour

1 recipe Pâte Sucrée (see recipe,
   page 307)

½ cup Frangipane (see recipe,
   page 304), made with
   almonds

2 large eggs, lightly beaten

If you are looking to dazzle your family and friends, a freshly baked plum tart topped with your favorite summer smash-in ice cream (see page 135) is a combination that can't be beat. In the restaurant, we garnish the tarts with coarse sugar to give them an extra bit of sweetness and crunch. Unfortunately, coarse sugar can be difficult to find at the grocery store, so instead I suggest sprinkling regular granulated sugar on the tarts before putting them in the oven. This will still add a bit of crunchy sweetness.

IN A BOWL, toss together plums, ½ cup of the sugar and cinnamon; set aside.

Line a large baking sheet with parchment paper or a silicone mat. Lightly sprinkle with flour and set aside.

On a lightly floured surface, divide pâte sucrée into 8 equal portions. Using a floured rolling pin, roll out into eight 7-inch rough circles. Transfer to prepared baking sheet. Spoon 1 tbsp frangipane in the center of each dough circle and spread out evenly, leaving a 2-inch border. Place a scant 1 cup of plum wedges in the center of each circle. Lift border of pastry up over filling, letting pastry fall naturally into folds. Brush sides with egg and sprinkle with the remaining sugar. Refrigerate for 10 minutes. (*Make ahead: Cover and refrigerate for up to 2 hours, or freeze in an airtight container for up to 3 weeks. Increase baking time by 5 minutes if baking from frozen.*)

Preheat oven to 350°F, with rack placed in the bottom third. Bake tarts until filling is bubbly and crust is golden brown, about 45 minutes. Let rest for 5 minutes before serving.

Watermelon and Ginger

Serves up to 20, depending on the size of the watermelon

1 large piece gingerroot (about 5 inches long), cut into 1-inch lengths

1 watermelon, cut into quarters lengthwise, then into 1-inch slices

I consider the perfect summer dessert to be a giant slice of juicy watermelon. The idea of trying to improve on something that comes out of the garden so wonderfully sweet may seem absurd, but if you want to try something a little more creative for guests, a hint of ginger may be just the thing.

RUB CUT SIDES of ginger all over each watermelon slice.

Whiskey Peaches and Cream

This is my favorite recipe from my favorite pastry cookbook: *In the Sweet Kitchen* by Regan Daley. Her recipe for Whiskey Peaches is so outstanding that I modified it slightly and now serve it to customers every summer in a number of different ways. Feel free to come up with your own variation!

My favorite peaches to use for this recipe are White Lady peaches. The sugar will help draw the natural juices out of the peaches, creating the sauce. The easiest way to serve these yummy peaches is over your favorite ice cream or topped with unsweetened Crème Fraîche (page 302). Alternatively, you could make Whiskey Peach Shortcakes by substituting these peaches for the strawberries in the shortcake recipe on page 136.

IN A BOWL, gently toss peaches, sugar, whiskey and vanilla seeds until peaches are coated. Cover and refrigerate for at least 1 hour or overnight to draw out as much juice as possible.

Serves 6

6 to 8 freestone peaches (about 1 lb), thinly sliced
3 tbsp granulated sugar
2 tbsp whiskey (your favorite variety)
1 vanilla bean, split lengthwise and seeds scraped out

Whole Wheat Focaccia

Makes 1 flat loaf

6 cups whole wheat flour
   (preferably Red Fife), divided
2 tsp dry instant yeast
2 tsp salt
3 cups water
1 cup extra-virgin olive oil,
   divided
2 cups all-purpose flour (approx.)
1 plum (Roma) tomato, thinly
   sliced
1 tbsp chopped fresh rosemary
Kosher salt
Cornmeal for dusting

We understand that it may not be possible for everyone to plant, grow, harvest and process their own Red Fife wheat. What we do suggest is that you look for organic whole wheat flour at your local grocery store. Focaccia is an easy one-rise bread that is great for sandwiches or can be sliced for crostini.

IN A LARGE BOWL, combine 4 cups of the whole wheat flour, yeast and salt.

In another bowl, combine water and ½ cup of the oil; add to flour mixture. Using a spoon, gradually work in the remaining whole wheat flour and all-purpose flour until dough pulls away from the sides of the bowl.

Turn out onto a lightly floured surface and knead until dough is smooth and elastic, about 10 minutes. Place in a large greased bowl, turning dough to grease all over. Cover with a tea towel and let rise in a still oven, with light on and door closed, until doubled in size, about 1½ hours.

Punch down dough and place on a greased baking sheet that's been dusted with cornmeal. Press or roll out dough to fill baking sheet. Pour the remaining oil over dough and work it with your fingertips to create dimples all over the bread. Let rest for 30 minutes. Meanwhile, preheat oven to 400°F.

Cover dough with tomato slices and sprinkle with rosemary and salt to taste. Bake until golden and crisp, about 30 minutes. Let cool slightly before serving.

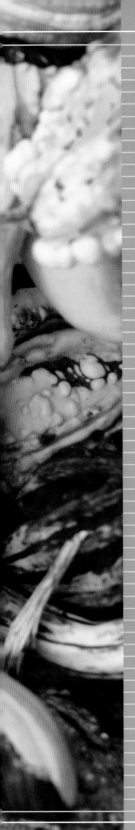

WHAT TO EAT

FALL

Almost imperceptibly, the glory of summer

becomes the dignity of autumn. I'm never quite sure how I know, but long before the leaves change or the geese fly south, I sense that some of the urgency has gone out of the weather. One day the angle of the light has changed. Another day the ceiling of the sky seems farther away, a deeper blue. The crickets grow silent at night, and the hum of other insects dies away in the afternoons. The nights grow cooler. And then it is autumn.

Of course, it's not as simple as that on the farm. Plump tomatoes keep appearing into October, and corn is still sweet and crisp into September. But somehow our cravings run ahead of the season. One day we realize we crave a soup—or at least our clients at the restaurant do. Mushrooms are back, and suddenly their earthy richness seems like just the thing. Apples are falling off the branches, as though the trees don't want them anymore, and their crisp tartness now seems preferable to the juicy sweetness of plump summer fruit.

I think of autumn as a time to really start cooking. The point of summer dishes is to do as little as possible. The food is already delicious; really, you just want to avoid interfering with its intrinsic taste. But in fall, you want something richer. You start coaxing out new flavors, achieving different textures, combining things to create a dish that didn't grow out of the ground on its own. I see it as a time to get a little more creative. I love the Jerusalem artichokes and black kale that Chris grows, but I'm not going to toss them on a plate the way I would a glorious August tomato.

Even when the weather does turn decisively and brittle stalks are all that remain of the reckless growth of summer, the bounty of the harvest has hardly disappeared. In fact, it is piling up all around us. Instead of the fleeting crops of July, we now have foods that endure (in fact, the autumn harvest yields foods that can safely be thrown across the room). A pile of zucchini induces a kind of anxiety: you have to think of a way to eat it right away. But a pile of squash inspires a reassuring confidence—you're looking at weeks of delicious

meals. If the summer harvest is about living and eating in the moment, the fall crops are about the pleasure of knowing that things are taken care of.

Perhaps no other foods represent the autumn harvest quite like the "three sisters": grain corn, beans and squash. Not the most glamorous sisters, to be sure. But they have great personalities. For one thing, they store well. North American settlers learned from First Nations farmers how to make it through the brutal winters; without cellars full of the three sisters, they would have starved. For another thing, they abide by one of my cardinal rules: what grows together, goes together. Just like basil and tomatoes, or oranges and olives (if only oranges and olives grew in Canada!), beans, corn and squash seem to have been made for each other. Planted together, the beans replace the nitrogen the corn strips from the soil, while the squash

provides ground cover to keep down weeds. In a meal, the corn provides the starchy backbone, the beans offer protein and the squash contributes a rich sweetness. I will probably never pass up duck confit in favor of the three sisters. But then, cooking is not an either/or project, at least not over a span of time like a season. And if you're interested in the relationship of earth to table, you can do a lot worse than the sisters.

Still, when we all gathered at the end of the harvest to celebrate the year, it wasn't squash we ate, or corn or beans. It wasn't turkey, either (though there were turkeys waddling around nearby). It was pizza.

If I were to ask anyone who worked on the farm all year—and that includes all of the restaurant staff—what they remember as the highlight of the year, I think they'd all name the harvest pizza party. I think Chris would say the same thing. To me, that means we've created something pretty special with our farm-restaurant collaboration. It's not something you can easily measure, and perhaps I'm being a little romantic about it, but I love the fact that everyone who pitched in over the sometimes back-breaking weeks could come together to take part in celebrating our success.

When I think of it, I'm reminded of that (largely forgotten) social moment in traditional farm life, the barn raising. All those collaborators, whose expertise is for the most part in something else, gathering to make something great, something none of them could have done on their own. In that sense, the sous-chef or server who shows up to pull weeds is not unlike the farmer from down the road who takes time off from his own fields to help his neighbor raise a beam. And once the roof is on, all the people who got their hands dirty gather around a table to enjoy the moment of completion.

That's our pizza party. It's not a fancy affair. But it is very much an earth-to-table moment, since we're all gathered behind the barn, just around the corner from the ducks and chickens wandering around (at least until twilight, when they all head to bed). Horses stand quizzically by the fence, wondering what all the fuss is about. Only a few yards away are the nearly empty fields, where a few leaves

of hardy salad greens push into the cool October night and an acorn squash or two wait to be harvested. A little farther away, cows and pigs cluster at the edge of a tiny copse of trees. This is a quintessential farm dinner.

Except for a few details. A band is tuning up near the shed roof Chris has erected over the wood oven, which has been taken off bread duty for the night. Bettina and I have rolled out dozens of circles of pizza dough, and dishes of toppings line two long tables: peppers, mushrooms, mozzarella, arugula, Chris's sausage, zucchini, tomatoes, goat cheese, chicken, bacon, onion, olives, chorizo, Swiss chard, basil, and much more. Coolers are overflowing with ice and beer. Another table is soon covered with corks and empty wine bottles.

Tonight the amateur farmers are amateur chefs as well—and those of us who are chefs every other day of the year, well, we take our place in line along with everyone else. Everyone inches along the table, judiciously (or recklessly) arranging cheese and vegetables and sausages on their circles of dough, preparing them for Chris to slide into the smoking oven. Chris shakes his head at some of the ambitiously piled pizzas, despairing of ever getting the heavier ones off the plate and onto the wooden paddle he'll use to get them into the heat. But it all seems to go off without a hitch, and all the pizzas emerge spectacularly. They're fragrant and bubbling and slightly blackened around the edges. People sample each other's, or share with those who have to wait. The mood is more than collegial. When people gather around a table this way, they are friends.

Bettina's Wheat Story

Our first wheat harvest was a bust. The weather turned very wet in August, and the kernels started to germinate. In other words, the crop was pretty much lost. Good thing it wasn't left up to me to carry on the last remaining seeds of a species. And good thing there was no village depending on our agricultural acumen. Farming, we were reminded once again, is serious business.

But the following year was awesome. Chris had an amazing field of amber grain positively glowing under the hot blue sky. We had a great harvest day.

There wasn't much we could do to help the wheat along once it had begun to grow, so we'd spent the summer hoping for the best and waiting eagerly for the right moment to bring it in. Farming is a little like cooking, in that timing is crucial. Harvest the wheat too soon, and it's green and all but impossible to mill. Wait too long, and the berries start to sprout. Chris can tell the wheat is ready when the

Red Fife wheat long before it becomes Bettina's bread.

berries fall off the stems fairly easily and are hard. He presses them with his fingernail; if it hardly makes a dent, the wheat is ready.

Jeff and I were keen to avoid a repeat of the previous year's disappointment, so we were ready one Tuesday morning when Chris called to say it was time to harvest the wheat. We drove out to the farm as quickly as we could. The morning was already hot and buzzing with grasshoppers.

The dry stalks rattled and rustled as we readied the combine for what seemed—to me, at least—to be a watershed moment. For most of the morning, Chris rattled on about how dangerous the combine was. He cautioned us with hair-raising stories about farmers dismembered by the merciless machinery, all the while working away merrily with his hands, arms and even his head in all the places he seemed to be warning us about. I tried to stand at least ten feet away at all times.

When the combine was deemed ready to bring in the wheat, Jeff and I took turns driving while Chris made adjustments on the fly. At first, all we seemed to be harvesting were crickets and grasshoppers, along with some ragweed. Careful inspection of the bin revealed that there were a few kernels of wheat sprinkled among the stuff we wouldn't be turning into bread.

We laughed for a bit at our sad harvest of bugs and weeds, but were quick to solve the problem. Our settings were off. Once again, Chris was up to his armpits in what certainly looked like the most dangerous part of the machine. In any case, he was cheerfully recounting farm lore, watching us squirm as he tossed out comments like "That's where people get totally wrapped up and found days later." But after one pass, everything seemed to be working properly, and Chris remained in full possession of all his limbs.

The combine is actually a fairly simple machine that cuts the stalk, strips the wheat berries, then sifts out everything that is not wheat (that is, everything that is not the size of a wheat berry). And as for the grasshoppers that had us so worried, Chris made the very important point that on a conventional farm, where they use pesticides, there wouldn't be any insects to laugh at because they would all have been killed much earlier in the season.

The combine rattled through the field like a long-lost cousin of the Zamboni, churning up clouds of dust, shooting a stream of wheat out of its curved beak and leaving a row of amber stubble in its wake.

It was a very satisfying day. And it was apparent that we actually had something we were going to be able to use. All jokes aside, it was pretty amazing to see the hopper fill up with seeds and to know that we had enough to turn into bread.

When the field was clear and the combine had shuddered to a halt at the treeline, the silence came rushing back, then the birdsong, then the swish of cars out by the road. We made our way back to the farmhouse just as the shadows lengthened enough to tell us that evening was on its way, but well before the blue sky had darkened or the heat of the afternoon had abated. Dust and chaff had stuck to Jeff's and Chris's sweaty brows, and I had to assume I looked the same. When I took my gloves off to drink a beer on the farmhouse deck, my hands looked strangely pale and clean at the end of my dusty arms.

FARMERS' MARKETS

Since I support Slow Food, you won't be surprised that I advocate slow shopping as well.

That's how I go about my business at a farmers' market. I don't plan to get in and out quickly; I plan to linger and find out what's going on. The shopping list you go in with may be provisional—you want some tomatoes, for example, or some salad greens. But you're sure to come across something you didn't expect—perhaps you didn't know it was in season, perhaps you just hadn't thought of it, perhaps you've never tried it.

That's one of the most enticing things about a farmers' market. You may not have had a craving for honey made by bees that have been feasting on blueberry blossoms, or for sausages made from Berkshire hogs, or for a creamy local Brie. But there it is. And now you know what you're having for dinner.

The food isn't the only thing that's going to make you feel satisfied by a trip to the farmers' market. I really want these businesses to succeed, and I'm always pleased to do my part to help that happen.

Tips for Your Next Trip to the Market

DON'T WORRY ABOUT ORGANIC VERSUS NON-ORGANIC. You are at a farmers' market, so the moral battle is won. Ask questions: some farmers who do not practice organic agriculture for various reasons still practice sustainable agriculture.

TASTE, TASTE, TASTE. Most stalls want you to try their wares. You are not committed to buy. Go to the market with an open mind.

BRING CASH (IN SMALL BILLS). These farmers and beekeepers and artisans aren't going to take credit or debit cards. They'll have a cash box, and I encourage you to do your best to fill it.

TAKE YOUR KIDS. These are the times we reminisce about as adults, even though we didn't appreciate them in the moment.

TRY SOMETHING NEW. If it looks good but you don't know what to do with it, ask. That's what the farmer is there for. Asking about preserving methods is a good idea as well. It is in season, so learn how to preserve that flavor.

BRING A COOLER and leave it in your car. It will keep those tender greens you came across fresh during the ride home.

BRING A CLOTH SHOPPING BAG (or five). Reuse, recycle. You know the drill.

BRING YOUR OWN COFFEE MUG. Most markets have a really great fair-trade coffee stall.

DAIRY

Blessed are the cheese-makers, that's what I say.

If there is someone in your neighborhood making cheese, chances are your local economy takes its food seriously. In the end, the best intentions to eat locally and seasonally depend on the availability of products worth eating, and the presence of a cheesemaker suggests that there will be other artisans and producers in the neighborhood.

Cheese, like wine, like charcuterie, like canning, is one of those wonderful accidents of culinary history in which the process of preserving something not only makes it taste *better* but transforms it into something absolutely wonderful. All of these things together—a glass or two of wine and a plate of charcuterie, tart pickles and robust cheese—is my idea of heaven.

Cheese is one of those things that gets adulterated when someone makes a whole bunch of it at once and then ships it around the country. I'm speaking, of course, of the bright orange stuff known as "cheddar" (presumably because of its slight similarity to the hard, sharp-tasting cheese made in the village of Cheddar, England). If the only cheese you had ever tasted was the waxy, bright orange slabs stacked in supermarkets, you might wonder why people get so excited by cheese, why the French go to the trouble of making 246 varieties of the stuff, and why some people find it so difficult to imagine going without it. But once you've had a gentle Chavignol or a ripe Morbier with a wine equal to the occasion, the mystery will have been admirably cleared up.

It used to be that the most "local" cheese we could get for

the restaurant came from Quebec, where a healthy cheese culture and an exemption from federal rules prohibiting raw-milk cheese (as if all the best cheese, including the Parmesan the politicians and bureaucrats sprinkle on their spaghetti, weren't made from raw milk) has sustained a large number of excellent *fromageries*. But I am delighted that there is now someone in my neighborhood I can turn to.

Ruth Klahsen is a veteran chef (and a graduate of the Stratford Chefs School, which is just down the road), so she knows what she likes and what to look for. She makes soft, young, herb-rolled ewe's-milk cheese and hard, assertive Toscano at Monforte, her unpretentious cheesery. The milk she uses comes from local Mennonite shepherds—about as local, nonindustrial and sustainable as it gets.

I see Ruth's business as a crucial link in our local food culture. She is supporting healthy, sustainable agriculture and is herself a producer of food that nourishes both those who eat it and the local economy as a whole. She is part of a renaissance of artisanal knowledge, a node in a small network of people and businesses who together comprise a sort of parallel food system.

In this context, I have to mention Mapleton Dairy, where we get our ice cream. And I do mean ice cream, not the mysterious aerated stuff we're all familiar with. Traditional ice cream is another of the old-school foods that has been so diminished by years of imitation that we forget how glorious the original was.

Mapleton's ice cream is so dense and rich that a few small spoonfuls are often enough to satisfy any craving. And when it melts, it turns into crème anglaise—unlike "ice cream," which never really melts at all. I once discovered a small slab of "ice cream," perfectly preserved in its little dish, hours after it had been set aside in the heat of the kitchen. Embalmed in stabilizers and lecithin, it looked as though it had just come out of the fridge.

Dairy is big business, like any other. But even in a world in which Holsteins saturated

with growth hormones are hooked up to computerized milking machines that look as though they belong on the set of a science-fiction movie, milk and cheese have somehow managed to cling to the innocence of a time when dairy was delivered to your front step each morning. That world is of course long gone, but good cheese and ice cream are still out there. You just have to find them.

Top photo: Monforte's ricotta cheese.
Bottom photo: Chris Krucker and a ManoRun goat.

CHEF DAN BARBER

If Dan Barber seems a little professorial for a cook, he comes by it honestly. He sits on the advisory board of Harvard Medical School's Center for Health and Global Environment. This is a guy who wants to get the word out.

And it's not just theory with Barber. His NYC restaurant Blue Hill was nominated "Best New Restaurant" by the James Beard Foundation and rated one of "America's Best Restaurants" by *Gourmet* magazine. In 2007, he was himself identified as Chef of Merit by *Bon Appétit*. Clearly, Barber knows his way around a kitchen.

Blue Hill's reputation is for local, seasonal food, and much of it comes from the Stone Barns Center for Food and Agriculture, a not-for-profit farm and educational center only thirty miles north of Manhattan. Barber serves on the board

of directors and has another restaurant on-site. I had long wanted to see for myself how he had created an earth-to-table regime that produces such excellent results. I also wanted to get my staff jazzed about what we were doing at the Mill. I knew we were blazing a trail in our area, but how could I show my team that we were doing what only the best in the world were doing?

We decided to take some of our kitchen staff to Blue Hill at Stone Barns. It wouldn't be easy to get away from the restaurant for long; we had Monday off and could push into Tuesday, but that was it. Bettina had to be in the kitchen at 9 a.m. So we undertook the eleven-hour drive to NYC after service on Sunday night. (If we were going to take a road trip, we figured we might as well spend a night in Manhattan.)

We arrived in New York early in the morning, no one feeling very "Vegas, baby, Vegas!" anymore. We went to our hotel and took showers, but had to avoid the temptation to curl up in the fresh beds. We had a lot of living to do in two days.

We toured the usual sites in Manhattan, then went to the Spotted Pig, in Greenwich Village, for dinner. This is one of Mario Batali's restaurants (the chef is April Bloomfield, a Chez Panisse alumna). We had a two-hour wait for our table, which we cheerfully took advantage of by strolling around the Village, looking for a beer. We noticed that all of the other restaurants were pretty much dead. But the Spotted Pig was crammed! We sat at what barely passed for a table for five, elbow to elbow, soaking up the electric energy in the room and practically shouting over the sea of voices.

This place is famous for two things: burgers and gnudi. It was good for my cooks to see that something as common as a burger could be elevated to world-class heights—not a foie gras and truffle burger, just a burger.

Gnudi had been on our menu for about a year (see our recipe on page 60). It's a relative of gnocchi, basically a robust ravioli without the pasta wrapper—indeed, *gnudi* means "nude" in Italian. Scott, my line cook, had made them every day during that year and considered himself a bit of an expert (he's a cocky boy, but real talented). But the young expert was as speechless as everyone else when the master, Mario Batali, rolled in on his scooter, in his signature shorts and bright clogs, just like on TV! The room suddenly went quiet, all eyes on the guy they'd come hoping to see.

"Scott," I said, "why don't you ask him how he makes the gnudi."

It took only one more glass of liquid courage to convince him to approach Mario. Next thing I knew, they were out on the front stoop, sharing a cigarette and talking gnudi! Mario was incredibly gracious with his time, exactly the kind of guy I'd raise a glass with any time. My whole staff fell under his gregarious spell. I know that Alex, Bryan and Scott now treat all food, including burgers and fries, with the care they would give a fillet of beef.

The next day, after a pitifully short sleep and a desperate infusion of coffee, we headed to

compound may be small in comparison to, say, an Iowa corn farm, but it is dense with life and activity, and is truly inspiring.

Stone Barns relies on organic and biodynamic farming methods, using careful crop rotation and traditional soil-improvement techniques to keep the land amazingly productive. The center is a kind of dreamscape for people interested in the earth-to-table relationship. In addition to growing the food and serving it in Barber's restaurant, the center offers workshops on everything from gardening in your own backyard to wine tasting to lectures on climate change.

Stone Barns. Driving up to the farm on a foggy autumn morning was a little like entering a different world. Manorial stone buildings with leaded windows and old-world architecture stood clustered in the midst of a kaleidoscope of fields lined with trees in their autumn colors. Big black Berkshire pigs, which looked more like wild boars than the pink pigs we're used to seeing, sniffed and rooted purposefully in a copse of trees. The

Chris Krucker had caught up with us by this point, and he was particularly impressed by the greenhouses. I had wanted Chris to see first-hand what we could build together in the future, and the fully irrigated, climate-controlled greenhouses did the trick. Chris looked around enviously, just as I would do when we got a tour of the kitchen.

We met Barber for the first time at dinner. He's quiet,

thoughtful and very slim—pretty much the opposite of what you imagine a chef to be. It's easy to see that he is passionate about the need to change how people think about food, and frustrated that the playing field is so slanted against anyone who challenges the fast-food, fast-farming orthodoxy. He speaks with the ease of someone who has explained this all many times, weaving statistics and figures into his conversation as though it is the most natural thing in the world.

I had a thousand questions to ask him. But one thing I had to get out of the way was the biggest question: Why? There are easier ways to get good vegetables than to establish a sprawling (albeit lovely) organic compound or to follow the seasons. I know this from experience.

His answer turns our usual sense of food culture, which allows us to have whatever we want whenever we want it, upside down. He ascribes his pursuit of local, seasonal food to "hedonism." He waits for New Jersey and New York asparagus to come up because it will taste better than the Californian or Mexican asparagus he could have much earlier. For one thing, the local asparagus—ripened on its stalks rather than in the back of a rattling transport trailer—will actually *be* better. But there is more to it than that. Just waiting for the asparagus makes it taste better. As he puts it, "With restriction comes a greater pleasure when the produce finally arrives." Waiting for the appropriate season is itself a kind of sauce.

Hedonism may not be the most obvious guide in spring

and winter. He calls the span between mid-February and the beginning of May "root vegetable hell." But the reward is delicious and memorable: tender, seasonable asparagus crowds the menu. And then it is gone. He remembers that the last day he served it the previous year was June 28.

There are, of course, enough measurable, practical reasons for eating local food to fill an entire book (or at least an appendix to one; see page 308): your personal health, the health of the local environment and the local economy all depend on exactly the sort of things Blue Hill and Stone Barns are pioneering. But if it didn't taste good and feel good, no one would do it.

Barber bristles a little when I ask him what he would say to those who think that investing so much in the creation of the perfect carrot is somehow elitist. First, he says, it's not such a bad thing that the so-called elite is driving the shift toward sustainable agriculture (we share a laugh at the idea that cooks are considered an elite). In fact, it's a source of optimism. Pointing at the examples of feminism and the civil rights movement, he makes the case that "most trends or revolutions begin and flow *down* the ladder" as they are adopted more generally and become a new norm. We'd be much worse off if the elites were developing a taste for something even less sustainable than the lifestyles they (and we) are living right now.

Even so, the "elitist" label suggests that hedonists of the Blue Hill school of thought are out of touch with real life. Barber believes this assessment couldn't be more wrong. "Most people's perception of local, organic food is that it is expensive and therefore elitist or unattainable," he says. "I would say, the price of conventional food doesn't reflect the cost of production. The price you are

paying for food is not the full cost. This is very common in America, where the agriculture industry is heavily subsidized. Not to mention the external costs, like health care and environment, which are paid by taxes, rather than at the cash register."

He's quick to point out that these are not trivial costs. In the mid-1980s, Americans spent twice as much per capita on food as they did on health care. Twenty years later, while the percentage of income spent on food has dropped by half (to just over 8 percent), the percentage spent on health care has more than doubled (to just over 16 percent). In other words, cheap food is costing a lot of money.

Still, like Heston Blumenthal, Barber is infectiously optimistic about the future of sustainable food. "The end of cheap food is here. That could be a very good thing, or bad," he says. "It depends on what we as chefs and consumers are going to demand. Local, sustainable farms or more imports, empty calories and worse food." He thinks we will make the right choice. Even if his form of

hedonism is not enough to change our food system, simple economics might do the trick in an era when the price of a barrel of oil keeps rising.

For one thing, local food "will not only become more attractive, it could become more convenient"—and less expensive, since it won't have to be shipped as far. For another, it will be cheaper to produce. Small, balanced farms are in a better position to use the free inputs of sunlight and compost; factory farms depend on fertilizers and pesticides made from dwindling fossil fuel reserves. Feedlot beef, fattened on corn intensively farmed on fields drenched with fossil fuels, will struggle to compete with grass-fed (that is, solar-fed) beef in an economy marked by high oil prices (and high corn prices, as ethanol plants gobble up the

mountains of subsidized corn
that once seemed as inex-
haustible as the oil fields of the
Middle East). Soon, the small
farmer will start to look very
efficient.

Barber's scholarly but passionate approach to food and
food culture is infectious and
urgent, and it is easy to be swept
up in his arguments. But you
know he's right when you judge
him by his own standard: hedonism. The cooks in New York
were all jealous when they
heard we were going to eat at
Blue Hill at Stone Barns.

Dinner was a magical trans-
formation of the foods we'd seen
in the fields. Some vegetables,
like the baby carrots and
turnips, were served whole,

lightly dressed with vinaigrette.
Others were served as a custard
or puree. It was all simply
presented—unadorned but delicious. If hedonism is the idea
that the standard of ethical
judgment should be pleasure, by
the end of the meal I was ready
to do the right thing.

FALL RECIPES

Fresh Verbena or Mint Tea

Making tea from fresh herbs is as simple as pouring hot water over a handful of your favorite leaves and letting it steep for about 5 minutes. The longer you let it steep, the more flavorful your tea will be.

I was inspired by a summer trip to Amsterdam, where one of the more popular drinks on patios was fresh mint tea. Glasses packed with mint were brought to the tables, and the minty aroma would fill the air! It was really quite dramatic.

Verbena tea can be made right up until early winter, when verbena is still in the garden, just hanging on. And, perhaps surprisingly, mint will still be in the garden through the fall.

FOR VERBENA TEA: Pick a small handful of verbena leaves from the tips of the plant. You should have about ¼ cup. Wash thoroughly. Fill a teapot with boiling water to heat the pot. Drain, place the leaves in the pot, cover with 2 cups boiling water and let steep for 5 minutes. Serve piping hot, with about ½ tbsp honey.

FOR MINT TEA: Rinse 4 to 5 mint sprigs and place them upside down in a glass. Pour hot water over the mint and let steep for about 5 minutes.

Mulled Cider and Cranberry

Both apples and cranberries are at their best in the fall. This recipe brings together these two great autumn flavors to make a delicious warm drink.

IN A SAUCEPAN, combine cider, cranberry juice, sugar, brandy, nutmeg, cloves, cinnamon stick, lemon zest and orange zest. Heat over medium heat, just to combine flavors; do not boil. Strain and serve warm. Garnish with apple slices and cranberries.

Makes 6 cups

4 cups pure apple cider
1 cup cranberry juice
½ cup granulated sugar
2 tbsp brandy
½ tsp ground nutmeg
2 whole cloves
1 cinnamon stick
Grated zest of 1 lemon and
    1 orange
Apple slices and fresh
    cranberries

Heirloom Beet Salad with Feta and Pumpkin Seeds

Serves 4

2 bunches beets (about 4 lbs),
    mixed colors if possible

¾ cup extra-virgin olive oil,
    divided

½ tsp kosher salt

6 tbsp sherry vinegar

2 tbsp local honey

1 shallot, thinly sliced

4 oz feta cheese, crumbled

½ cup packed arugula leaves

¼ cup Toasted Pumpkin Seeds
    (see recipe, below)

Salt and freshly cracked
    black pepper

This is the only way to cook beets. Roasting the beets (rather than boiling them) allows them to keep their color and all of their flavor.

PREHEAT OVEN TO 400°F. Cut greens off beets, leaving about ½ inch of stem. Scrub beets and toss with 2 tbsp of the oil and salt. Place in a large roasting pan with 1 tbsp water. Cover tightly with foil and roast until beets are tender when pierced, about 40 minutes. (The roasting time will depend on the size and type of beet, so it's best to check them earlier.) Remove foil and let cool. Peel beets by slipping the skins off with your fingers. Slice beets into wedges and set aside.

In a medium bowl, combine the remaining oil, vinegar, honey and shallot. Stir in beets, cover and refrigerate for at least 2 hours or for up to 12 hours.

Drain dressing from the beets and place them on a serving platter. Sprinkle with feta, arugula and pumpkin seeds. Season to taste with salt and pepper.

Toasted Pumpkin Seeds

Makes 1½ cups

1½ cups green hulled
    pumpkin seeds

1 tsp extra-virgin olive oil

¼ tsp kosher salt

IN A LARGE CAST-IRON SKILLET, toast pumpkin seeds over medium heat, stirring constantly, until puffed and slightly brown, about 10 minutes. Drizzle with oil and sprinkle with salt, stirring to coat. Serve warm or at room temperature. (*Make ahead: Store in an airtight container for up to 3 days.*)

"The beet is the most intense of vegetables. Tomatoes are lusty enough, yet there runs through tomatoes an undercurrent of frivolity. Beets are deadly serious."

TOM ROBBINS

French Onion Soup

At the restaurant we have the luxury of being able to make our soups with wonderfully thick, rich stocks. This may be difficult to achieve at home so we suggest the addition of a little flour to help with the thickening process. If there is one item our regular guests will never let us take off the menu, this is it. The recipe can easily be halved for a smaller party.

IN A LARGE, HEAVY POT, heat butter and oil over medium-low heat. Add onions, cover and cook, stirring occasionally, until softened and translucent, about 20 minutes. Increase heat to medium-high and add sugar and salt; sauté, scraping up any brown bits from the bottom of the pot, until onions are softened and a deep, rich brown, about 15 minutes.

Reduce heat to medium, sprinkle with flour and cook, stirring constantly, for 2 to 3 minutes. Gradually whisk in 2 cups of the stock, then add the remaining stock and wine. Season to taste with salt and pepper. Simmer for about 30 minutes to blend the flavors. Taste and adjust seasoning with salt and pepper, if necessary.

Preheat oven to 425°F. Divide baguette cubes among 8 individual ovenproof bowls. Fill bowls with onion soup and sprinkle each with a thick layer of cheese. Set bowls on a large rimmed baking sheet. Bake until cheese is browned, about 8 minutes. Garnish with thyme.

Serves 8

3 tbsp unsalted butter

1 tbsp extra-virgin olive oil

3 lbs medium yellow onions (about 5), thinly sliced

1 tsp granulated sugar

1 tsp salt

1 tbsp all-purpose flour

8 cups Beef Stock (see recipe, page 296)

2 cups local dry red wine

Salt and freshly cracked black pepper

2 cups cubed baguette, toasted

4½ cups shredded Gruyère cheese (about 1 lb)

2 tsp minced fresh thyme

Crispy Halloumi Cheese
with Cortland Apple Chutney

Serves 4

**CORTLAND APPLE
CHUTNEY**

4 prunes, chopped

2 Cortland apples, peeled and
    cut into ¼-inch dice

1 dried apricot, chopped

½ cup lightly packed golden
    brown sugar

½ cup pure apple cider

2 tbsp cider vinegar

Pinch ground allspice

Pinch cayenne pepper

HALLOUMI CHEESE

1 cup all-purpose flour

Salt and freshly cracked
    black pepper

1 package (12 oz) Halloumi
    cheese, sliced vertically into
    eight 1-inch-thick pieces

3 tbsp extra-virgin olive oil
    (approx.), divided

SALAD

2 cups packed baby arugula
    leaves

¼ cup Dijon Vinaigrette (see
    recipe, page 295)

Salt and freshly cracked
    black pepper

I received this cheese and various other varieties from Monforte Dairy, which is owned and operated by Ruth Klahsen, a former instructor from my Stratford Chefs School days. Halloumi has been around in Greece for hundreds of years, but is finally catching on in the U.S. and Canada. It is made by hand from a mix of sheep's milk and goat's milk. The soft, springy, oval curd resembles fresh mozzarella and has a milky yet tangy flavor. A versatile cheese, it can be grated, grilled, marinated, fried or eaten as is. If you like a grilled cheese sandwich, you have got to try Halloumi cheese!

PREPARE THE CHUTNEY: In a saucepan, combine prunes, apples, apricot, brown sugar, cider, vinegar, allspice and cayenne. Bring to a boil over high heat. Reduce heat and simmer, stirring occasionally, until thickened to a syrup-like consistency, about 30 minutes. (*Make ahead: Let cool and refrigerate in an airtight container for up to 3 days.*) Makes 1 cup.

Prepare the cheese: In a shallow bowl, combine flour and salt and pepper to taste. Add cheese and toss gently to coat. In a skillet, heat 2 tbsp of the oil over medium-high heat. Add cheese, in batches, and cook, turning once, until golden brown on both sides, about 8 minutes per batch, adding more oil between batches as needed. Season to taste with salt and pepper.

Prepare the salad: In a bowl, toss arugula with vinaigrette and salt and pepper to taste. Place ½ cup of arugula on each plate. Top with 2 slices of cheese and 1 tbsp of chutney.

Watercress Salad with Warm Bacon and Apple Cider Vinaigrette

We are quite fortunate to have a small creek running through the restaurant's property, from which we harvest enough watercress for all our summer and fall dishes. Wild watercress is much spicier than the stuff found in grocery stores.

IN A LARGE BOWL, whisk together vinegar, cider and mustard. Add watercress and toss to coat.

In a skillet, heat oil over medium heat. Add bacon and cook, turning once, until crisp, about 12 minutes. Transfer to a plate lined with paper towels and let cool slightly, then crumble into small pieces.

Return crumbled bacon to skillet and add apple slices, tossing gently to coat; cook until apple is softened, about 5 minutes.

Pour bacon mixture over watercress and toss to combine. Divide among 4 plates and season to taste with salt and pepper.

Serves 4

2 tbsp cider vinegar
2 tbsp pure apple cider
1 tsp grainy mustard
2 bunches watercress (about
    10 oz), trimmed
2 tbsp canola oil
8 slices bacon (about 12 oz)
1 small apple, peeled and thinly
    sliced
Salt and freshly cracked
    black pepper

Spot Prawns with Chanterelles

Serves 6

1 lb spot prawns

Salt and freshly cracked
    black pepper

2 tbsp extra-virgin olive oil,
    divided

5 cups fresh chanterelle
    mushrooms (about 11 oz),
    halved

1 cup rice vinegar

⅓ cup butter, cut into cubes

1 tbsp minced fresh thyme

1 bunch watercress (about
    5 oz), trimmed

Spot prawns, from the west coast of North America, have an unbelievable true shrimp flavor—what shrimp is supposed to taste like. Spot prawns are one of the few types of shrimp we can feel good about purchasing. This is another recipe from Spencer's. I love it. Prawns are best cooked in the shell, but for ease of eating, you can peel them, leaving the tail portion on.

SEASON PRAWNS WITH salt and pepper to taste. In a skillet, heat half the oil over medium-high heat until very hot but not smoking. Add prawns and sear well on one side, about 3 minutes. Turn and cook until just cooked through, about 30 seconds. Using tongs, remove prawns to a plate; set aside and keep warm.

Reduce heat to medium and add the remaining oil to the pan. Add mushrooms and cook, without turning, until softened, about 6 minutes. Turn and cook until golden brown, about 3 minutes. Using tongs, remove mushrooms to the plate with the prawns.

Add vinegar to the pan and cook until syrupy, about 6 minutes. Whisk in butter, one cube at a time, whisking constantly. Do not let boil, or sauce will split. Stir in thyme and season to taste with salt and pepper. Reduce heat to low and add prawns and mushrooms, stirring to coat with sauce; cook until heated through, about 45 seconds.

Divide prawn mixture among 6 plates. Place a piece of watercress on top of each and drizzle with extra sauce.

La Bomba: A Spicy Condimento

This spicy condiment known as "the bomb" is also called "the Italian Viagra." You can use this as a sandwich spread, pasta sauce, pizza topping or part of an antipasto platter. I tend to just eat it with Bettina's foccacia. It never really lasts much longer than that.

IN A SKILLET, heat oil over medium-high heat until hot but not smoking. Add eggplant, fennel, roasted peppers, onion, artichoke hearts, olives, mushrooms and garlic; sauté until slightly softened, about 12 minutes. Add cayenne and paprika; sauté until spices are aromatic and vegetables are softened, about 2 minutes. Stir in vinegar and salt and pepper to taste. Scrape mixture onto a large baking sheet and let cool. Sprinkle with parsley and toss to combine. Can be stored for up to 1 week.

Makes 2 cups

2 tbsp extra-virgin olive oil
2 cups finely diced eggplant
1½ cups finely diced fennel
    (about 1 bulb)
¾ cup finely diced roasted red
    peppers (about 3)
¾ cup finely diced white onion
½ cup finely diced artichoke
    hearts (about 4)
½ cup finely diced drained
    green olives
½ cup finely diced cremini
    mushrooms (about 10)
3 cloves garlic, minced
¼ tsp cayenne pepper
¼ tsp smoked paprika
2 tbsp sherry vinegar
Salt and freshly cracked
    black pepper
½ cup minced fresh flat-leaf
    (Italian) parsley

Pizza Dough

Makes 4 6-oz. balls of pizza
dough, or one large ball

3 cups all-purpose flour

2 tsp dry instant yeast

1 tsp kosher salt

1½ cups water (approx.),
  divided

1 tbsp extra-virgin olive oil

1 tsp local honey

ManoRun Farm's wood-burning stone oven produces the most beautiful pizzas you have ever seen. If you don't have your own wood-burning clay oven at home, the results can be mimicked by the use of a pizza stone in a conventional oven. Pizza stones can be found at most specialty kitchen stores. Make sure the stone is very hot before you place the pizza on it. My wife, Julie, and I make so many pizzas at home that our pizza stone has become a permanent fixture in the oven. On the following pages, we have some great topping combinations for you to try!

IN THE BOWL of a stand mixer, combine flour, yeast and salt. Add 1 cup of the water, oil and honey. Attach the flat beater and the mixer bowl to the mixer and mix on low speed until incorporated. Remove the flat beater and attach the dough hook. Gradually add the remaining water, mixing on low speed, until dough pulls away from the sides of the bowl and hangs on the hook, about 5 minutes. (You may not need all of the water.)

Turn out onto a lightly floured surface and knead until dough is smooth and elastic, about 3 minutes. Place in a large greased bowl, turning dough to grease all over. Cover with a clean, damp towel and let rise until doubled in size, about an hour or more.

Divide dough into 4 balls. Work each ball by pulling down the sides and tucking them under the bottom of the ball. Repeat 4 or 5 times. On a clean surface, roll each ball under the palm of your hand until smooth and firm. Cover with damp towels and let rest until dough has relaxed and started to rise again, 15 to 20 minutes.

(You should be able to fit four small pizzas on one stone; if you prefer, you could also make one large pizza with one dough recipe.)

Potato and Rosemary Pizza

Serves 4

1 batch of pizza dough
  (see recipe, page 184)
8 oz buffalo mozzarella, thinly
  sliced
8 new potatoes (about 3 lbs),
  thinly sliced
2 cloves garlic, minced
1 red onion, thinly sliced
1 cup freshly grated Parmesan
  cheese or shredded Gruyère
  cheese
2 tbsp minced fresh rosemary
Extra-virgin olive oil
Salt and freshly cracked
  black pepper

At Pizza Bianco in Rome, my wife, Julie, and I discovered that less is more when it comes to pizza toppings: the higher the quality of the ingredients you use, the less you have to add. But be generous with the garlic and olive oil. If you wish, you can replace the red onion with Cipollini Onions (page 251).

PREHEAT OVEN TO 425°F and heat a pizza stone for at least 30 minutes.

On lightly floured surface, roll out dough into a 14-inch circle, letting it rest for 15 to 20 minutes.

Working quickly, remove hot stone from oven and slide dough onto stone. Arrange mozzarella on dough, then top with potatoes, garlic, onion, Parmesan and rosemary. Brush edges of dough with oil. Return stone to the oven and bake until edges of pizzas are golden and crispy, 15 to 20 minutes. Just before serving, drizzle with more oil and season to taste with salt and pepper.

Fresh Ricotta, Roasted Pepper and Basil Pizza

We get fresh ricotta from local sheep's milk cheesemaker Monforte Dairy. The difference between store-bought ricotta and fresh ricotta is like night and day. Fresh ricotta is so good that you don't have to do much to it to create a delicious recipe.

PREHEAT OVEN TO 425°F and heat a pizza stone for at least 30 minutes.

On a lightly floured cutting board, roll out dough into a 14-inch circle, letting it rest for 15 to 20 minutes.

Working quickly, remove hot stone from oven and slide dough onto stone. Arrange ricotta, Parmesan, roasted peppers and garlic on dough. Brush edges of dough with oil. Return stone to the oven and bake until edges of pizza are golden and crispy, 15 to 20 minutes. Just before serving, sprinkle with basil and salt and pepper to taste.

Serves 4

1 batch of pizza dough (see recipe, page 184)
1 cup fresh ricotta cheese, well drained
¼ cup freshly grated Parmesan cheese
3 sweet red peppers, roasted, peeled and thinly sliced
2 cloves garlic, minced
Olive oil
½ cup sliced fresh basil
Salt and freshly cracked black pepper

Squash, Sage and Pancetta Pizza

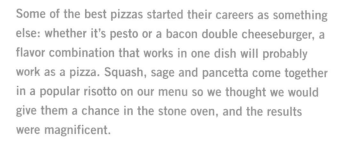

Serves 4

3 cups diced butternut or acorn
   squash (½-inch dice)
Extra-virgin olive oil
Salt and freshly cracked
   black pepper
1 cup diced pancetta
1 batch of pizza dough (see
   recipe, page 184)
10 fresh sage leaves
1 cup freshly grated Parmesan
   cheese

Some of the best pizzas started their careers as something else: whether it's pesto or a bacon double cheeseburger, a flavor combination that works in one dish will probably work as a pizza. Squash, sage and pancetta come together in a popular risotto on our menu so we thought we would give them a chance in the stone oven, and the results were magnificent.

PREHEAT OVEN TO 350°F. Place squash on a large rimmed baking sheet, drizzle with oil and season to taste with salt and pepper; toss to coat and spread out in a single layer. Bake until tender and caramelized, about 10 minutes. Set aside.

Increase oven temperature to 425°F and heat a pizza stone for at least 30 minutes.

Meanwhile, in a skillet, sauté pancetta over high heat until crisp, about 6 minutes. Drain and set aside.

On a lightly floured cutting board, roll out dough into a 14-inch circle, letting it rest for 15 to 20 minutes.

Working quickly, remove hot stone from oven and slide dough onto stone. Arrange squash, pancetta and sage on dough and sprinkle with Parmesan. Brush edges of dough with oil. Return stone to the oven and bake until edges of pizza are golden and crispy, 15 to 20 minutes. Just before serving, season to taste with salt and pepper.

Wild Mushroom and Roasted Corn Pizza

This combo is the best of both summer and fall! My favorite wild mushrooms are chanterelle and oyster.

PREHEAT OVEN TO 425°F and heat a pizza stone for at least 30 minutes.

On a lightly floured cutting board, roll out dough into a 14-inch circle, letting it rest for 15 to 20 minutes.

Working quickly, remove hot stone from oven and slide dough onto stone. Arrange mushrooms, corn, thyme, goat cheese and chili flakes on dough. Brush edges of dough with oil. Return stone to the oven and bake until edges of pizza are golden and crispy, 15 to 20 minutes. Just before serving, season to taste with salt and pepper.

Serves 4

1 batch of pizza dough (see
    recipe, page 184)
2 cups fresh wild mushrooms,
    torn into pieces
1 cup fresh corn kernels (see
    Grilled Corn, page 117)
2 tbsp roughly chopped fresh
    thyme
1 cup crumbled goat cheese
1 tsp chili flakes
Extra-virgin olive oil
Salt and freshly cracked
    black pepper

Make-Your-Own Pizza

At our harvest party, we set out bowls of ingredients, both fresh from the farm and exotic, and let our guests make their own pizzas.

PREHEAT OVEN TO 425°F and heat a pizza stone for at least 30 minutes.

On a lightly floured cutting board, roll out 1 batch of pizza dough (see recipe, page 184) into 4 8-inch circles, letting it rest if too elastic to work.

Working quickly, remove hot stone from oven and slide dough onto stone. Arrange toppings on dough. Brush edges of dough with extra-virgin olive oil. Return stone to the oven and bake until edges of pizza are golden and crispy, 15 to 20 minutes, depending on the choice of toppings (the more toppings, the longer it will take).

Tasty Toppings

TOMATOES: Use this versatile fruit to give inspiration. Try Tomato Confit (page 301), sliced heirloom tomatoes, cherry tomatoes, sun-dried tomatoes, smoked tomatoes and spicy tomato sauce.

CHEESES: Local cheese not only makes for delicious pizza, but you may introduce your guest to new flavors right on their doorstep. Try mozzarella, ricotta, Parmesan, Gruyère, hard cheeses such as pecorino or cheddar, and cream cheeses.

MEATS: Aside from ham and pepperoni, all forms of charcuterie make excellent pizza toppings. Try smoked fish, salami, prosciutto, sausage, smoked turkey and smoked chicken.

EXTRAS: Add even more flavor with capers, lemon zest, chili peppers, hot sauce, anchovies, olives and condiments such as La Bomba (page 183).

HERBS: Fresh herbs and lettuces add a real zing to even an ordinary pizza. We like arugula, Thai basil, tarragon and lemony sorrel. Add fresh herbs after the pizza comes out of the oven.

Roasted Pork Loin with Fennel

Serves 6

3-lb boneless center-cut pork
    loin roast
4 cloves garlic, minced
1 medium onion, minced
1 cup minced fennel bulb
1 cup fresh flat-leaf (Italian)
    parsley, minced
1 tbsp chili flakes
5 tbsp extra-virgin olive oil,
    divided
2 tbsp balsamic vinegar
Salt and freshly cracked
    black pepper
⅓ cup unsalted butter
2 sprigs fresh rosemary
2 sprigs fresh sage
2 sprigs fresh thyme

Because pork loin is a lean cut of meat, this recipe is all about maximizing its taste and preserving its moisture. For my kitchen, I buy whole pigs so I can use the skin as a wrap; this gives me loads of crispy crackling.

PLACE PORK ON A CUTTING BOARD, with short end of pork closest to you and fat side up. Starting at the right side, with your knife parallel to the board, cut loin in half, almost but not all the way through; open like a book. Starting in center of opened loin, with knife parallel to board, make short saw-like motions with knife and cut in half on left side, almost but not all the way through. Repeat on right side. Open flat.

In a bowl, combine garlic, onion, fennel, parsley, chili flakes, 3 tbsp of the oil and vinegar. Season to taste with salt and pepper.

Season pork loin all over with salt and pepper. Leaving a 1-inch border on one short side, spread garlic mixture over pork and pat down with the palm of your hand. Starting at the other short side, roll up tightly. Tie loin snugly, at 1-inch intervals, with kitchen twine. (*Make ahead: Wrap pork in plastic wrap and refrigerate overnight.*)

In a large skillet, heat the remaining oil over medium-high heat. Add pork roast and cook, turning, until it is a deep, rich golden brown on all sides, about 15 minutes. (Be patient: this searing process is important for flavor.) Meanwhile, preheat oven to 375°F.

Transfer roast to a rack fitted into a large roasting pan. Slather roast with butter and arrange rosemary, sage and thyme sprigs on top. Roast until a meat thermometer inserted in the center registers 140°F, about 1½ hours. Transfer pork to a cutting board, tent with foil and let stand for 10 minutes before slicing.

Pan-Roasted Mushrooms

Mushrooms have a high water content and must be cooked over high heat long enough to remove the excess moisture. I add a splash of water to the skillet to prevent them from burning before they can release their natural, flavorful juices. Undercooking mushrooms is a common mistake for both home cooks and chefs. I like to cook mushrooms until they are dark and crispy. They become sponge-like, soaking up the rich flavors of butter and herbs added in the cooking process.

HEAT A LARGE SKILLET OVER HIGH HEAT. Add oil and wait for 30 seconds. Add mushrooms and water. Cook, without stirring, until mushrooms are crispy and golden, about 8 minutes. Remove from heat and stir in butter, shallots, thyme, chives and garlic. Season to taste with salt and pepper.

Serves 4 as a side dish
or topping

3 tbsp extra-virgin olive oil
8 cups sliced wild mushrooms
   (such as chanterelle, shiitake, oyster or morel)
2 tbsp water
¼ cup unsalted butter
2 tbsp minced shallots
1 tbsp chopped fresh thyme
1 tbsp chopped fresh chives
1 clove garlic, minced
Salt and freshly cracked
   black pepper

Sweet Potato Gnocchi

Serves 6 as a main course

4 medium sweet potatoes (about
    4½ lbs)
4 medium Yukon gold potatoes
    (about 4 lbs)
3 cups all-purpose flour
2 tsp salt
¼ tsp freshly cracked
    black pepper
2 extra-large eggs, beaten
3 tbsp extra-virgin olive oil
¼ cup freshly grated Parmesan
    cheese
12 fried sage leaves (see tip)

Adding sweet potatoes to a gnocchi recipe makes it a little easier for the home cook to pull off, because sweet potatoes have less starch than potatoes, and a high starch content can make gnocchi dense and tough. The combination of sage and sweet potatoes is one for the ages.

PREHEAT OVEN TO 375°F. Place sweet potatoes and potatoes on a baking sheet and roast until soft, about 2 hours. Let cool slightly, then cut in half and scoop the flesh into a large bowl. (This should yield about 5 lbs of roasted potato mixture.)

Add flour, salt and pepper to the potato mixture and mix together until smooth. Make a well in the center and pour in eggs. Using a fork and starting in the center of the mixture, incorporate eggs into mixture.

Turn out onto a lightly floured surface and knead until a soft, slightly sticky, spongy dough forms, being careful not to work dough too much. Shape into a ball and place on a lightly floured cutting board. Cut ball into 8 pieces and cover with a clean tea towel. Dust a baking sheet with flour.

On a lightly floured surface, working with one piece of dough at a time and keeping the rest covered, roll each piece into a 20-inch rope, about ½ inch thick. Cut rope into 1-inch lengths. Using your thumb, roll each piece of dough over the back of the tines of a floured fork, leaving an indention from your thumb on one side and the markings from the fork on the other. Place gnocchi on prepared baking sheet. Repeat with remaining dough. (*Make ahead: Cover and refrigerate for up to 1 day, or freeze in an airtight container for up to 1 month.*)

>>>

Meanwhile, bring a large pot of salted water to a boil over high heat. Plunge half the gnocchi into the boiling water. Once they float to the surface, cook for 1 minute longer. Using a slotted spoon, transfer to a baking sheet or plate and continue cooking the remaining gnocchi. Drizzle with oil and toss to coat. Sprinkle with Parmesan and fried sage leaves.

TIP: There is such a thing as "tough herbs" or winter herbs, like sage or rosemary. These hearty herbs that keep growing well after the first snowfall can handle being fried—the result is crispy and delicious. In a small frying pan heat ½ cup of canola oil until hot but not smoking. Add herbs and cook until crispy, about 30 seconds, and remove from oil using tongs. Transfer to a plate lined with paper towel and use as needed.

Braised Short Ribs

Serves 6

6 beef short ribs (about 7 lbs)

Salt and freshly cracked
    black pepper

⅓ cup extra-virgin olive oil,
    divided

2 cups chopped onions (½-inch
    chunks)

1 cup chopped carrots (½-inch
    chunks)

1 cup chopped celery (½-inch
    chunks)

3 cloves garlic

2 dried bay leaves

2½ cups local hearty red wine

1½ cups port

2 tbsp balsamic vinegar

6 cups Beef Stock (see recipe,
    page 296)

Citrus Gremolata (see recipe,
    page 57)

Fresh bay leaves, for garnish

Chefs love working with gnarly cuts of meat. They make the most flavorful, succulent dishes, perfect for a cool evening. At the restaurant, we serve short ribs with creamy Apple and Parsnip Puree (page 200).

SEASON SHORT RIBS generously with salt and pepper. In a large skillet, heat 3 tbsp of the oil over medium-high heat until smoking. Add short ribs, in batches, and cook, turning occasionally, until a deep, rich golden brown on all sides, about 15 minutes per batch, adding more oil between batches as needed. Using tongs, transfer ribs to a large Dutch oven as completed; set aside. Preheat oven to 325°F.

Reduce heat to medium and add the remaining oil, onions, carrots, celery, garlic and bay leaves to the skillet. Sauté until vegetables begin to caramelize, about 5 minutes. Add to the Dutch oven.

Add wine, port and vinegar to the skillet, stirring to scrape up any brown bits on the bottom of the pan. Bring to a boil and cook until reduced by half, about 10 minutes. Add to the Dutch oven.

Add stock to the skillet and bring to a simmer. Pour over short ribs. (The stock should just cover the ribs; if it doesn't, add more stock until the ribs are covered.) Cover with a tight-fitting lid.

Bake until meat is very tender and yields easily when pierced with a knife, about 2 hours. Using tongs, transfer ribs to a serving platter and keep warm.

Strain liquid from Dutch oven into a saucepan. Bring to a boil and cook until reduced by three quarters, about 25 minutes. Season to taste with salt and pepper. Pour over ribs and garnish with gremolata and fresh bay leaves.

Apple and Parsnip Puree

Serves 6

6 parsnips (about 4 lbs), peeled
    and coarsely chopped

2 tbsp unsalted butter

1 cup chopped onion

2 green apples (such as Granny
    Smith), peeled and chopped

¾ cup sour cream

Salt and freshly cracked
    black pepper

Parsnips are so delicious! In the restaurant, I pick them out of the roasted root vegetables as they cool on the racks. Here is a way to introduce them to fussy eaters— just tell them it's mashed potatoes!

IN A LARGE POT of boiling salted water, cook parsnips until very tender, about 15 minutes. Drain, reserving ¾ cup of the cooking liquid, and set aside.

Meanwhile, in a large skillet, melt butter over medium-high heat. Add onion and apples; sauté until apples are tender and slightly golden, about 10 minutes. Remove from heat.

In a food processor, working in batches, puree parsnips, onion mixture and sour cream until smooth. Transfer to a bowl and stir in reserved cooking liquid. Season to taste with salt and pepper.

Roasted Fennel Gratin

Fennel is such an underrated vegetable. It is so versatile that, for a chef, living without it would be unthinkable. I use it raw, shaved paper-thin; diced and slowly cooked in olive oil; or roasted, as in this recipe.

PREHEAT OVEN TO 375°F. In a large bowl, toss fennel with oil until well coated. Spread out in a single layer on a large rimmed baking sheet. Roast, turning occasionally, until softened, about 30 minutes. Remove from oven, leaving oven on, and sprinkle with thyme and salt and pepper to taste.

In a bowl, combine bread crumbs and Parmesan.

Spread tomato confit in the bottom of a large baking dish, followed by an even layer of roasted fennel. Top with the bread crumb mixture and dot with butter. Bake until golden brown, about 20 minutes.

Serves 6 as a side dish

5 fennel bulbs, sliced in half and then into wedges, core trimmed away
2 tbsp olive oil
¼ cup minced fresh thyme
Salt and freshly cracked black pepper
1 cup fresh bread crumbs
1 cup freshly grated Parmesan cheese
2 cups Tomato Confit (see recipe, page 301)
¼ cup unsalted butter

Colcannon Potatoes

My friend Chris Haworth, the chef at our sister restaurant, Spencer's at the Waterfront, introduced me to Colcannon potatoes. It was Chris, by the way, who first introduced us to the family at ManoRun Farm. This dish is a great way to introduce Brussels sprouts to your family.

PLACE POTATOES IN A SAUCEPAN and add enough cold salted water to cover by 1 inch; bring to a boil over high heat. Reduce heat and simmer until potatoes are tender, about 30 minutes.

Meanwhile, in a skillet, heat 1 tbsp of the oil over medium heat. Add bacon and sauté until slightly crisp, about 4 minutes. Add Brussels sprouts, wine and thyme; cook until Brussels sprouts are tender and wine has evaporated, about 8 minutes. Remove from heat.

Drain potatoes and, while still steaming, add to bacon mixture. Add milk, butter and chives. Using a fork, lightly mash potatoes until crushed but still chunky. Season to taste with salt and pepper.

Serves 6

5 medium Yukon gold potatoes
     (about 2½ lbs), cut into
     1-inch chunks
3 tbsp extra-virgin olive oil,
     divided
¾ cup finely chopped smoked
     bacon
1½ cups finely sliced Brussels
     sprouts (about 5)
¼ cup local dry white wine
2 tbsp finely minced fresh thyme
1¼ cups 2% milk
½ cup unsalted butter
¼ cup finely minced fresh
     chives
Salt and freshly ground
     black pepper

Duck Confit

Serves 6

4 muscovy duck legs

3 dried bay leaves

3 star anise, slightly broken

1 cinnamon stick, broken into
four pieces

2 tbsp kosher salt

1 tbsp thyme leaves (about 20
sprigs)

2 tsp freshly ground
black pepper

5 cups Chicken Stock (see
recipe, page 297)

1 cup pure apple cider

½ cup minced flat-leaf (Italian)
parsley

Salt and freshly cracked
black pepper

Duck confit is one of my earliest memories of food heaven. It was a revelation that food could taste so good. Traditionally, the duck is braised in copious amounts of duck fat. I have altered the recipe to braise the legs in chicken stock—still delicious, but a little less heart-stopping.

We pot this duck in glass jars and cover it with duck fat to seal in the flavor. Packed this way, it can be stored in the refrigerator for up to one month.

Serve with bread crostini, or in a tart watercress salad.

IN A MEDIUM BOWL, combine duck legs, bay leaves, star anise, cinnamon, salt, thyme and pepper. (Make sure duck legs are completely covered with seasoning.) Cover and refrigerate for at least 6 hours or overnight.

Brush seasoning off duck legs. Place skin side up in a 12- by 4-inch baking dish. Preheat oven to 350°F.

In a saucepan, bring stock and cider to a simmer over high heat. Pour over duck legs, just covering them. Cover dish with foil and bake until duck is very tender and nearly falling off the bone, about 2½ hours. Remove pan to a wire rack. Using tongs, transfer duck to a cutting board. Remove the meat from the bones and coarsely chop. Discard bones.

In a bowl, combine duck meat and parsley. Season to taste with salt and pepper. Serve immediately, or pack into a jar and top with the fat that rose to the surface of the stock during roasting. (The fat helps seal in flavor and will solidify after chilling.)

White Truffle Risotto with Cauliflower

Make this dish when wild mushrooms become available at your local farmers' market. The greater the variety of mushrooms, the more flavor your risotto will have—each mushroom adds its own complex flavor, aroma and color. In the restaurant, we use foraged wild mushrooms. While in Italy, I had the opportunity to purchase a beautiful Italian white truffle, so I jumped at it.

IN A LARGE SKILLET, melt 2 tbsp of the butter over medium-high heat. Add mushrooms, cauliflower, a pinch of salt and a splash of water; sauté until liquid is evaporated and mushrooms appear dry, about 15 minutes. Transfer mushroom mixture to a plate and set aside.

In the same skillet, melt 2 tbsp of the butter over medium heat. Add shallots and pancetta; sauté until shallots are softened, about 2 minutes. Stir in rice until well coated (do not let brown). Stir in wine and cook, stirring constantly, until liquid is absorbed. Stir in ½ cup stock and cook, stirring constantly, until stock is absorbed. Continue adding stock, 1 cup at a time, stirring constantly until absorbed before adding more. It will take about 20 minutes to incorporate all the liquid.

Stir in mushroom mixture and cook until vegetables are tender and rice is creamy, about 5 minutes. Stir in the remaining butter, cheese, parsley and thyme. Season to taste with salt and pepper. Let stand for 2 minutes.

Ladle risotto into warm bowls and garnish with shaved truffle or drizzle with truffle oil.

Serves 4

¾ cup unsalted butter, divided
5 cups wild mushrooms (such as oyster or shiitake), thinly sliced
3 cups small cauliflower florets
2 shallots, finely diced
¼ cup diced pancetta
1½ cups Arborio rice
1 cup dry white wine
4 cups hot Chicken Stock (see recipe, page 297), divided
1 cup grated Parmigiano-Reggiano cheese
1 tbsp minced fresh flat-leaf (Italian) parsley
1 tsp minced fresh thyme
Salt and freshly ground black pepper
Shaved fresh white truffle (as much as you can afford), or 2 tsp white truffle oil

Apple Tarts

Serves 8

1 package (1 lb) frozen all-butter
    puff pastry

½ cup Frangipane (see recipe,
    page 304), made with
    hazelnuts

3 large Granny Smith or Young
    Golden Delicious apples
    (about 2 lbs), thinly sliced

¼ cup granulated sugar

1 tsp ground cinnamon

3 tbsp unsalted butter

There are certain dishes a chef is never able to take off the menu. This is one of those items, which suits me just fine—it's an absolute cinch to prepare and even easier to bake to order. You too can assemble the tarts beforehand and bake them to order for your guests. We like to serve the tarts with Caramel Sauce (page 305) and ice cream.

Don't complicate this dessert by trying to make your own puff pastry. It can be purchased at the grocery store for a reasonable price. Be sure to buy the "all butter" variety, and look for puff pastry that has already been rolled out into sheets, making your job even easier.

USING A 4-INCH ROUND cookie cutter, cut puff pastry into 8 circles. Place circles on a rimmed baking sheet lined with parchment paper. Using a 3-inch round cookie cutter, score another circle inside each. (Just score the circle—do not cut through the dough.)

Spread 1 tbsp frangipane in the middle of each circle, filling the score mark. Arrange apple slices on top of frangipane, making circular layers until apples are about 1½ inches high. (*Make ahead: Wrap in plastic wrap, then in foil, and freeze for up to 6 weeks. When cooking from frozen, increase cooking time by 7 minutes.*)

Preheat oven to 375°F. In a small bowl, combine sugar and cinnamon.

Dot the top of each tart with butter and sprinkle with cinnamon-sugar. Bake until crispy and golden brown, about 20 minutes.

Sweet Mediterranean Pizza

Why leave dessert out of all the pizza fun? Sweet toppings such as honey or corn syrup are delicious on pizza dough. You could even simply brush the dough with butter and sprinkle with cinnamon-sugar.

PREHEAT OVEN TO 425°F and heat a pizza stone for at least 30 minutes.

On a lightly floured cutting board, roll out dough into a 14-inch circle, letting it rest if too elastic to work.

Working quickly, remove hot stone from oven and slide dough onto stone. Drizzle dough with 1½ tbsp of the honey and sprinkle with pistachios. Brush edges of dough with oil. Return stone to the oven and bake until edges of pizza are golden and crispy, 15 to 20 minutes. Just before serving, drizzle with the remaining honey.

Serves 4

1 ball of pizza dough (see recipe, page 184)
1 cup local honey, divided
1 cup ground or chopped pistachios
Extra-virgin olive oil

Mile-High Pumpkin Pie

Serves 8

SHELL

½ recipe Pâte Brisée (page 306)

PUMPKIN FILLING

¼ cup cold water

1 packet (½ oz) powdered
   unflavored gelatin

1 cup cream cheese, softened

½ cup granulated sugar

½ cup whipping (35%) cream

2 cups roasted pumpkin (see tip,
   page 214)

1½ tsp salt

2 tsp ground cinnamon

1 tsp ground cloves

1 tsp ground ginger

½ tsp ground nutmeg

MILE-HIGH MERINGUE

1 cup pure maple syrup

3 large egg whites

1 tsp cream of tartar

This pumpkin pie recipe uses a no-bake method for the filling. I have been disappointed by pumpkin pie recipes that seem to "bake down" to scarcely no filling. By excluding eggs and firming up the pie with gelatin, you can fill the pie as high as you want and get the most out of the best part!

PREPARE THE SHELL: Preheat oven to 350°F. On a lightly floured surface, roll out pâte brisée to fit a 9-inch pie plate. Trim edges to leave a 1-inch overhang; fold edges under, and crimp with your fingers by pinching the dough. (Alternatively, you can use a lightly floured fork to crimp, or cut out shapes with the remaining dough and decorate the edges.)

Line shell with parchment paper round, and fill with pie weights. Chill for 15 minutes. Transfer to oven, and bake for 15 minutes. Remove pie weights and parchment paper. Bake for 15 to 20 minutes more, until golden. Remove from oven and set aside.

Prepare the filling: In a small bowl, combine cold water and gelatin; let bloom for 10 minutes.

In a stand mixer fitted with paddle attachment, cream the cheese and sugar until smooth. Add cream and mix until incorporated, stopping the mixer occasionally to scrape down the sides. Add pumpkin, salt, cinnamon, cloves, ginger and nutmeg; beat until smooth. Set aside.

In a small saucepan, cook gelatin mixture over low heat, stirring until gelatin is completely dissolved, about 1 minute. Add to pumpkin mixture and mix until well combined.

Pour filling into prepared pie shell, cover and refrigerate for at least 1 hour or overnight.   >>>

Prepare the meringue: In a saucepan, heat maple syrup over high heat until it registers 250°F on a candy thermometer, about 20 minutes.

Meanwhile, beat egg whites and cream of tartar until stiff peaks form. Gradually add maple syrup in a slow, continuous stream, beating until whites puff up and take on a glossy shine, about 10 minutes.

Preheat broiler. Dollop meringue mixture over pie and, with the back of a spoon, make large, swooping curls. Place on a rimmed baking sheet and broil until meringue is golden brown, about 10 minutes.

TIP: To make 2 cups roasted pumpkin, cut a 1½-lb pumpkin in half and remove seeds. Spray pumpkin with vegetable oil and place flesh side down on a baking sheet lined with parchment paper. Roast in a 350°F oven until soft to the touch, about 1 hour. Let cool completely, then scrape the flesh from the skin.

Pumpkin Seed Brittle

When making this recipe, it is important to move quickly. The hot sugar will start to set once you have added the seeds and baking soda. It's not a particularly difficult recipe—just be sure to read it through before you begin.

GREASE A BAKING SHEET with butter or line it with a nonstick mat (such as silicone) or parchment paper. Set aside.

In a medium saucepan, combine sugar, water, corn syrup and butter. Bring to a boil over high heat. Boil until mixture is almost reddish in color, about 20 minutes. Remove from heat and stir in pumpkin seeds, baking soda and salt. Working quickly, using a heatproof spatula, spread mixture onto prepared baking sheet (be careful— the mixture will be very hot). Let cool completely. Once cool, break into pieces. (*Make ahead: Store in an airtight container for up 1 week.*)

TIP: You can easily substitute peanuts or any nuts, such as pecans, for the pumpkin seeds.

Makes 1 lb

1⅓ cups granulated sugar

½ cup water

¼ cup corn syrup

3 tbsp unsalted butter

1½ cups Toasted Pumpkin
  Seeds (see recipe, page 174)

½ tsp baking soda

¼ tsp salt

Roasted Autumn Fruits with Torched Sabayon

When you try this recipe, make sure your fruit pieces are all about the same size. This will allow you to roast it all at the same time. Also, when choosing apples and pears, look for firm green varieties. In the restaurant, we use a blowtorch to brown the sabayon. Try it at home! Blowtorches are available at many kitchen equipment stores.

PREPARE THE FRUIT: Preheat oven to 400°F. On a baking sheet, combine grapes, plums, pears, apples, sugar and butter; toss to coat and spread out in a single layer. Bake until soft, about 15 minutes. Let cool.

Meanwhile, prepare the sabayon: In a large, stainless steel bowl, whisk together egg yolks and sugar. Set over a pot of simmering water (the bowl should not touch the water). Pour in wine and whisk vigorously to incorporate air until mixture has doubled in volume and is thick like whipped cream, about 10 minutes. You can use an electric mixer if it's easier.

To assemble: Divide fruit among 6 dessert plates. Spoon sabayon over fruit. If desired, quickly wave a blowtorch over the surface to brown the sabayon.

Serves 6

FRUIT

20 red or green grapes

3 large plums, cut into wedges

2 medium pears, cut into wedges

2 medium green apples (such as Granny Smith), cut into wedges

½ cup granulated sugar

½ cup melted unsalted butter

SABAYON

6 large egg yolks

3 tbsp granulated sugar

¼ cup late harvest sweet wine

Wheat Berry Beer Bread

Makes 2 loaves

3 cups dark rye flour

2 tsp dry instant yeast

4 cups bread flour, divided

1 cup cooked wheat berries
(see tip, below)

1 bottle (12 oz) dark ale, at room
temperature

1 egg, lightly beaten

½ cup mild (light) molasses

¼ cup unsalted butter, melted

1 tbsp granulated sugar

2 tsp salt

Milk

Wheat berry bread is very hearty and very dense, perfect for the fall season. At the restaurant, we proof the dough in a floured basket, or couronne, to give the bread its characteristic patterned crust.

IN A BOWL, whisk together rye flour and yeast; set aside.

In another bowl, mix 3¾ cups of the bread flour, wheat berries, ale, egg, molasses, butter, sugar and salt until well combined. Using a spoon, gradually work in rye flour until dough pulls away from the sides of the bowl.

Turn out onto a lightly floured surface and knead until dough is smooth and elastic, about 15 minutes. Place in a large greased bowl, turning dough to grease all over. Cover with a tea towel and let rise in a still oven, with light on and door closed, until doubled in size, about 2 hours.

Punch dough down and turn out onto a lightly floured surface. Divide in half, roll each half into a round ball and place on a baking sheet lined with parchment paper. Cover with tea towels and return to still oven until doubled in size, about 1 hour.

Preheat oven to 375°F. Brush tops of dough with milk and dust with the remaining bread flour. Using your sharpest knife, slash tops three times, no more than ½ inch deep. Bake until dark golden brown, about 30 minutes. Let cool on wire racks.

TIP: To cook wheat berries, in a saucepan, bring 1 cup wheat berries and 2 cups water to a boil. Reduce heat to medium and cook until berries are soft to the touch and skins are beginning to peel off, about 20 minutes. Drain and let cool. (*Make ahead: Cover and refrigerate for up to 4 days.*)

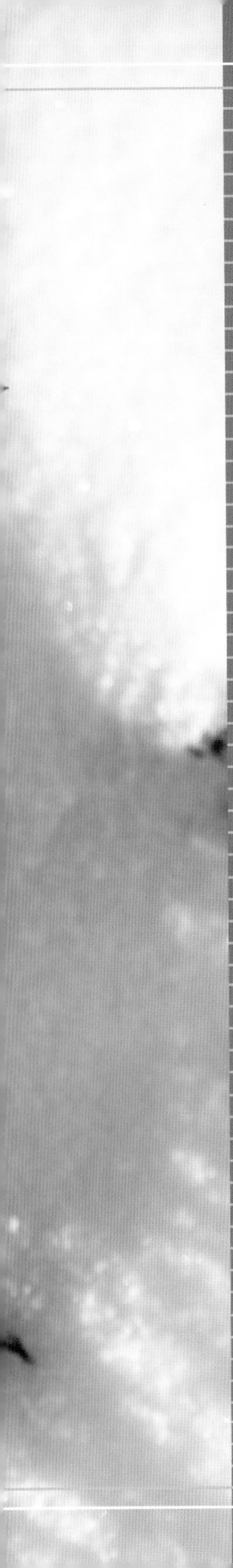

BACON

BEETS

CARROTS

WHAT TO EAT

WINTER

CHARCUTERIE

CHEESE

CITRUS

DRIED BEANS

ENDIVE

HOT CHOCOLATE

PARSNIPS

PRESERVES

SHELLFISH

VENISON

It is a testament to the pleasure of watching

seasons change that I enjoy even the shift from autumn to winter. The farm, of course, is a completely different place. The fields seem huge and featureless, where only recently they were riotously alive and stalks of grain were swaying in the breeze. The trees and windbreaks are skeletal and black against the white snow. The barn looks like an art installation, lifted out of its familiar context. Inside, the cows and horses shuffle in their pens, their breath smoking in the cold.

As a cook, I don't miss summer's bounty at all when the snow is on the ground. When the wind is howling outside, I want something that comes from the field by way of the larder. I want something wholesome, hearty, nourishing and probably fatty. And I'd like it with bread, please. (I think of wheat as a sort of battery charger, soaking up the sun's energy all summer and storing it for those dark days when we really need it.) I long for rich braises in the winter; my thoughts turn to red wine, to celery root and the whole family of root vegetables tucked away in the cellar. And I am so addicted to stews and other one-pot dishes that my wife opened our dishwasher one winter day and remarked that there was nothing in it but bowls and spoons.

That probably wasn't quite true, however. I'm sure there must have been at least a couple of knives in there, since I don't generally go very long during the winter months without eating cheese or charcuterie, two foods that not only provide comforting richness when your body is begging for calories, but also stand for everything reassuring about seasonal, local and artisanal eating.

Bettina, Chris and Jeff planning the year's crops.

For me, charcuterie is fast food. Nothing is easier for the home cook than preparing a charcuterie plate. Charcuterie is all around us—bacon, sausage, cold cuts and ham, to name a few—but if you're not familiar with the real thing, don't let childhood memories of macaroni-and-cheese loaf turn you off. *Real* charcuterie is a craft that takes years to master.

There are some rules to follow when making a charcuterie plate. First, find a deli that makes a high-quality product. Second, serve a few different styles of charcuterie: spicy, soft and salty. All you need to accompany it is a fruity red wine, pickles for an acidic counterpoint and crunch, a pot of Dijon mustard and some bread. This makes the perfect appetizer, light lunch or (in a chef's case) late-night snack.

All of these things—the meat, the pickles, the mustard and of course the cheese—are delicacies that were laid away. They all represent a way of setting aside some of the farm's bounty to be eaten later. There is a special form of contentment that comes from knowing the larder and the cellar are full. But each of these delicious foods also tastes radically different from the way it would have tasted when it came off the field.

Of course, there was a time not long ago when these transformations were imposed upon the food to make it last. Refrigeration did not exist, nor were supermarkets stocked to satisfy just about every conceivable whim. You made sausage so your meat wouldn't go bad; you made preserves to, well, preserve your produce; you made cheese to turn your milk into food that could be tucked away. Even wine and beer seem to have been developed as much for storage as for the good cheer they yield to those wise enough to drink them. So here's to winter, for forcing humanity to invent some of the most enticing things anyone can put on a table. We don't *have* to make sausages and cheese and wine anymore, but the world would be a drearier place without them.

In any case, winter still forces us to be creative. As a cook, you're transforming food, whether it's by braising or caramelizing it, or by working with foods that have already been transformed through canning or freezing. Blueberries, for example, burst when they freeze, producing a sweet, pulpy liquid that's perfect for sauces or vinaigrettes. This may seem like a small thing, but it would never come up in the summer.

I love the way these new constraints and opportunities get channeled into our menu: apples, Jerusalem artichokes, eye-watering

horseradish—anything the market or farm throws at me. This is the real earth-to-table moment. Cookbooks are selected, pages are flipped and ideas start to simmer. This is when the sketches start. We have a few whiteboards that become the center of action. The cooks get involved, adding opinions and suggestions for the dish that will ease the flow of service. Flow of service is crucial: dishes must be spread throughout the stations—grill, sauté, pivot, hot and cold appetizers and pastry. Cooking methods are taken into consideration, something that might determine or be determined by the cut of meat, chicken or fish.

Once a dish makes the cut in the kitchen, it must pass the final test: the servers. No one has the power to make or break a new dish quite like the service staff. If they're not on board, you might as well cancel the whole process, because it's highly unlikely they'll be recommending the dish to the customer. Which is all the more reason to have them involved from the very beginning—especially if the very beginning was back in the spring, when we were all out in the fields.

It's all a cycle, of course. While winter is, in a sense, the end of the cycle, it's also the beginning. As the sun is setting early, we're sitting around a table, going through seed catalogs and talking about what we're going to plant in the spring.

Bettina, Jeff and Chris planning the year's menus.

Bettina's Wheat Story

Nothing illustrates the amount of work that goes into a loaf of bread quite like answering a knock at the receiving door one winter day to see a farmer standing there with forty pounds of wheat berries in a grain bag (and reminding me that there are forty more waiting for me at the farm).

It has also become very clear to me through the process of growing and harvesting wheat just how much I love to make bread. I'm not yet a master baker, but I love the learning process. It's full of trial and error and the unexpected.

There is something about the prospect of turning a dusty bag of wheat into loaves of bread that made me wonder what I was supposed to do with it all.

The answer, of course, was to grind it. But me? That seemed crazy. I could make bread out of it eventually, but I thought it was best to leave the grinding to someone else. I made a few phone calls and discovered that the closest mill that would process our rogue grain was about three hours away. As reluctant as I was to undertake a drive like that for a bag of flour, the local mills weren't exactly begging for our business. Since our grain didn't come from a commercial field, millers were skeptical about our wheat—they didn't want us contaminating their mills. Fair enough, I figured, though the irony that we might just as easily have worried that our organic heirloom flour might be contaminated by genetically modified, chemically grown wheat from an industrial farm was not lost on me.

Drive or no drive, if we were going to send our wheat to a

commercial mill, we would have to get it cleaned first—professionally. Chris would probably argue that the wheat *had* been cleaned professionally, by him. He had winnowed it by tossing handfuls of wheat berries into the air in the expectation that the bugs and chaff would drift away on the breeze.

I had no doubt that Chris had winnowed the wheat, but when I started to make batches of Wheat Berry Beer Bread and cooked out the berries, about half the volume was oats. I really like oats, so this was fine with me. But I knew it would be much less fine for the mills I was trying work with.

In the end, we decided to use Chris's home mill, which looked like it had been built thirty years ago. It was very heavy and finicky, and I resisted until I actually looked inside the grinder to see how it worked. When I saw the two stone wheels working hard to grind the wheat, I was hooked. I loved it. It was definitely a temperamental little machine, but with a little patience, it ground the wheat just fine.

Once the wheat has been ground to a powder, it has to be sifted to remove the husks and any other foreign particles. It took a bit of work (if you are dispirited by a little arm-numbing work, baking might not be your vocation) before I had enough flour to make a loaf

  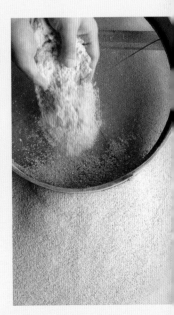

of bread, but once I had a substantial pile I couldn't wait. My love of bread-making stems from the fact that you can't rush the process—but in this instance, I was looking for some immediate results.

I decided to make a basic whole wheat loaf with a whole wheat poolish (a yeast bread starter that helps to improve the bread fermentation and flavor). The whole endeavor took about eight hours, and I'm sure that, to most people, the resulting bread tasted just like all the other Red Fife wheat loaves I had made in the past. But to me, it was the most perfect loaf ever baked.

We roll bread every day at the restaurant, sometimes up to seventy-five loaves. It's a process that intimidates a lot of people, even fellow chefs, but once you understand the basics of fermentation, it's a piece of cake (no pun intended) and very satisfying work. I'm spending a lot more time these days working on bread recipes, trying to get the most flavor out of the flours. I often shake hands with a doughy, dusty hand, quickly wiped on a doughy, dusty apron.

We now use Red Fife every day in the restaurant's whole wheat bread. It's in our whole wheat pasta as well. The pasta is actually a better showcase for the wheat, because all whole wheat breads need to be made with some white flour to work. Pasta does not, so you get a much truer taste of the Red Fife in a plate of handmade pasta—except that it's all mucked up by yummy garlic, olive oils and seasonal veggies.

I have to admit that we didn't grow enough of our own wheat to make all this bread and pasta. To meet our needs, we have to buy our fair share of commercial Red Fife. Only in the last year or so have we been able to buy it commercially from a supplier. (The grower is Marc Loiselle, who supplied our first seeds.) We're just glad there is enough demand for Red Fife that it has become a viable commercial concern.

A while ago, Jeff and I were talking about how we would know when Red Fife had taken its rightful place in the wheat pantheon. We decided that the best indication would be seeing it on Jamie Kennedy's menu in Toronto. Little did we know that our favorite wheat's moment had already arrived. The next week, when we ate at Jamie's, there it was on his menu: Red Fife Sourdough Loaf.

The process of planting, harvesting and milling the wheat is a complete cycle, and we were fortunate to have the means to pull it off. I doubt many people who read this book are going to grow their own wheat. But that wasn't really the point when we started. We just wanted to trace the journey from the spring earth to the table.

If you set about making your own bread, there are few things to be aware of. Assuming you don't grow your own, the flour you choose to work with should be organic, or at least unbleached. There is no need for a crazy chemical like bleach in your food. True, flour has a yellow tint when it is first harvested, ground and sifted. The idea behind bleaching the flour was to create pristine white loaves. Unfortunately, the bleach removes more than just the yellow tint; texture and flavor are also affected. Organic white flour may have a little yellowness to it, but that will be more than made up for by the superior taste.

I once heard a story about a professional baker who would start work every day at 3 a.m. and bake all morning. When he was finished his shift, he would pick out the most beautiful loaf he had made that day and take it home to his family, and they would all enjoy it together at supper. I think this is a really nice story. Now imagine how great he'd feel if he had grown the wheat.

PLANNING A HERB GARDEN

To me, herbs (and I am talking about fresh herbs) are a great source of inspiration. When someone asks, "What was in that?" a herb is usually the answer. When someone says, "Mine didn't taste as good at home," they probably didn't use the right herbs, or any at all. Most home cooks and, dare I say, professionals don't use herbs enough.

Some herbs have a deep, heavy scent; others are the definition of fresh and light. Have you ever found yourself in a herb garden in full bloom? It's magical. I especially love the association between herbs and season. Chives speak of spring; basil says summer; sage is the aroma of autumn. And winter is the season to start planning the next year's garden.

The smell of herbs is sometimes stronger than their taste— and our sense of smell is a major factor in our sense of taste. One avant-garde restaurant in Spain, called elBulli, serves shrimp cooked in butter with branches of rosemary on the side of the plate. You are instructed to smell the rosemary and eat the fish; the rosemary is so powerful that a mere whiff helps you experience your dinner in a whole new way.

Herbs fall into two categories. On the one hand, we have the stronger varieties: rosemary, thyme, bay and sage. They can stand cooking without deteriorating. On the other, we have the more delicate varieties, such as chervil, basil, tarragon and chives, which should be added to dishes only at the end of cooking or just before serving.

Avoid using dried herbs (except for bay leaves). They are often stale and have harsh, bitter flavors. Eating dried herbs is a little like eating dried salad.

Fresh herbs are the best, and most are very easy to grow, be it in a garden or on a windowsill. If you don't have a big yard, you can plant a variety of herbs in a nice arrangement of pots on your back patio or balcony.

The first thing to think about when planning your herb garden is location. Full sun is best for herbs, but in my experience, most herbs will grow in partial shade. They may not grow as fast as those planted in full sun, but they will do just fine. Avoid locations that get no sun at all.

When you have decided on a location for your herb garden, it's time to figure out which herbs you'd like to grow. Ask yourself why you want to grow herbs. Is it for cooking, teas, potpourri, fragrance or a combination of all these? For instance, I have learned that I don't really use mint, except in teas for my wife. So I don't need to grow much. Whatever your reason for growing herbs, it will help you decide which herbs to grow. If it's for cooking, which herbs do you currently use? You can grow these, plus others that have caught your interest in the past. I can't get enough of basil, so I tend to plant at least four varieties.

Here's what I think every herb garden should have. Others will certainly have different priorities, but here's what I grow:

THYME (LEMON AND PINEAPPLE): You can get so many interesting varieties of this perennial, it seems a waste to grow plain old thyme.

TARRAGON: This distinctive herb loves chicken and lemon. It's best used as the only herb in a sauce or garnish.

ROSEMARY: You can plant this perennial as a stand-alone bush. The streets of Berkeley, California, are lined with big, fragrant rosemary bushes (more proof that the place is in the same neighborhood as Nirvana).

SAGE: Turkey and squash love this fall herb. *I* love sage that has been deep-fried to a crisp chip.

CHIVES: Chives and their flowers are so spring! The bigger they get, the more pronounced their oniony flavor. That's another way of saying that chives go well with everything.

SORREL: This large, lemony leaf is not well known, but is very nice pureed into soups or sauces for fish.

CHERVIL: A very delicate leaf, but an incredibly hardy plant, chervil is always the last herb standing in my garden, even after the frost. It's used in French dishes, but is primarily a fancy-pants garnish.

FLAT-LEAF (ITALIAN) PARSLEY: Parsley is the workhorse of my kitchen. We use it on everything from steaks to soups. Officially, it is a biannual, but it flowers in the second year and should be replanted. Parsley is too often used as a garnish, rather than as a flavoring.

CILANTRO: Some love it; some hate it. I love it. Cilantro is the most popular fresh herb in the world. It defines Indian, Thai, Chinese and Mexican cuisines, all very distinct. Don't use too much, or your food will taste soapy.

WHOLE FORESTS OF BASIL: Basil is an annual that can be easily grown from seed. It is the definition of summer, and it goes best with tomatoes, corn, olive oil and garlic.

A word on mint: it's a weed and will take over your garden. I've seen it take over whole lawns (which smelled great when they were mowed, I have to admit). At the restaurant, we plant mint in its own bed, so it doesn't impinge on the other herbs.

You should also know that herb flowers are edible and add a real zip to salads and flavored butters. Chive flowers enhance our recipe for Scrambled Eggs with Chives and Caviar (page 51).

Once you have chosen the herbs you want to grow, it's time to decide how you will plant them. First, make a list of the herbs you will be using, leaving space for descriptions of height, foliage and/or flower color, and spacing requirements. (To find these requirements, look the plants up in a gardening reference book or look on the seed packets.) Decide what shape of bed you'd like and what size. Keep in mind that an island bed (one that can be accessed from

all sides) should be no wider than five feet, and a border bed (one that can be accessed only from the front) should be no wider than two and a half feet.

Now take a piece of paper and a pencil and sketch in the shape of the bed. Look at your list of herbs and place them in the bed according to height, keeping in mind which plants would complement each other. Write in the names of the plants on your sketch. If you change your mind about something, simply erase and change it. You may even want to go so far as to use colored pencils to color code or to indicate the color of the plants. You can use this sketch as your planting guide.

The planning process can be just as enjoyable as planting and caring for the herbs. It also enables you to get to know your plants before they are planted. There is no time of the year quite like winter for imagining a herb garden bursting with life, buzzing with dizzy bees and drenching the summer breeze with its aroma.

Winter thyme

MEAT

It is not easy to talk about meat. On the one hand, nothing inspires longing for food quite so much as a juicy steak just off the grill, or a beautiful herb-roasted chicken, or spicy barbecued pork ribs (my personal favorite). On the other hand, while any host would be proud to serve homegrown lettuce or tomatoes, the idea of butchering their own meat doesn't hold much appeal for most people I know. In fact, many people are put off their dinner by the sight of a carcass hanging in a butcher's shop.

One way to negotiate the dilemma of being disgusted by the same foods we can't help craving is to close our eyes to the things we would rather not think about. Personally, I prefer to think the question through, and I go out of my way to introduce the cooks in my kitchen to what Alice Waters calls "the moral dimension of pleasure." (Of course, there is a third option for those troubled by the dilemma of meat: giving it up. But that is not the path for me.)

Every once in a while in a busy restaurant, a harried cook will toss a piece of meat into the trash. Perhaps it had been overcooked, or dropped on the floor. Whenever I see that, I tell the cook, "If you had killed that chicken, you would have been more careful." I usually get a confused look in return, but it's an important point for me: no animal should be killed for food, only to be treated so carelessly that it has to be thrown out.

I've seen the intelligence in animals' eyes, and watched them tend to their offspring. You don't have to be an animal rights activist to feel an innate sympathy for all animals, or ambivalence about the ones whose destiny leads to the kitchen. But the ethical response to this sympathy is not necessarily to forgo the pleasure of meat. And ignoring the whole problem by looking for meat that comes in tidy cellophane packages not only leaves your own questions unanswered but probably leaves the animals worse off, since supermarket meat is raised and slaughtered in conditions that can only be described as horrific. If you have any concerns about the ethics of eating meat, ignoring them only makes things worse.

The only way to deal with these misgivings is to meet them head-on. I was discussing this issue with one of my brightest young chefs, Alex. We were talking about the idea that we kill by proxy every single day of our lives. If you eat meat, she thought aloud, should you not be willing to kill an animal? If not, shouldn't you be a vegetarian?

Alex was later discussing our restaurant's philosophy with her father, and he quickly put the ethical challenge in very practical terms. Through his work in the construction business, he knows many European

immigrant men, some of whom buy and kill rabbits regularly. We soon had an invitation: Would we like to participate?

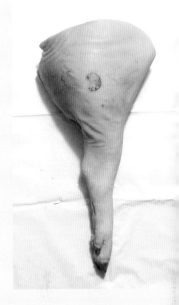

I have killed and prepared many animals: chickens, pigs, fish, geese and once, by accident, a deer. I remember them all—their trust or their fear, their sheer vitality, the steamy breath of ducks quacking nervously in a cold barn. But rabbits pose a unique ethical problem: they're about as cute as an animal can get. I can say that a cardboard box with a few nervous bunnies huddled at the bottom is a powerful lesson in the moral dimension of dinner. The cooks were horrified by the prospect of killing anything so adorable, and it seemed as though everyone was waiting for someone else to propose turning around and going home. And if we had not been cooks, perhaps we would not have gone through with it. But we *are* cooks, and we handle animals all day. If anyone is capable of understanding that leaving those rabbits in their box would not save them, it was my team.

We went through with it, of course. Not without qualms, and

not without wondering if we would ever be finished. But it was soon over, and once it was, we all came away with a more powerful respect for, and an urgent sense of responsibility to, the animals we cook and eat every day. That meant we had to make use of the whole rabbit. Alex kept the pelts, and we even braised, breaded and fried the ears, which we tossed in a salad.

Of course, we don't usually get our meat for the restaurant in cardboard boxes from friends of the staff. Like everyone else, we get our meat from suppliers. (Though I do butcher my own pigs.) And as we do with all of our sourcing, we make every effort not only to find the best product available but also to support the local economy. When it comes to procuring meat for the kitchen, finding the right supplier means finding someone who shares your ethical priorities. We were lucky our research led us to Forsyth Farm.

We are also lucky that what tastes better so often *is* better. I doubt anyone would disagree that fresh, local, organic lamb tastes better than frozen cuts

shipped from the other side of the planet (I'm always happy to see a green meadow dotted with grazing sheep in my neighborhood). What I love about our relationship with the Forsyths is that what is good for the farmer is also good for the animals.

"There's more to a lamb than just the rack," says Shane Forsyth. (Just as there is more to a cow than a tenderloin, and more to a chicken than a skinless breast, I add.) The fetishization of premium cuts makes life hard for producers, since they are raising whole animals, while shoppers and diners want only a small part. This puts obvious pressure on farmers to lower costs and encourages all of us to think of the animals as no more than commodities. As Shane puts it, "You'd think these lambs were walking racks."

When we started doing business with the Forsyths, we asked what we could do to improve their business. The answer came quickly: buy the whole animal—don't just cherry-pick the good cuts.

I wouldn't have it any other way. Wasting most of an animal is not an option for us, and neither is trying to coerce a farmer or artisan into a business relationship that benefits only one party. But this is not only the ethical high ground, it's the culinary high ground as well. The gnarly off-cuts are infinitely more flavorful than the so-called choice bits; properly prepared braised short ribs or osso buco beat a tenderloin hands-down. And they're cheaper, too. This brings me back to the importance of learning to cook: cuts such as lamb shank do require a certain amount of knowledge of cooking technique to bring them to the ethereal state they are capable of. It's not a question of making do with second-best; some of the most delicious dishes in the world *call for* the less exalted cuts. But if you don't know how to cook, you are damned to eternal steak grilling.

The way I see it, I have a moral obligation to use the whole animal, nose to tail, and this happens to be more gastronomically interesting than obsessing over premium cuts— and much more economical. I use the Forsyths' lambs in Spring Lamb Shoulder (page

64) and Braised Lamb Shanks (page 250), and I would miss these dishes if I were limited to cooking only racks.

I am not suggesting that there are easy answers to the ethical questions raised by eating meat. I am not even suggesting that there are clear answers, though difficult ones. But the way we frame the questions is at least a start, and I do not think it is a mistake to begin with one of our best emotions: sympathy. No dimension of the earth-to-table philosophy hits home with the immediacy of the respect for animals this sympathy engenders. It is easy enough to dismiss the thoughtlessness of monoculture (see page 309) or the unaccounted cost of food miles. But no one can morally ignore the plight of living, breathing animals for the sake of a backyard barbecue.

CHEF THOMAS KELLER

THE FRENCH LAUNDRY, YOUNTVILLE, CALIFORNIA

I began cooking four years before *The French Laundry Cookbook* came out, and my well-thumbed first edition is among my most prized possessions. I cannot exaggerate the effect the book had on me as I was figuring out how to cook. Reading it, I realized in a new way that food comes from *somewhere* or *someone*. Not that I had ever doubted the existence of farmers—I just hadn't really thought about them at all, or considered that their work, and that of other producers, could be part of the story of food. By spotlighting some of his suppliers in his book, Thomas Keller opened up for me and a generation of cooks a new perspective on food. I happen to think his cookbook is the best ever published.

So I was eager to meet the chef himself, and was thrilled when his assistant agreed to block off some time for him to meet with us. (And equally thrilled when *her* assistant actually booked the appointment.) I have to admit, we were also excited to be heading to Napa Valley in the middle of the Canadian winter.

Bettina and I drove up to Napa Valley from San Francisco, enjoying the spectacle of farmland already springing to life and trading lines from *Sideways*. As work goes, it gets a lot worse than heading to Yountville to talk to the man named "America's Best Chef" by *Time* magazine and "Best Chef" by the James Beard Foundation (in fact, he was the first person to be honored in this way in consecutive years).

Keller is famous for his ability to coax flavors and intense colors out of each ingredient, and for his sense of humor. His menu offers many witty and refined versions of comfort food:

Fish and Chips (red mullet with *palette d'ail doux* and garlic chips), Macaroni and Cheese (butter-poached lobster and orzo) and his most copied dish, Coffee and Doughnuts (cappuccino semifreddo with cinnamon doughnuts). The prospect of chatting with Thomas Keller doesn't seem like work at all—I can't think of anything I'd rather be doing.

I didn't want to be late for our meeting, and we ended up arriving at the French Laundry quite early. We sat in the meticulously groomed outdoor garden, amid the lemon trees, and caught glimpses of Keller coming and going as he went about his business. By the time he sat down with us, I felt as though I already knew him.

This sense of familiarity was perhaps increased by the fact that he looked exactly like his author photo. He is tall and slender, and carries himself with the cool composure of an aristocrat. His chef's coat was a radiant, wrinkle-free white. It is difficult to imagine him with so much as a hair out of place.

Attention to detail is what he and his restaurants are known for, and we enjoyed it ourselves when our coffee arrived. Keller has commissioned a signature blend of coffee beans for the restaurant and has had the grinding and brewing machines specially calibrated. The brew was served in a pristine sterling silver pot, accompanied by a small ewer of heated milk. Keller's hackles seemed to go up at the sight of his off-duty server appearing at our table in street clothes, but I certainly didn't enjoy the coffee or the conversation one bit less.

It was this fastidious and world-famous attention to detail that convinced me I had to make the trip to Yountville. It's pretty easy to make the case that there is no one better equipped to talk to about what constitutes good food. Keller is the only American-born chef to hold multiple three-star ratings from the Michelin Guide: both the French Laundry and his New York restaurant, Per Se, have been awarded the highest

ranking. So if he says that local, seasonal produce is best, no one is really in a position to disagree.

It has to be said that cooking and eating seasonally and locally is a lot easier in Napa Valley than pretty much anywhere else in North America, possibly the world. It all started with Alice Waters and Chez Panisse—ground zero for local, sustainable agriculture. Now it is the new normal, as Keller points out. In fact, he finds the idea that eating this way might be inconvenient a little ridiculous. "Just look in the supermarket," he says. (Sure enough, when we do, we find that fresh, local produce dominates the store, crowding out the dry foods and snacks. If only all stores were like this!)

Keller makes the same point as Heston Blumenthal and Dan Barber: when people start demanding good food, they'll get it. Evidently, people around here have been demanding it a little longer and perhaps a little louder. And now they've got it. It's up to the rest of the world to catch up.

When I point out that his mechanism for improving our food culture could be criticized as elitist, he barely bats an eye. "It *is* elitist," he says. "Good food costs more to make and therefore is more expensive." The important thing, he argues, is not the *cost* of food, but its *value*. We do not really value good food, so we get cheap food. However expensive a meal might be at the French Laundry, we all have something to learn from the people who eat there: no one questions the value of the food he serves. The citizens of wealthy countries with mature food cultures, such as France, Italy and Japan, tend to spend far more of their disposable income on good food than we do. Are they elitist, or do they simply value food?

Keller stresses that the experience of eating is as important as the food itself. "A great

meal is not about filling yourself up," he says. A great meal is marked by the company you share it with, the environment you enjoy it in, the pleasure you derive from the confluence of all these elements. If you try to measure all this with a criterion as crude as price, you will inevitably get it wrong. If you instead enjoy the experience, value the ingredients and respect the producers, you may find that the increase in price is more than offset by the many advantages this way of cooking and eating offers.

Not least among these advantages is a food economy that supports the people who produce the food. Cheap food is to a large degree subsidized by the farmers themselves. As recently as 1950, farmers got about fifty cents of every retail food dollar. Now they get about ten cents. When we go looking for local, artisanal fare, and reward those men and women who are going about their work thoughtfully, we end up not only with great food but with a better, fairer food system. For example, Keller sources his butter from Animal Farm, a tiny farm in Vermont—not exactly around the corner from the French Laundry, it's true, but still a small-scale, sustainable, humane enterprise that can only benefit farmers and butter-lovers in that part of Vermont.

Keller insists that even those of us on a limited budget should look for food artisans or quality growers whose products suit our needs. "Source less expensive but still artisanally produced dried beans, for example, or off-cuts of meat," he says.

The Future of Food

Thomas Keller predicts that as people pay more attention to the food they shop for and eat, the farmers and artisans who produce it will begin to get their due. "It is time for the farmers to shine as chefs do," he says. He has always shared the spotlight with the men and women who contribute to the experience of the food he serves, and he arranged for us to meet a couple of them.

TUCKER TAYLOR:
THE BEST FARMER IN THE WORLD

Tucker Taylor runs the small farm (or huge garden) where the French Laundry grows its vegetables. He's a soft-spoken, bearded Georgian whose brown overalls and wraparound sunglasses make him look like a snowboarder. Like Keller, Tucker values attention to detail, and it shows in his tidy rows of greens, all meticulously labeled and carefully mulched with straw to keep down weeds. When we told him that being the farmer for the best restaurant in the world must make him the best farmer in the world, he laughed uncomfortably. It seemed he preferred to offer advice on our own restaurant garden than to accept accolades. Fair enough. But these are Michelin three-star vegetables. The French Laundry takes its pick of the most exalted of the daily harvest, then Bouchon gets its turn, then Ad Hoc. Tucker feeds a lot of pretty discerning diners.

THE JACOBSENS:
THOMAS KELLER'S LONG-TIME PRODUCE SUPPLIER

It is impossible not to like the Jacobsens and get caught up in their enthusiasm for the food they grow. You can tell they love having a sprawling Eden in their backyard. Peter, a retired dentist, kept pulling vegetables out of the ground and offering them to us so we could taste their sweetness, or earthiness, or juiciness. "This one tastes like candy," he says. "These are the limes we serve with tequila." (We were very interested in the Meyer lemons, a fruit that is nearly impossible to source in Canada, but he was much more interested in showing us his limes.) This could have gone on for ages, as the Jacobsens grow ten varieties of figs, thirty types of tomatoes and a wide variety of edible flowers. We were getting an impromptu version of the French Laundry's tasting menu, before it was cooked.

His most recent success shows that he knows what he's talking about when he says more modest food can be extraordinary. Keller intended Ad Hoc to be a temporary restaurant, but it quickly became a local sensation and he had to make it a permanent fixture. The place is bustling, informal and cheerfully unpretentious. The servers wear jeans and Ad Hoc bowling shirts, and the set menu of classic American fare—which changes every day, according to what is available—is just as relaxed. In fact, the night we were there, the menu featured the very foods Keller had mentioned only a few hours earlier: beans and cheaper cuts of meat. Dinner began with a tureen of ham hock soup large enough for seconds and thirds. The rich broth was fortified with lardons of bacon, two types of beans, chunks of carrot and wilted broccoli rabe leaves— pure comfort food. The second course was perfectly grilled skirt steak with a sauté of mushrooms, peppers and marble-sized new potatoes tossed in garlic and olive oil. But much like the playful menu at the French Laundry, this informality belies the careful thought and world-class ingredients that go into

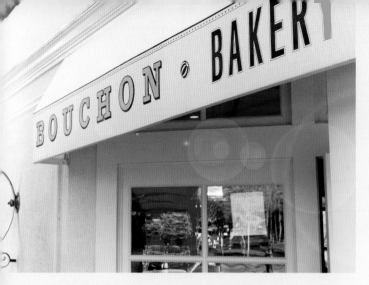

the food. The produce comes from the same gardens that supply the French Laundry and Bouchon, Keller's other restaurant in the area.

(Bouchon is Keller's version of a Paris brasserie. Stepping into Bouchon is like stepping off the Champs-Elysées. It is magical. We had only enough time to stop in for a quick bite, as it was not really on our itinerary, but I knew the famous curved zinc bar would have a whack of oysters on offer. So we plunked ourselves down and drank local sparkling wine and slurped oysters for a moment's escape. Just to make conversation, we mentioned to the bartender that Bettina had spent time in the kitchen at Per Se, and we got a staff discount!)

We came away from Ad Hoc bursting with ideas and talking excitedly about how his restaurant proves the argument Keller had made that afternoon. The meal we had enjoyed so immensely was the result of the process he had described.

Pioneers such as Alice Waters and Thomas Keller (to say nothing of the local wineries, which have really come of age in the last couple of decades) have helped to create a culture of excellence and pleasure, in which humble fried chicken, bean soup or fish and chips can be a culinary delight and local farmers and artisans can be celebrated and rewarded.

Winter Salad

Serves 8

3 Belgian endives, cored and
broken into leaves

1 head radicchio, leaves torn
from ribs and finely sliced

1 bunch watercress (about 5 oz),
trimmed

1 head blonde frisée, cored and
broken into leaves

1 tbsp snipped chives (½-inch
pieces)

⅓ cup Dijon Vinaigrette (see
recipe, page 295)

1 cup crumbled blue cheese

1 cup candied hazelnuts (see
recipe, page 271)

Salt and freshly cracked
black pepper

Salads are still seasonal in winter. Winter greens are
hearty and bitter, so they go well with rich blue cheese
and sweet candied nuts.

IN A LARGE BOWL, using your hands, toss together
endives, radicchio, watercress, frisée and chives. Pour in
vinaigrette and toss gently until greens are lightly but
evenly coated. Add blue cheese and nuts; toss gently, making sure not to break up cheese more than it already is.
Season to taste with salt and pepper. Serve immediately.

Bay Scallops with Broccoli Rabe

The East Coast of North America has long produced these sweet tender mollusks, available from late September through March. They should have a sweet briny smell and no fishy fumes. Scallops are no trouble to prepare once you get the knack of working quickly over high heat. Use a heavy skillet and wait until its very hot before the scallops go in the pan.

IN A LARGE POT of boiling salted water, cook broccoli rabe until stems are just cooked, about 5 minutes. Using tongs, remove rabe and plunge into a large bowl of ice water to stop the cooking. Drain and set aside.

Meanwhile, in a large skillet, heat half the oil over high heat. Reduce heat to medium-high and add half the scallops; cook until golden and crisp on the bottom, about 6 minutes. Turn and cook until golden and crisp on the other side, about 3 minutes. Transfer to a plate and keep warm. Wipe out skillet and repeat with the remaining oil and scallops.

In the same skillet, reheat the oil left in the pan. Add garlic and chili flakes; sauté until garlic is golden, about 1 minute. Add broccoli rabe and stock; cook over medium-high heat until rabe is heated through and tender, about 2 minutes. Stir in lemon juice and season to taste with salt and pepper.

Divide scallops among 6 plates and top with broccoli rabe.

Serves 6

2 lbs broccoli rabe
⅓ cup canola oil, divided
2 lbs large-sized bay scallops (about 12 scallops per lb)
3 cloves garlic, minced
1 tsp chili flakes
¼ cup Chicken Stock (see recipe, page 297)
¼ cup freshly squeezed lemon juice
Salt and freshly cracked black pepper

Roasted Fingerling Potato Salad with Watercress and Horseradish Dressing

Serves 4

2 lbs fingerling potatoes, peeled

3 tbsp extra-virgin olive oil

3 tbsp dry white wine

1 tbsp fresh thyme leaves

1 tsp salt

2 bunches watercress (about
    10 oz), trimmed

DRESSING

¼ cup extra-virgin olive oil

¼ cup sour cream

2 tbsp red wine vinegar

1 tbsp freshly grated horseradish
    root

Salt and freshly cracked
    black pepper

Potatoes are something that I have planted in my garden at home. There is really something special about digging a few potatoes from the cold earth with your hands. It is almost surprising to find them under the plant. I prefer to roast potatoes whole "in their jackets," which allows them to retain all the flavor and even adds a bit of char to the skins. Horseradish and potatoes have a real love for one another; try some horseradish on french fries.

PREHEAT OVEN TO 450°F. In a medium bowl, toss potatoes, oil, wine, thyme and salt. Spread out in a single layer on a baking sheet and bake until very tender, about 40 minutes.

Prepare the dressing: In a large bowl, whisk together oil, sour cream, vinegar and horseradish. Season to taste with salt and pepper. (*Make ahead: Cover and refrigerate for up to 5 days.*)

Add warm potatoes to dressing and toss to coat. Divide among 4 plates and top each with a handful of watercress.

Braised Lamb Shanks

Serves 4

4 small lamb shanks (each
    about 8 oz)
Salt and freshly cracked
    black pepper
3 tbsp extra-virgin olive oil
4 cloves garlic
2 stalks celery, roughly chopped
1 carrot, roughly chopped
1 onion, roughly chopped
1 leek (white and light green
    parts only), roughly chopped
1 sprig fresh thyme
1 sprig fresh rosemary
1 dried bay leaf
2 cups dry red wine
4 cups Beef Stock (see recipe,
    page 296)

We feature lamb shanks on our winter menu at the restaurant. As a chef, I gravitate toward cheap cuts of meat, like lamb shanks. They are very flavorful, and I hope to inspire you to use a variety of meat cuts.

Our lamb comes from Brenda and Shane Forsyth, who own a lamb farm. I have developed a relationship with them over my time as the chef at the Ancaster Old Mill. I try to help farmers and work with them: rather than buying only prime cuts, as some chefs do, I buy a whole lamb and use as much of the animal as possible. We usually purchase about four lambs a week, and I use both the popular and unpopular cuts.

GENEROUSLY SEASON LAMB with salt and pepper. In a large skillet, heat oil over high heat until smoking. Add lamb and cook, turning, until golden brown on all sides, about 10 minutes. Using tongs, transfer lamb to a large Dutch oven and set aside.

Reduce heat to medium and add garlic, celery, carrot, onion, leek, thyme, rosemary and bay leaf to the pan. Sauté until vegetables are golden brown, about 8 minutes. Add wine and cook, scraping up any brown bits from the bottom of the pan, until reduced by half, about 5 minutes. Add stock and bring to a boil. Meanwhile, preheat oven to 325°F.

Pour everything over lamb. (Liquid should cover shanks; if it doesn't, add water or more stock until covered.) Cover and bake, turning every 20 minutes, until meat is very tender and yields easily when pierced with a knife, about 3 hours. Remove meat, strain sauce, and reduce by half. Serve lamb in a shallow dish, dressed with sauce, ideally with Cipollini Onions (opposite).

Cipollini Onions

Cipollini onions are usually harvested in the fall and are available primarily in specialty markets through fall and winter. The flesh is pale yellow, and the skins are thin and papery. Cipollini onions are sweet and have more residual sugar than the garden-variety onion. They have a distinctive shape—small and flat—so I like to serve them whole, alongside chicken, fish and lamb on a large family-style platter.

IN A LARGE POT of boiling salted water, cook onions, immersed in water, until peels are starting to break, about 2 minutes. Drain and peel.

In a skillet, heat butter and oil over medium heat until foaming, about 2 minutes. Add onions and sugar, tossing to coat. Add port, increase heat to medium-high and cook until reduced by half, about 3 minutes. Add stock, lower heat to simmer and cook until onions are tender and glazed, about 30 minutes. Season to taste with salt and pepper.

TIP: If you can't find cipollini onions, you can substitute pearl onions.

Serves 4

24 cipollini onions (about 12 oz)
3 tbsp unsalted butter
1 tbsp extra-virgin olive oil
1 tbsp granulated sugar
1 cup port
2 cups Chicken Stock (see
    recipe, page 297)
Salt and freshly cracked
    black pepper

Braised Pork Belly

Serves 4

2 lbs boneless pork belly

4 cloves garlic

1 onion, roughly chopped

3 stalks celery, roughly chopped

1 sprig fresh thyme

1 sprig fresh rosemary

1 dried bay leaf

4 cups Chicken Stock (see
   recipe, page 297)

½ cup soy sauce

½ cup mirin (rice wine)

1 tbsp packed brown sugar

Salt and freshly cracked
   black pepper

Pork belly is uncured, unsmoked bacon. It has recently become a cult favorite at restaurants, and why not—it is delicious. We pair the belly with Pickled Fennel (page 127) to contrast the rich meat with sweet and sour fennel . . . so good. Add a green salad on the side, and your meal is complete.

PREHEAT OVEN TO 225°F. Place pork belly skin side up in a medium ovenproof casserole dish and score skin with a sharp knife. Scatter garlic, onion and celery over and around pork belly. Add thyme, rosemary, bay leaf, stock, soy sauce and mirin to the casserole dish. (Liquid should come halfway up pork; if it doesn't, add water.) Cover tightly with foil and bake, stirring occasionally and basting pork with liquid, until very tender, about 6 hours.

Increase oven temperature to 500°F. Sprinkle top of pork with brown sugar and salt and pepper to taste; bake uncovered until top is golden and skin is crisp, about 20 minutes. Let cool, then cut into slices. Strain sauce and drizzle over meat.

Maple, Molasses and Beer Bean Pot

This dish overlaps winter and spring. When the maple syrup is fresh, it is technically spring, but it's still quite cool out. Try serving this with the pork belly on the facing page—the two dishes pair very well. This is a big enough recipe to serve at a party, but the flavors develop overnight so it makes great leftovers.

IN A LARGE BOWL, combine black, white and red beans with 14 cups of water and let soak overnight. Drain and rinse.

In a large pot, combine beans with 8 cups of salted water. Bring to a boil; reduce heat and simmer until beans are softened, about 40 minutes. Drain and set aside.

In a small bowl, combine chipotles with 1 cup of boiling water and let steep for 30 minutes. Remove chilies from water, reserving water, and finely chop. Set aside.

In the same large pot, sauté bacon over medium-high heat until browned and crisp, about 7 minutes. Add onions and sauté until softened, about 15 minutes. Stir in beans, chipotles, chipotle water, garlic, cayenne and cumin. Reduce heat to medium and add brown sugar, cider, maple syrup, molasses and beer. Cook, stirring occasionally, until beans are very tender, about 3 hours. Season to taste with salt and pepper.

Serves 12

2 cups dried black beans
2 cups dried white kidney beans
2 cups dried red kidney beans
2 dried chipotle peppers
1 lb double-smoked bacon, cut into ¼-inch pieces
2 large Spanish onions, finely chopped
5 cloves garlic, minced
1 tsp cayenne pepper
2 tbsp ground cumin
1 cup packed brown sugar
1 cup pure apple cider
¾ cup pure maple syrup
3 tbsp blackstrap molasses
2 bottles (each 12 oz) local dark beer
Salt and freshly cracked black pepper

Venison Pub Pie
with Chestnuts and Parsnips

During the late fall and early winter, chestnuts can be found fairly easily at the grocery store. For those who are interested in foraging for their food, chestnuts are also all over the ground at this time of year. It can be a little tricky to get the nuts out of their shells once they have been roasted, but have no fear—they get chopped into little bits before going into the pie, so smash away! Venison is available at specialty butcher shops and farms.

IN A LARGE SKILLET, heat 4 tbsp of the oil over medium-high heat. Add pancetta and sauté until crispy and golden brown, about 4 minutes. Reduce heat to medium and add garlic and onion; sauté until softened, about 10 minutes. Add parsnips, carrot, celery and chestnuts; sauté until softened, about 15 minutes. Transfer mixture to a 12-cup ovenproof casserole dish.

In a large, shallow dish, combine flour and salt and pepper to taste. Add meat and toss to coat. In clean large skillet, heat 4 tbsp of the oil over high heat until smoking. Add meat, in batches, and sauté until browned on all sides, about 10 minutes per batch, adding more oil between batches as needed. Transfer to casserole dish and toss with vegetables. Stir in water, wine and vinegar.

Preheat oven to 400°F. Wrap juniper berries and bay leaves in cheesecloth or a coffee filter, tie with string and add to the casserole dish. Place dish on stovetop and bring to a boil over high. Remove from stovetop. Cover loosely with foil and bake, stirring occasionally, until meat is tender, about 1½ hours.

Meanwhile, roll out pâte brisée to ¼-inch thickness and cut to fit top of casserole dish. Remove dish from oven and discard juniper berries and bay leaves. Carefully

Serves 6

¾ cup extra-virgin olive oil, divided

4 oz pancetta or smoked bacon, chopped

2 cloves garlic, minced

1 medium red onion, chopped

2 large parsnips, finely chopped

1 large carrot, finely chopped

1 stalk celery, finely chopped

1 cup roasted chestnuts (see tip, page 256), finely chopped

¼ cup all-purpose flour

Sea salt and freshly ground black pepper

2 lbs venison stewing meat, cut into 1-inch chunks

3 cups water

1 cup dry red wine

3 tbsp sherry vinegar

1 tbsp juniper berries, crushed

2 dried bay leaves

½ recipe Pâte Brisée (page 306)

1 egg yolk, lightly beaten

>>>

place pastry over dish and brush with egg yolk. Return to oven and bake until pastry is golden and crisp, about 20 minutes.

TIP: To roast chestnuts, using a sharp knife, score an X along the flat side of each chestnut, cutting all the way through to the meat. Cover chestnuts with cold water and let soak for 15 minutes. Drain and spread out on a large rimmed baking sheet. Roast in a 400°F oven, stirring occasionally, until peels have curled along cut marks, about 12 minutes. Let cool, then remove outer and inner peels.

Calf's Liver with Cavolo Nero

Cavolo nero is an Italian cabbage with dark green leaves and a good, strong flavor. When traveling along the country roads of Tuscany, you will see the tall stalks and long, narrow leaves of the cavolo nero plant in every little garden plot.

If the slices of calf's livers you buy are thicker than ¼ inch, you will have to increase the cooking time slightly. Serve with Double Crispy Onion Rings (page 258).

BRING A POT of heavily salted water to a boil. Meanwhile, remove leaves from the cavolo stalks. If the leaves and stalks are large, trim them into manageable pieces. Blanch stalks until just tender, about 3 minutes; drain and pat dry. Plunge leaves into boiling water for 1 minute; drain and pat dry. Cut stalks into thin strips. Set leaves and stalks aside.

Season liver with salt and pepper to taste. In a large skillet, heat oil over medium-high heat until very hot but not smoking. Add liver and sear well on one side, about 20 seconds. Turn and sear the other side for 10 seconds for medium-rare, or until desired doneness. Using tongs, transfer liver to a plate, cover and set aside.

Add vinegar to the pan and cook until reduced by half and syrupy, about 4 minutes. Remove from heat and add butter, one cube at a time, whisking constantly until melted. Do not let boil, or sauce will split. Stir in pine nuts and cranberries. Return liver to pan and heat through.

Divide cavolo nero leaves and stalks among 6 plates. Place a piece of liver on each and drizzle with sauce, nuts and cranberries.

TIP: Soaking the cranberries in warm water for a few minutes plumps them up and softens their flavor slightly.

Serves 6

1 small bunch cavolo nero (about 10 stalks) or Swiss chard
6 slices calf's liver (each about 3½ oz and about ¼ inch thick)
Salt and freshly cracked black pepper
2 tbsp extra-virgin olive oil
1 cup balsamic vinegar
⅓ cup unsalted butter, cut into cubes
3 tbsp toasted pine nuts
3 tbsp dried cranberries, soaked in warm water (see tip)

Double Crispy Onion Rings

Serves 6

Canola oil

3 large Vidalia or other sweet
onions (about 2 lbs)

2 cups buttermilk

3 cups all-purpose flour

½ cup cornmeal

1 tsp cayenne pepper

1 tsp salt

Freshly cracked black pepper

I like to let the onions sit in the buttermilk for about 10 minutes before coating, which gives the onion time to soak up the tart goodness of the milk. Be sure to have all your guests at the table for this one as the rings will go soggy quickly.

IN A LARGE, HEAVY POT, heat 3 inches of oil over high heat until it registers 300°F on a candy/deep-fry thermometer, or until a cube of bread turns golden in 20 seconds.

Meanwhile, cut onions into ½-inch-thick slices and separate into rings. Pour buttermilk into a bowl, add onion rings and let sit for 10 minutes. In another bowl, combine flour, cornmeal, cayenne, salt and black pepper to taste.

Working with 4 to 5 onion rings at a time, shake off excess buttermilk. Toss in flour mixture and shake off excess. Repeat both steps again. Carefully transfer onions to the hot oil and fry, turning occasionally with tongs, until golden brown, about 3 minutes per batch. Transfer to a plate lined with paper towels and sprinkle with salt to taste. Serve immediately.

Hanger Steak with Beet Horseradish Relish

I love this dish for its character. You know you have good beet horseradish relish if it makes you cry! It works well and complements the steak.

There is only one hanger steak per beef steer. It "hangs" from the last rib when the animal is suspended during the butchering process. It is prized for its tenderness and deep, satisfying flavor. Like the flank steak, it is a coarse-grained cut, so it can be chewy if cooked past medium-rare. It is the traditional cut of steak, called an onglet, served in French bistros as steaks frites—so serve it with shoestring fries. Take the battery out of your smoke alarm before you start—you want a really hot pan when searing meat.

IN A LARGE POT of boiling salted water, cook beets until tender, about 1½ hours, boiling the whole time. Drain and, while still warm, using a tea towel, remove skins. Let cool and grate beets into a bowl. Toss with horseradish.

In a saucepan, combine vinegar, sugar and salt. Bring to a boil over high heat. Pour over beet mixture and toss to coat. Cover and refrigerate for at least 24 hours or for up to 3 days.

Pat steak on both sides with a paper towel. Season both sides generously with salt and pepper. In a large cast-iron skillet, heat oil over high heat until smoking, about 7 minutes. Add steak and cook, turning once, until golden brown, about 8 minutes. Let rest for 5 minutes before slicing. Serve with beet horseradish relish on the side.

Serves 6

10 medium red beets (about 4 lbs), trimmed
½ cup freshly grated horseradish root
2 cups rice vinegar
½ cup granulated sugar
2 tsp salt
3-lb hanger steak (about 1¼ inches thick)
Salt and freshly cracked black pepper
½ cup extra-virgin olive oil

One-Pot Fish Soup with Rouille

Serves 6

2 tbsp extra-virgin olive oil
4 cloves garlic, minced
1 large onion, minced
1 leek (white part only), finely
    chopped
1 cup finely chopped fennel
    bulb, fronds reserved
1 tbsp tomato paste
Salt
2 cups dry white wine
9 cups Fish Stock (see recipe,
    page 298)
3 lbs mixed skinless white-
    fleshed fish fillets (such as
    striped bass, tilapia or
    Pacific halibut), cut into
    2-inch pieces
1 lb mussels, cleaned and
    debearded
Pinch saffron threads
Salt and freshly cracked
    black pepper
½ cup Garlicky Rouille (see
    recipe, page 294)

Easy and delicious, this recipe can be a warm winter lunch or an elegant dinner appetizer. The freshness of the fish is important. Take the time to find a good fish counter and ask lots of questions, such as when fresh fish arrives at the store.

IN A LARGE STOCKPOT, heat oil over medium-high heat. Add garlic, onion, leek, fennel and tomato paste, stirring to combine. Season to taste with salt and sauté until vegetables are softened, about 8 minutes.

Add wine and cook until reduced by half, about 4 minutes. Add fish stock and bring to a boil. Add fish, mussels and saffron; reduce heat to medium, cover and simmer until mussels have opened and fish is opaque and flakes easily with a fork, about 8 minutes. Do not let boil. Discard any mussels that have not opened. Season to taste with salt and pepper.

Divide soup among 6 bowls and garnish each bowl with fennel fronds and 1 tbsp rouille.

TIP: Cleaning mussels is important, though most cultivated mussels have already been cleaned for you. If by chance you come across a mussel with the beard still attached, you can either cut it off with a knife or pull it off from tip to hinge. Be sure to do this right before cooking, as mussels will die shortly after their beards have been removed.

TIP: Throw out any mussels with broken or cracked shells and always wash with cold water—washing with warm water will kill the mussel and you want to be sure it is alive when you cook it.

Salt-Baked Arctic Char

Serves 6

3-lb Arctic char, cleaned

4 sprigs flat-leaf (Italian) parsley

1 sprig fresh rosemary

1 bunch fresh tarragon
   (about 1 oz)

¼ bunch fresh chives
   (about ¼ oz)

1 lemon, sliced

3 organic egg whites

¼ cup water

1 box (3 lbs) kosher salt

Although this is a real showstopper when served at a party, it's surprisingly easy to prepare. Arctic char can be quite slimy and tricky to handle. We suggest running the fish under cold water before trying to handle it—there is nothing worse then a slimy fish slipping around in your hands. If you can't find Arctic char, trout would make a good substitute. Serve with Aïoli (page 292) and Winter Salad (page 246).

PREHEAT OVEN TO 400°F. Rinse fish under cold water and pat dry. Stuff cavity with parsley, rosemary, tarragon, chives and lemon slices.

In a bowl, whisk together egg whites and water until frothy. Add salt and mix well. Spread 3 cups of the salt mixture along the bottom of large rimmed baking sheet and set fish on top. Completely cover fish with the remaining salt mixture (it should form a layer about ½ inch thick). Bake until an instant-read thermometer inserted in the center of the fish registers 135°F and salt is very hard, about 50 minutes. Let rest for 15 minutes, then break salt crust with a spoon and peel back the skin.

Rabbit Stew
with Herbed Dumplings

Serves 6

2 small rabbits (each about
    1½ lbs), cut into 6 pieces
    each
Salt and freshly cracked
    black pepper
¼ cup all-purpose flour
½ cup extra-virgin olive oil,
    divided
2 medium onions, cut into
    ¼-inch chunks
2 cups pure apple cider
8 cups Chicken Stock (see
    recipe, page 297) or
    rabbit stock
4 sprigs fresh thyme
3 sprigs fresh rosemary
1 dried bay leaf
1 large carrot, cut into ¼-inch
    chunks
1 stalk celery, cut into ¼-inch
    chunks
4 cloves garlic, minced
1 leek (white and light green
    parts only), cut into ¼-inch
    chunks
½ cup finely chopped pancetta
½ cup dried currants
Herbed Dumplings (see recipe,
    page 269)

This dish was the inspiration of one of my chef apprentices, Alex Feswick. Creating it was quite an experience, both for us and for others from our kitchen. Animals are killed for food each day, but to actually see the process changes you. It instills a profound respect for the animal, and a desire to use as much of the animal as possible.

This dish is also important to me because Alex was inspired by her day-to-day work with me to learn more about the earth-to-table philosophy. This is a fundamental part of my job as a chef: to teach and inspire my customers, my friends and family, and the people I work with, from fellow chefs to apprentices to farmers. A dish like this one serves as testimony that I have had an impact on someone's life.

SEASON RABBIT PIECES generously with salt and pepper, then dust with flour, shaking off and discarding excess. In a large skillet, heat 2 tbsp of the oil over medium-high heat until smoking. Add rabbit pieces, in batches, and cook, turning, until a deep, rich golden brown on all sides, about 12 minutes per batch, adding more oil between batches as needed. Using tongs, transfer rabbit to a large pot and pour off fat from skillet.

Reduce heat to medium and add 2 tbsp of the oil to the skillet. Add onions and sauté until they begin to caramelize, about 10 minutes. Add cider and bring to a boil; boil until reduced by half, about 10 minutes. Add stock.

Pour stock mixture over rabbit and add thyme, rosemary and bay leaf. Cover and simmer over medium heat for 1½ hours. Transfer rabbit to a large bowl. Strain liquid and discard solids. Set rabbit and liquid aside separately. >>>

In clean skillet, heat the remaining oil over high heat. Add carrot and celery; sauté until soft and golden brown, about 15 minutes. Add garlic, leek, pancetta and currants; sauté until vegetables are softened and fragrant, about 6 minutes.

In pot, combine rabbit, strained liquid and vegetable mixture. Cook over medium-low heat, turning rabbit to coat with sauce, until heated through. Season to taste with salt and pepper. Add dumplings and cook about 7 minutes. Serve in cooking vessel.

Herbed Dumplings

This is the dumpling recipe that goes with the Rabbit Stew (page 266). The cooking time for the dumplings is 10 minutes, which leaves them slightly underdone, the assumption being that they will finish cooking and plump up when you add them to the stew. If you choose to serve them as a side dish, add 7 minutes to the cooking time.

IN A LARGE BOWL, stir together flour and salt.

In another bowl, whisk together eggs and milk. Whisk into flour mixture until smooth. (The batter will be quite sticky and stiff.) Stir in chives, parsley and pepper. Cover and refrigerate for at least 30 minutes or for up to 2 hours.

Bring a pot of salted water to a simmer over medium heat. Using a soup spoon, scoop out spoonfuls of batter and gently slip into simmering water. Continue scooping batter until water is slightly crowded with dumplings. Cook until dumplings are floating on top of the water, about 10 minutes. Using a slotted spoon, transfer dumplings to a colander to drain. Repeat with any remaining batter.

Place dumplings in a bowl and toss with butter. Immediately add to hot rabbit stew.

Serves 6

2 cups all-purpose flour

1 tsp kosher salt

2 large organic eggs, lightly beaten

¾ cup whole milk

¼ cup minced fresh chives

¼ cup minced fresh flat-leaf (Italian) parsley

¼ tsp freshly cracked black pepper

¼ cup unsalted butter, chopped into small pieces

Roasted Root Vegetables

Serves 6 as a side dish

1½ lbs celery root (about 1),
   peeled and cut into ½-inch
   pieces

1 lb parsnips (about 3), peeled
   and cut into ½-inch pieces

1 lb small turnips (about 4),
   peeled and cut into ½-inch
   pieces

1 lb red onions (about 2), cut
   into wedges

8 oz carrots (about 2 medium),
   cut into ½-inch pieces

4 oz Jerusalem artichokes (about
   6), halved

¼ cup canola oil

¼ cup minced fresh thyme

Salt and freshly cracked
   black pepper

This dish symbolizes the winter season for me. It is easy and colorful, and highlights many of my favorite fall vegetables. Roasting brings out the flavor and sweetness of each of these vegetables. For consistent and even cooking, make sure they are all cut to the same thickness and size.

Parsnips are one of my favorite vegetables, though not many people gravitate toward them. Try them! As for the small turnips, look for them at your local farmers' market. If you can't find them, just cut larger ones into wedges, but small turnips are sweet enough to eat raw.

PREHEAT OVEN TO 375°F and line a large rimmed baking sheet with parchment paper.

In a large bowl, combine celery root, parsnips, turnips, onions, carrots and artichokes. Add oil and toss to coat.

Spread vegetables out in a single layer on prepared baking sheet. Roast, turning occasionally, until softened and slightly caramelized, about 30 minutes. Sprinkle with thyme and salt and pepper to taste.

Candied Nuts

The size of the nuts is quite important in this recipe. Nuts that are the same size, such as pecans and walnuts, can be baked together. Be careful if you want to add smaller nuts or peanuts; the cooking time will be quite different, so these should be baked separately.

You can package candied nuts to give out as presents, or leave out a bowl for friends and family to snack on. They can also be tossed into salads or sprinkled into soups.

PREHEAT OVEN TO 350°F. In a bowl, combine brown sugar, water, salt and nutmeg to make a paste. Stir in nuts until completely coated with sugar mixture.

Spread nuts out in a single layer on a baking sheet and bake, stirring every 10 minutes, until sugar looks crumbly and nuts are toasted and very aromatic, about 30 minutes. Remove from oven and stir. Let cool completely before serving. (*Make ahead: Store in an airtight container for up to 1 week.*)

Makes 3 cups

½ cup packed brown sugar

2 tsp water

½ tsp salt

Pinch ground nutmeg

3 cups raw nuts (such as pecans, almonds, cashews, hazelnuts and/or walnuts)

Apple Cider Muffins

This recipe was given to me by Karen DeMasco, founding Pastry Chef at Craft restaurant in New York City and someone I consider a role model. Not only is she the star of the kitchen at a young age, she is quick to smile and just as quick to lend a hand. These muffins are unpretentious and unique, not unlike Karen herself, and every guest at Craft is given one to take home after dinner to enjoy the next morning. I spent a week working at Craft in 2007, and made these signature muffins a couple of times. I loved the idea that they would be spreading out all over Manhattan by the end of the evening.

PREHEAT OVEN TO 350°F. Butter and flour a 12-cup muffin tin. In a medium bowl, whisk together white sugar, brown sugar and oil. Add eggs and whisk to combine.

In another bowl, sift together flour, baking soda, salt and cinnamon. In a third bowl, whisk together apple cider, sour cream and vanilla.

In 3 additions, add flour mixture and apple cider mixture to sugar mixture, folding with a spatula to combine. Fold in apples then pour batter into muffin cups. Fill the cups about ¾ of the way to the top. Bake, turning halfway, until muffins spring back to the touch, 20 to 25 minutes. Remove from oven and cool on a rack.

Makes 12 muffins

1 cup white sugar

1 cup dark brown sugar

¾ cup grapeseed or vegetable oil

3 large eggs

2¼ cups all-purpose flour

1½ tsp baking soda

1 tsp kosher salt

1 tsp ground cinnamon

1 cup pure apple cider

¾ cup sour cream

1½ tsp pure vanilla extract

2 medium apples, peeled and grated (ideally crisp baking apples, Granny Smiths or Mutsus)

Bread and Butter Pudding

I serve this pudding as the dessert for our Sunday suppers all winter long. I bake it in a cast-iron frying pan and serve it steaming. The aroma of the sizzling maple syrup wafts through the whole restaurant. It may be a simple dish, but this is a dessert that really turns guests' heads.

PREHEAT OVEN TO 350°F. Place currants and cherries in a bowl and cover with hot water; set aside for between 10 minutes and an hour.

Place bread cubes in a shallow 16-cup baking dish and set aside.

In a bowl, whisk together eggs and sugar. Stir in cream, nutmeg, vanilla, lemon zest, lemon juice, orange zest and orange juice.

Drain dried fruit and sprinkle evenly over bread cubes, along with pecans. Pour in egg mixture, making sure bread is completely saturated. Cover with foil.

Place baking dish in a large roasting pan, place in oven and pour in enough hot water to come halfway up sides of dish. Bake for 45 minutes. Remove foil and bake until golden and puffed, about 15 minutes. Pour maple syrup over top. Let stand for at least 20 minutes before serving.

Serves 6

¼ cup dried currants
¼ cup dried cherries
16 cups cubed day-old bread (preferably real-butter croissants or brioche)
6 eggs
1 cup granulated sugar
3 cups whipping (35%) cream
1 tsp ground nutmeg
1 tsp pure vanilla extract
Grated zest and juice of 1 lemon and 1 orange
¼ cup chopped pecans, toasted
¼ cup maple syrup

Sticky Toffee Pudding

Serves 6

2 cups Medjool dates, pitted

2 cups water

1½ tsp baking soda

½ cup packed brown sugar

2 tbsp unsalted butter

3 large eggs

¼ cup mild (light) molasses

2 tbsp corn syrup

¼ tsp pure vanilla extract

½ cup all-purpose flour

1 tsp baking powder

1 tsp salt

This classic British pudding is another recipe brought to us by Chris Haworth. He put it on the menu at Spencer's at the Waterfront the day it opened and he has not been able to take it off since—people love it! It is best when served warm, with a little Caramel Sauce (page 305), or try a dollop of Crème Fraîche (page 302).

IN A SAUCEPAN, combine dates and water. Bring to a boil over high heat. Reduce heat and simmer until dates are very tender and water has almost entirely evaporated, about 30 minutes. Remove from heat and stir in baking soda. Transfer to a blender (or use an immersion blender) and puree until dates are just a little chunky.

Preheat oven to 325°F and grease a 6-cup muffin tin.

In a medium bowl, cream brown sugar and butter. Beat in eggs, molasses, corn syrup and vanilla until combined. Stir in flour, baking powder and salt. Stir in date mixture.

Divide mixture evenly among prepared muffin cups. Bake until tops spring back when touched, about 35 minutes. Let stand 5 minutes before serving.

Spiced Hot Chocolate

Makes 6 cups

6 cups whole milk

2 cinnamon sticks

1 vanilla bean, split lengthwise
and seeds scraped out

1 Thai chili pepper, halved

10 oz milk chocolate, chopped

2 tbsp local honey

1 tbsp ground walnuts

Whipped cream

The Mayans got it right when they spiced their chocolate. A hint of heat adds satisfying complexity to the rich sweetness of the chocolate. Adding a couple of cubes of homemade marshmallow (opposite) makes you forget the wind howling outside.

In a saucepan, heat milk, cinnamon sticks, vanilla bean and seeds and chili pepper over medium heat until bubbles appear around the edges, about 10 minutes. Reduce heat to low and add chocolate and honey; cook, whisking occasionally, until chocolate is melted and honey dissolves, about 3 minutes. Remove from heat.

Strain hot chocolate and discard solids. If chocolate is too thick, thin with a little more milk. Serve in small cups and offer ground walnuts and whipped cream as garnish.

Marshmallows

Marshmallows are a great option when we are craving something sweet in the winter months. In the past, marshmallows were made from the root of the marshmallow plant. Today, they are made with gelatin and often with whipped egg whites. This particular recipe does not have any egg whites in it. They tend to complicate things because they are not fully cooked (raw eggs can carry salmonella bacteria). This egg-free choice is sweet and delicious and will settle any winter cravings for a sugar treat.

Makes 40 large squares

1 cup cold water, divided
3 tbsp powdered unflavored
    gelatin (three ½-oz packets)
2 cups granulated sugar
½ cup corn syrup
1 tbsp pure vanilla extract
¼ tsp kosher salt
Icing sugar, for dusting

GREASE A 13- BY 9-INCH baking pan with butter and dust with icing sugar. Set aside.

In a small bowl, combine ¾ cup cold water and gelatin; let bloom for 10 minutes.

Meanwhile, in a saucepan, combine sugar, corn syrup and ¼ cup water. Bring to a boil over medium heat. Boil until bubbles start to become bigger in size, about 5 minutes.

Place gelatin mixture in the bowl of a stand mixer. Attach the whisk attachment and the mixer bowl to the mixer and set to medium speed. Gradually drizzle syrup mixture over gelatin. Add vanilla and salt. Once mixture begins to fluff up, increase speed to high and mix until very fluffy, about 7 minutes.

Pour mixture into prepared pan and, using a lightly oiled spatula, spread out evenly. (The marshmallows will be quite sticky and difficult to spread.) Dust top with icing sugar and let set overnight.

Using a sharp knife or pizza wheel, cut into squares. Dust each marshmallow all over with icing sugar before serving. (*Make ahead: Store in an airtight container for up to 1 week.*)

Oatmeal Molasses Bread

At the restaurant, on any given day, we will make up to 70 loaves of bread. Oatmeal Molasses Bread stands out as a little bit sweet, with a thin crust and a hearty oatmeal flavor.

IN A LARGE BOWL, combine boiling water, 1 cup of the oats, butter and molasses; let cool until lukewarm.

In another bowl, whisk together 2 cups of the flour, brown sugar, salt and yeast. Add to oat mixture, stirring well to combine. Using a spoon, gradually work in the remaining flour until dough pulls away from the sides of bowl.

Turn out onto a lightly floured surface and knead until dough is smooth and elastic, about 12 minutes. Place in a large greased bowl, turning dough to grease all over. Cover with a tea towel and let rise in a still oven, with light on and door closed, until doubled in size, about 1½ hours.

Punch down dough and turn out onto a lightly floured surface. Divide in half and press each half into a 12- by 9-inch rectangle. Starting at a narrow end, roll up into a cylinder and pinch along the bottom to smooth and seal. Cover with tea towels and let rise in still oven until dough no longer springs back when lightly pressed, about 40 minutes. Brush tops with egg wash and sprinkle with the remaining oats.

Preheat oven to 350°F. Bake loaves until they are golden brown and sound hollow when tapped on the bottom, about 50 minutes. Turn out onto wire racks to cool.

Makes 2 loaves

2 cups boiling water
1¼ cups quick-cooking rolled oats, divided
¼ cup melted unsalted butter
¼ cup mild (light) molasses
6 cups all-purpose flour (approx.), divided
⅓ cup packed brown sugar
2 tsp kosher salt
1 tsp dry instant yeast
1 large organic egg, whisked with 1 tbsp water

WHAT TO KNOW

CONCLUSION

PAY FOR GOOD FOOD

EXPLORE

JOIN A CSA

PLANT A GARDEN

PICK ONE FOOD

ENJOY

And so it begins again.

Having gone through the cycle of the seasons, we end up in spring after the lean days and long nights of winter. And each spring, we've learned a little more. We're a little better prepared for the year ahead. We may even be a little wiser.

This sense of progress is important—vitally important. As I look back over the year, I am struck by how much I learned just by doing and experimenting and talking. In addition to the cycle of the seasons, I realize, there is a straight line of progress.

I see this in my conversations with chefs and farmers who see the earth-to-table relationship more or less as I do, and I can't help noticing how invigorating these ideas are. It's not as though an emphasis on old-fashioned-sounding values such as freshness or excellence, or a return to traditional methods of raising and preparing food have locked these men and women into some sort of time warp. On the contrary, these are the people who are shaping the future of food and food culture. The great innovators are the ones who are strengthened by their inheritance.

It seems strange that developing a sustainable way of cooking and eating would be thought of as cutting edge. It has to be one of the most common sense "radical" ideas of all time. Anyone who thinks about it for five minutes, as Michael Schwartz said, would conclude that we have to figure out a way of eating that benefits the environment, the local economy and those who enjoy the food.

I'm the first to admit that I didn't invent this stuff. Not even close. Like many of the people featured in this book, I took much of my inspiration from Alice Waters and my time at Chez Panisse. It is probably impossible to exaggerate her influence on me and on an entire generation of cooks. More than one person I've come across has suggested that we're "standing on the shoulders of giants."

This link between the work of pioneers and the work now going on in kitchens and fields is probably nowhere more clear than at L'Etoile, in Madison, Wisconsin. This small restaurant was built on the earth-to-table philosophy in 1976 by Odessa Piper. She has since become something of a Midwestern Alice Waters, garnering praise from *Gourmet, Bon Appétit, Food & Wine, Wine Spectator* and the *New York Times,* among many others, not to mention a James Beard Foundation award for "Best Chef: Midwest."

From the very beginning, L'Etoile has been a node in a network of local farmers and artisans (each season's menu features food from dozens of different producers), and has forged a partnership with the local farmers' market. The restaurant has gone out of its way to help sustain the people that supply it, and as a result the Madison area has a very sophisticated and robust food culture. If you are interested in how what we eat affects the world around us, the model of L'Etoile can only be heartening, and I find it refreshing to see that the finest food in the world can be found in your own backyard.

But that's just part of the story. The stewardship of the L'Etoile tradition has now passed to executive chef-owner Tory Miller and his sister Traci, and the transition has left the ideas and their practical implications unadulterated and even strengthened. Tory is warm and laughs easily, but when I ask him how he sees his role, he has a serious answer: "I see myself as a partner with the farming community, a coproducer."

TORY MILLER
Executive Chef

Like any good chef, he is motivated by taste and the desire for excellence, and that means eating locally and seasonally: "It doesn't sit on a truck before you eat it. Better ingredients mean better taste." But he is quick to point out that the relationship works both ways. Good farming leads to good cooking, but good cooking also leads back to good farming and good citizenship. He views his work in the kitchen as a "delicious promotion of a way of life that is threatened by industry, rapid urbanization and the spreading consumerist mentality."

Like Matthew Dillon and Dan Barber, he sees education as the crucial next step in developing a sustainable food culture, and as soft-spoken and thoughtful as he is, he lets his exasperation show when the conversation turns to the popular misconception that eating good food is elitist. "If you think it is elitist to protect the environment, the economy, your community . . . then perhaps this way of eating isn't for you," he sighs.

But he is as optimistic as other chefs around the country, and he has reason to be. His career and his restaurant are proof that we are making progress from generation to generation, just as I manage to learn a thing or two from year to year. He believes that sustainable cooking and eating will soon be the mainstream. He points to organic sections in supermarkets as evidence that people are thinking carefully about their health and their food dollars. And once they think about it, he believes, change can happen in only one direction.

That was certainly my experience. When I was chatting with Heston Blumenthal, he asked, mock-accusingly, "You just stumbled onto this, didn't you?" I wasn't embarrassed to say yes. When I began thinking about these issues years ago, I started my journey down the path this book has traced. When I thought hard about the quality of the produce in my kitchen, I was drawn to small-scale, local farmers. When I thought about the ethical implications of meat, the logical thing to do was to seek out farmers who were asking the same questions and acting accordingly. The more I learned about factory farming and what might be called factory eating, the more I found myself in the company of others (some of them chefs, many of them not) who wondered whether there might be a better way of doing things. It was a little like a roller-coaster ride: there were lots of twists and turns, but there was never any doubt about where I would end up.

It turns out that the questions are often enough to see you through. You don't need to start with the answers; you figure things out as you go along. You incorporate new ideas, new techniques, new habits as they become available or practical. It gets simpler all the time, though there is always more to learn. I cringe when I think of all that has been forgotten in only a few decades. There are so many farmers who can't farm without chemicals, men and women who can't cook without microwaves. When privatization gutted the Russian economy in the 1990s, many families saved themselves from starvation by relying on their backyard gardens. I often wonder how we North Americans would fare in a similar situation.

The consequence of forgetting is that very few of us can choose to eat the way we want (assuming that we even think enough about eating to want something other than conventional, industrial-scale food). It seems to me that understanding food, and knowing how to cook it, is a basic freedom.

It is also, first and last, a matter of pleasure. Nothing can challenge the flavor of local, seasonal food. And nothing can compare to the satisfaction of a meal at the family table, or the aroma of the kitchen, or the collective effort of washing up. Weeding your garden and harvesting its produce is a quiet joy all its own. And learning how to do any of these things is a pleasure in itself. I won't mislead you—what I'm describing is work, and for many of us it is axiomatic that convenience is preferable to work. No doubt about it, work can be dreary and tedious. But convenience can be dreary and tedious too. And it will never taste as good, will never benefit your neighbors, and will probably never do anything but harm the planet.

In the end, I'm just a chef. The only thing I'm an expert on is cooking food, and even there I figure I'll always have more to learn. I'm not a farmer, not an economist, not a nutritionist or an environmentalist. But I am an eager student of food and its role in the world, and so, even though I am certainly no giant, here is the view from my shoulders.

PAY FOR GOOD FOOD. There are many ways to make this point, and everyone I've spoken to has made it in one way or another: good food isn't expensive; conventional food is cheap. You'll always get what you pay for, and no one wants to pay for food that is nutritionally inferior, economically draining and environmentally unsustainable.

EXPLORE. There's a lot of food out there that you're not eating simply because you've never thought of it. Wander around farmers' markets and ask questions. Wander through fields and ditches—and definitely ask questions before eating the mushrooms you find. See what artisans are in your area: cheesemakers, bakers, winemakers, butchers. They will probably knock your socks off.

JOIN A CSA. Part of the appeal of local, seasonal eating is shortening the link between farm and table. Unless you are a farmer, a share in a CSA is about as close as it gets, and about as *good* as it gets for both you and the farmer.

PLANT A GARDEN. Nothing will attune you to the earth-to-table experience more than growing your own food (particularly if you have a composter in your backyard). You'll pay attention to the changes in the seasons, and to the relationship of the food to the soil. A head of lettuce cut from your garden will not only be tastier than one carried home in plastic from the supermarket, it will be precious to you in a way you probably won't be able to imagine before you've spent several weeks nurturing it and protecting it from weeds and bugs. And you can't imagine how proud you'll be when you serve it to your family and friends.

PICK ONE FOOD. There is no reason to think of this as an all-or-nothing proposition. None of the chefs in the book, including me, source *all* of their food locally. Start where you feel comfortable, and before long you'll find you are drawn to do more and more. This is not about sacrifice.

ENJOY. In the end, no one would pursue the earth-to-table philosophy if it didn't taste better. In this case, what tastes right *is* right. So make sure you enjoy your meals, and the rest should take care of itself.

In the meantime, it is spring again.

The preserves and root vegetable have run out, but the time has come to think of ramps and asparagus, and all the tender things that emerge as the snow withdraws. Chris will be calling soon to tell us to get over to the farm to help get the seedlings into the still-cool earth, and though our next crop of Red Fife is no more than a bag of seed set aside after last year's harvest, it too will soon be sown.

We are looking forward to another earth-to-table year, more eagerly attuned to the modulations of the seasons, a little more prepared for the things that may well go wrong, our imaginations already conjuring the meals that await us.

BASIC RECIPES

Aïoli

Makes 1 cup

1 clove garlic, roughly chopped
¼ tsp salt
1 large organic egg yolk
½ tsp Dijon mustard
1 cup extra-virgin olive oil

The garlic you buy here is crucial—use only fresh garlic from the farmers' market. Older garlic is too strong for this recipe, considering that aïoli is basically pureed garlic. Traditionally, there is no egg in aïoli, but we add one for a little extra richness and consistency.

Take your time when incorporating the oil; if it is added too quickly, the aïoli will split and you'll have to start all over again. If you find the aïoli too thick, add 1 tbsp water halfway through the mashing and stirring process to loosen it.

USING A MORTAR AND PESTLE, mash garlic and salt to a paste-like consistency. Stir in egg yolk and mustard. Add oil in a slow, steady stream, mashing and stirring slowly until well combined and emulsified.

Mayonnaise

When you make mayonnaise at home, the flavor is fresh and very rewarding. We use egg yolks from free-range chickens. When making mayonnaise, it's important to add the oil very gradually: start with a few drops and slowly build up to a continuous drizzle. You can use this recipe as a base mayonnaise and add flavorings, such as fresh herbs, mustard or lemon zest, as you desire.

IN A BOWL, whisk together egg yolks, vinegar, mustard, salt and lemon juice. Gradually drizzle in oil, whisking constantly until thick and emulsified. Season to taste with salt and pepper. (*Make ahead: Transfer to an airtight container and refrigerate for up to 5 days.*)

TIP: To successfully pour oil and whisk at the same time, it can help to place a damp towel under your bowl to prevent it from spinning.

Makes 2 cups

2 large organic egg yolks
2 tsp white wine vinegar
1 tsp Dijon mustard
Pinch salt
Juice of ½ lemon
1½ cups canola oil
Salt and freshly cracked
    black pepper

Garlicky Rouille

Makes ½ cup

¾ cup coarse fresh bread
   crumbs
3 tbsp water
1 clove garlic, roughly chopped
½ tsp kosher salt
½ tsp cayenne pepper
3 tbsp extra-virgin olive oil

Rouille, which means "rust" in French, is a versatile sauce that can be used to garnish fish soup, dolloped on top of bistecca or spread on baguette slices for a late-night snack. Some variations of this recipe include egg yolks or red peppers, but this is the real deal.

IN A SMALL BOWL, combine bread crumbs and water; set aside.

Using a mortar and pestle, mash garlic, salt and cayenne to a paste. Mash in wet bread crumbs. Add oil in a slow, steady stream, mashing and stirring quickly until well combined. (*Make ahead: Place in an airtight container and refrigerate for up to 1 week.*)

Dijon Vinaigrette and Red Wine Vinaigrette

These are very basic vinaigrettes and the ones we use most at the restaurant. The "vinaigrette" is also the most versatile sauce in any kitchen. The formula is simple, and the modifications are endless. Feel free to experiment with different oils and vinegars—just keep in mind that while quality oils and vinegars will cost more, you get what you pay for.

DIJON VINAIGRETTE In a bowl, combine shallot, rice vinegar and sherry vinegar; let stand for 15 minutes. Whisk in sugar and mustard. Add oil in a slow, steady stream, whisking until well blended. Season to taste with salt and pepper. (*Make ahead: Cover and refrigerate for up to 1 week.*)

RED WINE VINAIGRETTE In a bowl, whisk together vinegar, shallots, mustard, salt and pepper; let stand for 10 minutes. Add oil in a slow, steady stream, whisking until well blended. (*Make ahead: Cover and refrigerate for up to 2 weeks.*)

DIJON VINAIGRETTE

Makes 1 cup

1 shallot, minced

2 tbsp rice vinegar

2 tbsp sherry vinegar

2 tsp granulated sugar

1 tsp Dijon mustard

1 cup extra-virgin olive oil

Salt and freshly cracked
    black pepper

RED WINE VINAIGRETTE

Makes 3 cups

1 cup red wine vinegar

2 tbsp minced shallots

1 tbsp Dijon mustard

1 tsp kosher salt

1 tsp freshly cracked
    black pepper

2 cups canola oil

Beef Stock

Makes 8 cups

4 lbs beef bones (necks, shanks,
  knuckles, oxtails or a mixture
  of these)

1 tbsp local honey

2 medium yellow onions, halved
  lengthwise

2 bulbs garlic, halved

2 carrots, roughly chopped

2 stalks celery, roughly chopped

8 cups water

1 cup local dry red wine

2 tbsp tomato paste

10 whole black peppercorns

2 dried bay leaves

2 whole cloves

2 sprigs fresh thyme

Try to get bones that still have a good quantity of meat on them. The bones add body to the stock, but the meat adds flavor. Toss the bones with a little bit of honey at the beginning to help the browning process and add more flavor.

PREHEAT OVEN TO 400°F. Spread bones in a large roasting pan and toss with honey. Roast, turning occasionally, until golden and caramelized, about 1 hour. Stir in onions, garlic, carrots and celery; roast until vegetables are caramelized, about 30 minutes.

Transfer bones and vegetables to a large stockpot and add water; bring to a boil over medium-high heat. Skim off any foam. Stir in wine, tomato paste, peppercorns, bay leaves, cloves and thyme. Reduce heat and simmer, stirring occasionally, until slightly thickened, about 5 hours.

Strain stock through a cheesecloth-lined sieve into a large bowl and discard solids. Let cool to room temperature. Cover and refrigerate until fat congeals on the surface, about 8 hours; remove and discard fat. (*Make ahead: Transfer to airtight containers and refrigerate for up to 3 days or freeze for up to 4 months.*)

Chicken Stock

Don't shy away from making your own stock—it is one of those things that make your cooking ethereal. Having homemade stock in your freezer will also allow you to tackle many recipes on the spur of the moment, which is the point of seasonal cooking. Browning the bones as per Beef Stock, without the honey, before beginning the recipe will give you are darker, more flavorful stock, but remember, not all recipes call for a "roasted" chicken flavor. We leave it up to you to decide how you will be using your chicken stock.

IN A LARGE STOCKPOT, combine bones and water. Bring to a boil over medium-high heat. Skim surface to remove any scum. Reduce heat to medium-low and stir in onions, carrots, celery, wine, peppercorns, bay leaves, cloves and thyme. Simmer, uncovered, for 3 hours.

Remove bones from stock and discard. Strain stock through a cheesecloth-lined sieve into a large bowl, pressing vegetables to extract as much liquid as possible. Discard solids. Let cool to room temperature. Cover and refrigerate until fat congeals on the surface, about 8 hours; remove and discard fat. (*Make ahead: Transfer to airtight containers and refrigerate for up to 3 days or freeze for up to 4 months.*)

Makes 6 cups

4 lbs chicken bones (necks, backs, breast bones, wings, etc.)
6 cups cold water
2 medium yellow onions, halved lengthwise
2 carrots, roughly chopped
2 stalks celery, roughly chopped
1 cup local dry white wine
10 whole black peppercorns
2 dried bay leaves
2 whole cloves
2 sprigs fresh thyme

Fish Stock

Makes 6 cups

2 tbsp olive oil

4 cloves garlic, minced

1 large onion, minced

1 leek (white part only), finely
   chopped

1 cup finely chopped fennel bulb

1 tbsp tomato paste

1 cup local dry white wine

3 lbs mixed white-fleshed fish
   bones (such as monkfish,
   striped bass, cod or halibut)

5 cups cold water

We tend to buy our fish whole, which gives us really fresh bones to make stock. Freshness is key here, as the water will take up the true flavour of the fish—less-than-perfect fish will yield less-than-perfect stock. Ask your local fishmonger when they have the freshest bones. Bring the stock to a near-boil as rapidly as possible and don't cook for more than 20 minutes.

IN A LARGE STOCKPOT, heat oil over medium-high heat. Add garlic, onion, leek, fennel bulb and tomato paste; sauté until soft, about 10 minutes. Add wine and cook until reduced by half, about 4 minutes. Add fish bones and cold water; bring to a near-boil, reduce heat and simmer, skimming occasionally, for 20 minutes. Do not let boil or the stock will be cloudy.

Strain stock through a cheesecloth-lined sieve into a large bowl and discard solids. Let cool to room temperature. (*Make ahead: Transfer to airtight containers and refrigerate for up to 3 days or freeze for up to 4 months.*)

Our Steak Sauce

Makes 2 cups

1 cup water

1 cup cider vinegar

¾ cup fresh apple juice

½ cup tomato paste

¼ cup minced pitted dates

3 tbsp blackstrap molasses

3 tbsp tamarind pulp

½ tsp ground cloves

½ tsp ground allspice

½ tsp ground cardamom

Salt and freshly cracked
    black pepper

This steak sauce is based on the classic brown sauce
famous in Britain and around the world. My head chef,
Bryan Gibson, whipped it up one day when a guest
requested steak sauce. Both sweet and sour, it's so good
with a fatty, salty steak.

IN A SAUCEPAN, combine water, vinegar, apple juice,
tomato paste, dates, molasses, tamarind, cloves, allspice
and cardamom. Bring to a boil over medium-high heat.
Reduce heat and simmer until slightly thickened, about 10
minutes.

Transfer mixture to a blender and puree until smooth.
Transfer to a bowl and let cool. Season to taste with salt
and pepper. (*Make ahead: Cover and refrigerate for up to 1
week.*)

Maple Mustard Sauce

Makes ¾ cup

½ cup Dijon mustard

¼ cup pure maple syrup

Here's a very fast and flavorful sauce that perfectly complements steaks, burgers and cheese.

IN A SMALL BOWL, combine mustard and maple syrup.
(*Make ahead: Cover and refrigerate for up to 1 week.*)

Fresh Horseradish Cream

I love the stinging heat of fresh horseradish root. It's fun to watch someone grating horseradish; it's like cutting onions, but ten times worse. In the restaurant's kitchen, we grate about 10 lbs at a time—major tears! The best way to grate horseradish is with a box grater, using the medium holes. Oysters and roast beef sandwiches will never be the same again.

IN A SMALL BOWL, combine sour cream, horseradish and vinegar. Season to taste with salt and pepper. (*Make ahead: Cover and refrigerate for up to 1 week.*)

Makes 1¼ cups

1 cup sour cream
¼ cup freshly grated
    horseradish root
2 tsp cider vinegar
Salt and freshly cracked
    black pepper

Tomato Confit

We use this sauce as a garnish for fish and keep it on hand to enhance the flavor of soups and stews. If you find it too acidic, you can add a pinch of granulated sugar to take out the bite!

IN A 5-QUART stainless steel pot, combine tomatoes and water (the water should just cover the bottom of the pot). Bring to a bare simmer over medium-low heat. Cover and cook, stirring once, until tomatoes are just softened, about 7 minutes; drain.

Force tomatoes through a coarse-holed food mill into a saucepan. Discard seeds and skins. Stir in garlic, basil and oil; bring to a simmer over medium heat. Simmer, stirring occasionally, until slightly thickened, about 25 minutes (sauce will appear paler and slightly creamy). Discard garlic and basil. Stir in salt.

Makes 2 cups

4 lbs very ripe plum (Roma)
    tomatoes (about 8), chopped
½ cup water
2 cloves garlic, crushed with
    the side of a knife
2 fresh basil sprigs
½ cup extra-virgin olive oil
2 tsp kosher salt

Crème Anglaise

Makes 3 cups

2 cups whipping (35%) cream
½ cup granulated sugar,
    divided
1 vanilla bean, split lengthwise
    and seeds scraped out
6 large egg yolks

This sauce can be used with any of your favorite desserts, but it goes especially well with Bread and Butter Pudding (page 275) and Sticky Toffee Pudding (page 276).

IN A MEDIUM SAUCEPAN, combine cream and half the sugar. Add vanilla bean and seeds. Bring to a boil over high heat. Remove from heat and let stand for 30 minutes, allowing vanilla flavor to infuse the cream.

In a bowl, whisk together egg yolks and the remaining sugar. Gradually whisk in cream mixture. (If the hot liquid is added too quickly, you may end up with scrambled eggs.)

Return mixture to saucepan and cook over medium-low heat, stirring constantly with a wooden spoon, until thick enough to coat the back of the spoon, about 5 minutes. Strain through a fine-mesh sieve into a bowl and discard vanilla. Let cool at room temperature for 30 minutes. Place plastic wrap directly on surface and refrigerate until chilled, about 4 hours (*Make ahead: Cover and refrigerate for up to 2 days. To serve, warm over low heat.*)

Crème Fraîche

Makes 2¼ cups

2 cups whipping (35%) cream
¼ cup buttermilk

Crème Fraiche is a thick soured cream with a rich and velvety texture and a nutty, slightly sour taste produced by culturing pasteurized cream with special bacteria. (However, in France, where it originated, the cream is unpasteurized so it naturally contains the bacteria necessary to transform it into crème fraîche.)

You can buy crème fraîche at specialty food stores, but it can be quite pricy. So you may want to try making your own. This really is simple; all you do is gently heat   >>>

heavy whipping cream (35% butterfat) with some butter-milk. It is ready when it has thickened to the consistency of creamy Jell-O. If you give it a shake it will jiggle. If it still looks a little runny after 24 hours, leave it another 8 to 12 hours but move it to a warmer spot. And don't worry about the cream going bad. As Regan Daley tells us in *In the Sweet Kitchen*, "The benign live bacteria in the but-termilk will multiply and protect the cream from any harmful bacteria." Once the crème fraîche has thickened sufficiently, cover and place in the refrigerator. It will con-tinue to thicken and take on a tangier flavor as it ages.

IN A PLASTIC OR STAINLESS STEEL BOWL, combine cream and buttermilk. Cover tightly with plastic wrap and label with time and date. Let stand in a warm spot (about 85°F), such as on top of the fridge or in a still oven with the light on, for about 12 hours. (The warmer the spot, the faster the process will go. However, if the spot is too warm, all the natural bacteria will be killed and there will be no reaction at all. It's the good bacteria at work here, keeping the cream fresh.)

Remove the cover. The mixture should jiggle like jelly; if it doesn't, recover and check again in 12 hours. When it looks and tastes right, transfer to a clean bowl, stir well, cover and refrigerate for up to 10 days.

TIP: For a sweet alternative, once the cream has thickened, stir in ¼ cup icing sugar and 1 tsp pure vanilla extract. Use in place of whipped cream on top of desserts.

Frangipane

Makes 1½ cups

1 cup unsalted butter, softened
½ cup ground hazelnuts,
    almonds or other flavorful nut
¼ cup icing sugar
¼ cup all-purpose flour
2 organic eggs

This is one of those recipes you can be creative with, and it's a make-ahead gem. Traditionally, frangipane is a thick paste made exclusively with almonds, but you can use any nut, as long as it is ground. I like to use hazelnuts. I've also made it quite buttery, which adds real flavor to any recipe the frangipane is used in. You'll want to use this particular version as a spread, not as a filling. It is very useful as a liner for most fruit tarts and pies, adding a nutty flavor and some buttery richness.

USING AN ELECTRIC MIXER, mix butter, hazelnuts, icing sugar, flour and eggs until smooth. (*Make ahead: Transfer to an airtight container and refrigerate for up to 2 weeks or freeze for up to 1 month.*)

Caramel Sauce

We serve this rich, creamy sauce with a number of our desserts. It is also fun as a dip for apples in the fall months. The darker the color, the richer the caramel flavor, so let it cook until it is a deep reddish brown. The addition of lemon juice at the beginning will stop crystals from forming.

IN A SAUCEPAN, combine sugar, water and lemon juice. Bring to a rolling boil over high heat. Boil until syrup is a deep reddish brown, about 20 minutes. Remove from heat and stir in cream and butter. Let cool completely, about 1 hour. The sauce will become quite solid once it has cooled, but 1 minute in the microwave on Medium (50%) will make it pourable again. (*Make ahead: Refrigerate in an airtight container for up to 2 weeks.*)

Makes 2 cups

2 cups granulated sugar

1½ cups water

1 tsp freshly squeezed lemon
   juice

1 cup whipping (35%) cream

¼ cup unsalted butter, cubed

Chocolate Sauce

Chocolate sauce is so easy to make, and it makes so many people so happy. The key to making a delicious chocolate sauce is using good-quality chocolate. Look for quality names such as Lindt or Callebaut, both of which can be found at fine food stores.

Pour this chocolate sauce over your favorite ice cream or use it to garnish desserts.

PLACE CHOCOLATE IN A LARGE BOWL. In a small saucepan, heat cream over medium heat until bubbles form around the edges. Pour cream over chocolate and stir constantly until smooth. (*Make ahead: Refrigerate in an airtight container for up to 3 weeks. To serve, warm in microwave on Medium [50%] for about 1 minute.*)

Makes 4 cups

1 lb good-quality dark chocolate
   (from a slab or bar), coarsely
   chopped

2 cups whipping (35%) cream

Pâte Brisée (Flaky Pie Dough)

Makes enough dough for a
9-inch double-crust pie

2½ cups all-purpose flour
2 tsp salt
½ tsp granulated sugar
1 cup cold unsalted butter
¼ to ½ cup ice water

This is one of my favorite dough recipes—it's buttery, flaky and delicious. I use it not only for sweet pies but for savory pies and tarts as well. The recipe asks that you grate the butter with a box grater, that way, you keep your hands off the butter, allowing it to stay chilled. The colder the butter, the better!

IN A BOWL, combine flour, salt and sugar. Using a box grater, grate butter into the flour mixture. Toss together, like a salad, using your fingers. Add water, a few tablespoons at a time, kneading dough until it comes together.

Turn dough out onto a lightly floured work surface. Divide in half and shape each half into a disk. Wrap in plastic wrap and refrigerate until chilled, about 1 hour. (*Make ahead: Wrap in plastic and refrigerate for up to 2 weeks or freeze for up to 3 months.*)

Pâte Sucrée

This dough has a texture and sweet taste that resembles cookie dough. I use it to make Plum Tarts (page 142). A reliable dough, it is firm and does not crumble or shrink in size when baked. When I need last-minute petits fours in the restaurant, I roll it out and use it to make cookies. I always have it on hand!

IN A BOWL, combine flour, sugar and salt. Using a box grater, grate butter into the flour mixture. Toss together, like a salad, using your fingers.

In another bowl, whisk together egg yolks and water. Add to flour mixture, a few tablespoons at a time, kneading dough until it comes together.

Shape dough into a disk, wrap in plastic wrap and refrigerate until chilled, about 1 hour. (*Make ahead: Wrap in plastic and refrigerate for up to 2 weeks or freeze for up to 3 months.*)

Makes 1 lb (enough dough for 8 tarts)

2½ cups all-purpose flour
3 tbsp granulated sugar
2 tsp salt
1 cup cold unsalted butter
2 large organic egg yolks
¼ to ½ cup ice water

Appendix

Good food is not expensive; conventional food is cheap.

I'm the first to admit it: I'm not an environmentalist.

For me, the proof of the tomato is in the eating. A local, seasonal, organic tomato tastes better than its alternative. So that's what I eat. I suppose if it were the other way around, I'd have to consider switching. Luckily, I don't.

And while many of the chefs I've spoken to use local produce at least in part because it is sustainable, just as many don't really care about the environmental benefits. David Kinch of Manresa, certainly one of the world's best chefs and among the most committed to very local sourcing, says he doesn't claim to be saving the world. He just wants good food.

Still, it's hard not to notice that food that tastes good happens to be much more sustainable than the fare offered up by global agribusiness. Sure, it's not difficult to understand the economies of scale at play in the vast infrastructure of factory farms and global distribution and retail networks, and it's not hard to see that as long as food energy is more expensive than fossil fuel energy, someone will be happy to profit by shipping food around the world, even if it means that it takes more calories to get a meal to your table than the food yields in nutritional energy. That's all simple economic theory, so we can't be too surprised that things have worked out this way.

But a reasonable person is free to wonder whether the whole thing is sustainable.

It's something of an understatement to say that it is not. One of the knocks against good food is that it is elitist—it's just too expensive for everybody to afford. Well, there is no getting around the fact that an organic carrot is going to cost you more than a genetically modified carrot pickled in pesticides and nitrogen fertilizer, particularly if you buy it in a supermarket (where organics are merchandized as premium product). But there is more to the story than the sticker on the bag.

You may pay less for the industrial carrots at the checkout, but does it not seem strange that the vegetable grown without the expensive inputs costs more than the one that has them? After all, there is a $30 billion global market for pesticides, and someone is paying for all those toxins. It's not the consumer, and it's not the producer. It's the taxpayer, who pays for the environmental cleanup, and it's whoever inherits the land we've used so recklessly. Add to these costs the billions that go toward subsidizing industrial agriculture, and that organic carrot is beginning to look pretty affordable (in addition to tasting better). Cheap food is not inexpensive.

If, like me, you are in this for the food rather than the science or the politics, or if you'd simply prefer not to be depressed, feel free to skip the next few paragraphs. But there is really no way I can make the case for good food without pointing out some of the many ways in which the cost of industrial agriculture is just too much to keep paying.

MONOCULTURE. One of the agricultural practices that leaves plants vulnerable to pests and viruses is monoculture—growing a single crop. The vast fields of corn and wheat we're used to seeing are, of course, unnatural, so it should be no surprise that they don't behave like natural ecosystems when it comes to supporting a variety of species or recycling nutrients. What might be a little more surprising is the drop in the genetic diversity of the crops themselves. About 60 percent of our plant-based diet comes from three crops: wheat, corn and rice. With this rush to standardization comes the abandonment of a huge variety of foods. According to the United Nations, monoculture farming has led to the loss of about 75 percent of the genetic diversity of the food we grew over the course of the twentieth century. To use one example, in 1950 there were thirty thousand varieties of rice grown in India. By 2015 there will be fifty. The same is true of livestock; every year, about 5 percent of the breeds disappear—that's six breeds each month.

This lack of genetic variability leaves us ridiculously vulnerable to outbreaks of disease. In fact, we've seen it before. History has shown how bad an idea it is to depend on a single crop: red rust on Roman wheat, ergot on European rye in the Middle Ages, blight on Irish potatoes in the eighteenth and nineteenth centuries all led to widespread calamity. Dependence on genetically identical livestock has had more recent implications: the 1997 avian flu outbreak in Hong Kong and the 2001 foot-and-mouth horror in Britain, and early indicators are that Bahamas could be next.

EROSION. The United Nations has estimated that we lose about 1 percent of our topsoil to wind and rain each year. If that doesn't seem like a lot, consider that since the Second World War, reckless farming has led to the loss of 550 million hectares of agricultural land. That's about 38 percent of the farmland in use today. In other words, we're losing soil faster than it's being replaced (it takes between two hundred and a thousand years to make an inch of topsoil). In the United States, soil is disappearing on average seventeen times faster than it is being replenished. The cost of soil runoff worldwide runs to hundreds of billions of dollars each year.

FERTILIZER. Plants need nitrogen—without it, there would be nothing. But it's possible to have too much of a good thing. When scientists discovered, in the early twentieth century, how to turn the atmosphere's nitrogen into fertilizer, food production boomed, and the globe's population shot up, calling for more food and therefore more fertilizer. Around the world, farms used seven times more fertilizer in 1995 than they did in 1960. The problem is, the more you use, the less good it does, since the fertilizer helps the crop but sours the soil. In 1980, one ton of nitrogen would get you 15 to 20 tons of corn. By 1997, the same amount would get you 5 to 10. If you're a farmer, you put on more fertilizer and corrupt your soil some more. If you're a fertilizer producer, you count your money; it is estimated that fertilizer applications will triple by 2050. And if you're a fish, well, you prepare to meet your maker. About half of the nitrogen applied by the farmer runs off the fields and ends up in rivers, lakes and oceans, where it fertilizes algae. The algae blooms and decomposes, in the process sucking up all the oxygen.

PESTICIDES. If fertilizer is self-defeating, pesticides are even worse. Like the use of artificial fertilizer, pesticide use has shot up from about zero at the end of the Second World War to about 11 million tons worldwide today. (And they're not evenly distributed. Here in Canada, with our massive grain exports, we dump nearly a ton of pesticide for each citizen.) But pesticide *doesn't even work*. In 1948, when chemicals were just coming into widespread use, about 7 percent of the pre-harvest crop was lost to insects. In 2001, by which time pesticide use had multiplied many times over, losses to insects had nearly *doubled* to 13 percent.

The reason it's so hard to get rid of pests is that you end up killing the things that eat them. About 67 million birds die each year from exposure to pesticides, and however you feel about the moral implications of killing that many birds, you have to concede that they would have been quite useful if they'd been around to eat the insects. Pesticides also kill predatory insects that eat pests; once they're out of the way, the surviving pests thrive. And many do survive, of course. Exposure to pesticides exerts immense evolutionary pressure to develop resistance to the chemicals. The result is a super-pest. In other words, these toxins do exactly the opposite of what they're meant to do. Meanwhile, they are accumulating in the soil and animal life, and they're exterminating crucial parts of the ecosystem such as soil biota (beneficial bacteria and fungi) and pollinators (honey bee populations are plummeting catastrophically, leaving farmers to wonder how they're going to pollinate $10 billion worth of crops).

MISTREATMENT OF ANIMALS. I will not explore the horrors of the feedlot, chicken battery or abattoir here. It is a subject best dealt with not in bullet points but in an outraged description of what animals must endure. And a cookbook is simply not the place to investigate something so ghastly. But the earth-to-table philosophy helps make sense of the paradox that we are repelled by the very food we lust after. It is possible to buy meat that has been organically reared and humanely slaughtered, pasture-fed and perhaps even known by name. If the farmer has nothing to hide, you have nothing to answer for.

CLIMATE CHANGE. Finally, the most pressing environmental problem of all: climate change. It is not difficult to see how conventional farming, shopping and eating contribute to our oversized carbon footprints. That flying in produce from the other side of the world might not be environmentally friendly is pretty clear, but the real culprit is not so much the distance traveled as the way the food was grown and distributed. First, though green, growing things generally counter climate change by soaking up carbon dioxide, an acre of industrially cultivated farm land is a net contributor to global warming. The greenhouse gases released by ploughing, the nitrous oxide created when fertilizer reacts with the environment, and the diesel-powered tractors that ply the fields all wreak havoc on the atmosphere. Moreover, the fertilizers and pesticides that drench most fields are manufactured from natural gas and oil respectively. (We put far more calories of fossil fuel energy into our energy than we get out in food energy.) Now take into account the fact that most food is shipped vast distances in trucks before it reaches the factory or distribution center it is destined for, that most shoppers have to drive to their local supermarket to pick up their food, and that supermarkets, with their open freezers and bright lights, use far more electricity per square foot that even factories do, and it is easy to see that we are going to have to find a new way to grow and distribute our food.

This list is not complete, but it's probably enough to make you wonder why anyone would want to go on eating as we're eating. It seems to me that if there are so many arguments against industrial farming, it shouldn't be up to traditional farmers or careful shoppers to defend their choice of food—the onus should be on the purveyors of industrial-scale, processed food to make the case for their product. If it's not better, and it's not cheaper, and it's not sustainable, then why would anyone buy it?

Acknowledgements

The Earth to Table project began four years ago. It was truly an innocent beginning. Over the years we developed a long list of local suppliers and our original intent was to connect the customers of the restaurant with this very unique catalogue of local farmers. We were going to highlight ManoRun Farm as the primary source of produce that came into the restaurant and encourage others to create similar relationships with local farms. Our experience with ManoRun had been wonderful (as I hope this book makes clear) and we wanted others to benefit from it. This beautiful book you are holding in your hand was originally destined to be a spiral bound resource guide that was only going to be sold out of the restaurant. No real thoughts of grandeur—we just wanted to share!

So, how on earth did we end up with such a cool book? It's really quite a story and it's been a lot of work. We have quite few people to thank.

The first person we would like to thank is Donna Dooher, owner of Mildred's Temple Kitchen. Donna has been a mentor for many years and was the first person we approached with this very simple idea. Since Donna is herself a published author, we thought she might have some idea as to where to begin. She suggested we start with photos documenting our experience with ManoRun Farm and to get ready for this idea to be really big. Donna's enthusiasm from the beginning gave our project a life of its own.

Two people were early influences on the style and content, John Bullock and Alisha Townsend. They too loved the idea and joined us for early mornings at the farm, listened to our stories to try to give us structure and direction. It was through our work with John and Alisha that a larger project really seemed to be taking shape. As for John, we still pester him weekly with any question we have to do with graphic design, whether he likes it or not.

He has become a good friend and we thank him for his continued support.

Alison Fryer of the Cookbook Store in Toronto was an early proponent and resource for us. I love cookbooks and have a vast collection, which is why I can't visit Toronto without stopping in for a look.

Next came Edward Pond and Claire Stubbs. Edward and Claire are a photography and food styling team that have worked on some of our favorite cookbooks. Both Edward and Claire had a beautiful vision for this book and their influence over how it turned out is obvious on every page.

Another important person on our journey was Sarah Davies. Sarah is highly respected in the publishing world, and many people referred to her as the one to meet if we wanted a publishing deal. Coincidently, Sarah is local to the restaurant. As soon as we met Sarah we knew she was special and that we were in good hands.

As rookie authors, we are grateful to the team at Random House Canada and Ecco for believing in us. The support of Anne Collins, Jennifer Shepherd, Kendall Anderson and Dan Halpern helped us realise our dream of making this book. Behind every pedestrian author is a terribly talented editor, and Nick Massey-Garrison, our editor and writer, helped us turn our half thoughts and incomplete ideas into beautiful prose. He is credited with how the book reads. Thanks also to Kelly Hill for this beautiful design.

We also would like to thank the very talented team at the Ancaster Old Mill and Spencer's at the Waterfront. Every one of them embraced the idea from the beginning with days worked on the farm, and contributions to recipes, particularly our General Manager, Kevin Marshall, and the Chef at Spencer's, Chris Haworth.

Extra special thanks to Bryan Gibson and Erin Schiestel. Bryan, our head chef, ran the kitchen and Erin ran pastry while Bettina and I were off writing this book.

Once all the recipes had been written, they then had to be edited and tested. For this we need to thank Kate Dowhan and Mike Vogt. Kate was invaluable in putting our rogue recipes into legible text. Mike was given the job of "recipe tester"—he took the edited recipes and made sure they worked, at the same time maintaining his role as Sous Chef.

We would like to thank our respective families for their love and support. Jeff's family: Julie, Brian and Judy, Brenda, Susan and Matt, Jen and Sean and all the girls Ella, Mya (Chuck), Grace and Anna, Kerry and Jay Johnson. And Bettina's family: Carolyn and Dieter, Chris, Stephen, Holly and Quinn.

Many thanks to all of the great chefs and food professionals who contributed their time to make this book better then we had ever thought possible: Heston Blumenthal, Thomas Kellar, Michael Schwartz, Matthew Dillon, Tory Miller, Dan Barber, Irene Hamburger, Jeffrey Alford, Naomi Duguid, Jamie Kennedy, Susur Lee, James Chatto, Judy Creighton, Michael Pollan, Katrina Simmons, Anne Yarymowich, J. Charles Grieco, Anita Stewart and Karen DeMasco, all of whom are doing extraordinary things.

We would like to thank Aaron Ciancone, his sister Leanne and the entire Ciancone family. As proprietors of the Ancaster Old Mill and Spencer's at the Waterfront, you are truly responsible for making this book a reality. Working with wonderful people like the Ciancone family makes each day a joy.

Chris Krucker and his lovely wife, Denise, daughters Naomi, Nakita and Keshia all have our gratitude for allowing us on to their farm to take pictures, and host parties and claim their son, Kaleb, as the star of this book. Our relationship with this family has gone far beyond Farm-Restaurant and had turned into something truly wonderful, and that's really what this is all about isn't it? Great relationships with extraordinary people.

Index

bees, 311
beets, 175
    Hanger Steak with Beet Horseradish
        Relish, 261
    Heirloom Beet Salad with Feta and
        Pumpkin Seeds, 174
    Pickled Beets, Shallots, Pearl Onions
        or Carrots, 132–33
berries, freezing, 90
Bertolli, Paul, 85
BEVERAGES
    Beer with Ice and Lime, 102
    Fresh Verbena or Mint Teas, 172
    herbal tea, 172
    Local Fruit Sangria, 102
    Mulled Cider and Cranberry, 173
    Sparkling Wine and Cherry Juice, 48
    Spiced Hot Chocolate, 278
    Watermelon Agua Fresca, 103
biodynamic farming methods, 166
Bistecca, 122
blight, 310
Bloomfield, April, 165
Blue Hill restaurant, 99, 161, 164, 166,
        168, 170
blueberries
    Blueberry Upside-Down Cake, 138
    freezing, 224
Blueberry Upside-Down Cake, 138
Blumenthal, Heston, 17–21, 41, 43,
        169, 240, 287
boiling water baths, 92–93
bok choy, planting, 29
Bon Appétit, 98, 164, 286
Bouchon restaurant, 244
Braised Lamb Shanks, 237, 250
Braised Pork Belly, 252
Braised Short Ribs, 198
Bread and Butter Pudding, 275
bread oven, 87–89
BREADS (*See also* DOUGHS; Red Fife
        wheat)
    Bread and Butter Pudding, 275
    fermentation, 228
    making your own, 229
    Milk and Honey Bread, 76
    Oatmeal Molasses Bread, 281
    sourdough, 88
    starter, 227
    stone-baked, 87–89
    Wheat Berry Beer Bread, 218
    whole wheat, 228
    Whole Wheat Focaccia, 146
    yeast-leavened, 88

brittle, pumpkin seed, 215
broccoli rabe
    Bay Scallops with Broccoli Rabe, 247
Brussels sprouts
    Colcannon Potatoes, 203
BSE (bovine spongiform encephalopathy),
    21
buffalo mozzarella
    Heirloom Tomato Salad with Buffalo
        Mozzarella, 107
Buttermilk Panna Cotta, 74–75
bycatch, 94

C
cabbage
    Calf's Liver with Cavolo Nero, 257
calf's liver (*See also* beef)
    Calf's Liver with Cavolo Nero, 257
Calf's Liver with Cavolo Nero, 257
Canadian Slow Food Ark of Taste, 33
Candied Nuts, 271
canning and preserving, 92–93
Caramel Sauce, 305
carbonara pasta, 20
carpaccio, vegetable, 108
carrots
    Pickled Beets, Shallots, Pearl Onions
        or Carrots, 132–33
    pickling, 90–91
    Roasted Root Vegetables, 270
catfish, buying, 97
cauliflower
    White Truffle Risotto with Cauliflower,
        207
caviar
    Scrambled Eggs with Chives and
        Caviar, 51
cavolo nero
    Calf's Liver with Cavolo Nero, 257
Center for Health and Global Environment
    (Harvard), 164
Chantilly Cream, 136, 137
charcuterie, 29, 160, 222
    charcuterie plate, 224
    pizza toppings, 191
Chavignol cheese, 160
cheap food. *See* conventional food vs.
    good food
cheddar cheese, 160
cheese
    Crispy Halloumi Cheese with Cortland
        Apple Chutney, 178
    Gnudi with Ramps, Morels and
        Fiddleheads, 60

salt, 15
Salt-baked Arctic Char, 264
Salt-Baked Arctic Char, 264
sangria, local fruit, 102
SAUCES. *See* DRESSINGS and SAUCES
scallops
Bay Scallops with Broccoli Rabe, 247
Scheckter, Jody, 41–43
Schormann, Bettina, 8–9, 12, 14, 15, 83, 86–89, 154–57, 238, 244
Schwartz, Michael, 98–100, 285
Scrambled Eggs with Chives and Caviar, 51
sea floor, damage to, 94
sea lice, 94
SEAFOOD, 94–97
Bay Scallops with Broccoli Rabe, 247
One-Pot Fish Soup with Rouille, 262
Spot Prawns with Chanterelles, 180
seeds
genetically modified, 33
planting, 34
servers, 225
shallots
New Potato Salad with Green Beans and Shallots, 105
Pickled Beets, Shallots, Pearl Onions or Carrots, 132–33
shopping locally. *See* local economy, supporting/protecting
Shortcakes with Chantilly Cream and Macerated Strawberries, 136–37
short ribs
Braised Short Ribs, 198
Korean-Cut Ribs with Honey and Soy Sauce, 127
shrimp
Spot Prawns with Chanterelles, 180
Sitka and Spruce restaurant, 44–46
Slow Food movement, 12–14, 31
Slow-Roasted Pork Shoulder, 66
Slow-Roasted Roma Tomatoes, 107
Smash-In Ice Creams, 135
smell, sense of, 230
smoked fish, 96
snails, 18
soil (*See also* composting)
erosion of, 310
microorganisms in, 40
traditional methods of improving, 40–41
sorrel
growing, 233
Sorrel Frittata, 69

Sorrel Frittata, 69
SOUPS (*See also* STOCKS)
Corn Soup, 116
French Onion Soup, 177
One-Pot Fish Soup with Rouille, 262
sour cream
Fresh Horseradish Cream, 301
sourdough bread, 88
sous vide (technique), 17
soy sauce
Korean-Cut Ribs with Honey and Soy Sauce, 127
Sparkling Wine and Cherry Juice, 48
specialists, 2–3
specificity of place, 36, 39
Spiced Hot Chocolate, 278
Spot Prawns with Chanterelles, 180
Spotted Pig restaurant, 165
Spring Lamb Shoulder, 64–65, 237
squash, 151–52
Squash, Sage and Pancetta Pizza, 188
Squash, Sage and Pancetta Pizza, 188
steak
Bistecca, 122
Hanger Steak with Beet Horseradish Relish, 261
Our Steak Sauce, 300
Sticky Toffee Pudding, 276
stinging nettles
foraging for, 37
Stinging Nettle Linguini, 63
Stinging Nettle Linguini, 63
STOCKS
beef, 296
chicken, 297
fish, 298
Stone Barns Center for Food and Agriculture, 99, 161, 164, 166–67
stone-baked bread, 87–89
storing
corn, beans, squash, 151–52
preserves, 92
Stratford Chefs School, 162
strawberries, 80, 82–83
freezing, 90
Shortcakes with Chantilly Cream and Macerated Strawberries, 136–37
striped bass, buying, 97
super-pests, 311
supermarkets, 6, 21, 36, 45, 96, 160, 224, 235, 240, 287, 308–9, 312
Sweet Mediterranean Pizza, 211
Sweet Potato Gnocchi, 196–97